THE AGE OF
INSANITY

THE AGE OF
──INSANITY──

Modernity and Mental Health

JOHN F. SCHUMAKER

Westport, Connecticut
London

Library of Congress Cataloging-in-Publication Data

Schumaker, John F., 1949–
    The Age of Insanity: Modernity and mental health / John F. Schumaker.
      p. cm.
    Includes bibliographical references and index.
    ISBN 0–275–97052–3 (alk. paper)
    1. Mental health.   2. Civilization, Modern—1950-   I. Title.
  RA790.S39 2001
    155.9′2—dc21   2001016360

British Library Cataloguing in Publication Data is available.

Library of Congress Catalog Card Number: 2001016360
ISBN: 0–275–97052–3

First published in 2001

Praeger Publishers, 88 Post Road West, Westport, CT 06881
An imprint of Greenwood Publishing Group, Inc.
www.praeger.com

Printed in the United States of America

The paper used in this book complies with the
Permanent Paper Standard issued by the National
Information Standards Organization (Z39.48–1984).

10 9 8 7 6 5 4 3 2 1

To Cheryl

Contents

Preface   ix

1.   Introduction: The Human Context of Modernity   1

2.   Megatrends in Identity, Consciousness, and Psychological
     Defense   13

3.   Materialism, Consumption, and Mental Health   29

4.   The Cultural Dynamics of Western Depression   51

5.   The New Anxiety   69

6.   Modernity and Interpersonal Health   83

7.   Spiritual and Existential Health   107

8.   Mental Health and the Physical World   139

9.   The New Mental Health Worker   169

Notes   179

Bibliography   197

Index   215

Preface

The initial idea for this book came to me after a lecture that I gave in 1995 at the University of Newcastle in Australia. The lecture itself dealt with the psychological toxicity of certain patterns of contemporary enculturation, most notably those related to materialism and consumerism. In my usual fashion, I tried to ruffle a few feathers by challenging the audience to question some of the cultural realities to which they had become accustomed. Afterward, a man in his late thirties said to me on his way out, "I want you to know that you just changed my life." He went on to say that he had a financially rewarding career, as well as all the trappings that make up the proverbial good life. But he added that he had been living for years with the nagging sense that his entire life somehow lacked meaning, substance, and grounding. In his words, his life was a sham. This man told me that, somewhere in the course of my lecture, he finally found the courage to make the radical changes that might help to bring him alive. Yet he never once made reference to anything that was actually *wrong* with him or his life.

Those comments reminded me of similar things I have heard from so many other people, including students, therapy clients, and acquaintances. In most cases, they talk about ill-defined forms of mental distress that cannot be traced to specific causes. Instead, it seems the good life of the modern consumer is often mocked by feelings of discontent, disorientation, and psychic numbness. Psychologists have a long tradition of understanding all forms of human behavior within the narrow context of isolated individuals. But the phenomenon that had captured my attention struck me more as the result of the generalized effects of modern living, or what one might call *modernity*.

It was at this point that I committed myself to writing a book about the interface of modernity and mental health. Among other things, it seemed worthwhile to describe the new types of existential disorders that often escape official diagnosis by mental health professionals who rely on traditional psychiatric labeling systems. This part of it would be an extension of my previous book *The Corruption of Reality*, in which I chronicle the growing difficulty of modern people in accessing the cultural sources of transcendence that, in earlier times, enabled members to resolve existential issues. But as the concept for this book matured, I came to realize that many other aspects of psychological well-being are also influenced by unseen macroscopic forces that express themselves through the unique cultural blueprints that have emerged in our current historical period, and that have become the new foundations for identity, consciousness, and emotion.

In addition to describing the emergence of new categories of psychopathology, I wanted to explain the dramatic increase in already existing disorders, such as clinical depression. I had always been intrigued by anthropological accounts of non-Western societies that appear to be psychologically immunized against mental disorders that are rampant in the Western world. A knowledge of the cultural structures of such groups can provide worthwhile points of comparison that enable us to better understand the deterioration of mental health in the West. Therefore, the book contains a number of detailed descriptions of cultures that are assembled in ways that lead to much different mental health outcomes.

In short, this book is a treatise on the mental health ramifications of modernity, with special emphasis on the cultural innovations that impinge upon people in the modern age. Although a good deal of this volume is an account of ways in which modernity has contributed to the often cited "mental health crisis" that exists today, I also touch on features of modernity that are potentially beneficial to our psychological welfare.

The definition of mental health that I employ includes, but goes beyond, the conventional diagnostic entities. In addition to exploring mental health in terms of the absence or presence of psychological symptoms, I delve into modernity's influence on such factors as the quality of interpersonal relationships, spiritual and existential health, intellectual health, and character formation. Although I have a background in clinical psychology, I have approached these and other topics from a wide perspective that draws on theory and research from diverse disciplines, including anthropology, sociology, cultural studies, religious studies, economics, consumer studies, and social philosophy. This in itself was challenging because of the different vocabularies and theoretical assumptions that prevail within these various disciplines. With my own writing, I strove for a generic style that could be accessed by people from a range of academic backgrounds.

This book continues my love affair with the "big picture," and with well-conceived generalizations that can provide contextual frameworks for more specialized approaches to knowledge. Some critics may argue that the modern person to whom I refer does not actually exist since everyone is at least a partial exception to the rule. But rather than being an attempt to tell the full story of separate individuals, this volume highlights the broader social arrangements and cultural configurations that establish proclivities, predispositions, and leanings. In many respects, it is about the cultural gravity of the modern era: that is, the way in which the cultural conditions of modernity cause individuals to gravitate toward certain values, attitudes, goals, and beliefs. Although the pull may not affect everyone equally, it nonetheless improves our understanding of many general mental health trends. Even our psychotherapeutic interventions with disturbed individuals can be guided to a large extent by the vision we gain from a broad-scale analysis of the general forces that act upon us at the moment.

I would like to express my appreciation to Anthony Marsella, Tod Sloan, and Martin Dorahy for their valuable insights and guidance.

CHAPTER 1

Introduction: The Human Context of Modernity

Our footprints through time track the story of a unique creature tempted incessantly to tamper with existing realities and prevailing orders. In the fifth century B.C., the Greek historian Herodotus described modernity as a demigod who mutters angrily at us, demanding that we entertain fantasy in place of dull rigid fact. Although we have always been modern in the sense of being an ongoing experiment with ourselves, the modernities that we compose can punish as well as reward. As we obey the command of this irascible demigod that resides within, we do not always foresee what sort of new age we are creating for ourselves. We cannot presume that the human being avails itself well of history, and the rich spoils of modernization ventures are often mocked by treacherous forces that are set in motion against us. Our latest experiment is a dramatic one that holds unprecedented potential for both reward and punishment. In this book, I explore our current modernization experiments in terms of their psychological benefits and costs, and of the growing number of claims that we have inadvertently steered ourselves into an Age of Insanity.

Our current version of modernity is often understood as a postindustrial order whose primary features are commodification, consumption, social marginality, technological encroachment, amplified organizational power, homogenized drives and tastes, deregulation of volition and emotion, in-comprehensible abstract systems, simultaneous communication, and the shift toward reflexive knowledge.[1] It is frequently depicted as an overwhelming force that detraditionalizes the world and sets in motion multiple out-of-control processes that require constant cultural, political, and institutional innovation. Other attributes of modernity that have been highlighted include ambiguity, fragmentation, impaired social memory, banality, pluralism, and the replacement of reality by images and fantasy.

Prevailing theories of modernity have been criticized on the basis of their overemphasis on knowledge and skill, and their neglect of emotional elements. Although modernity has the production of order as one of its basic operations, it has also been cited as a perpetrator of chaos, confusion, incongruity, and disquiet. But some scholars have perceived a distinct trend toward nonemotionalism under conditions of modernity and have started to speak in terms of *postemotional society* rather than *postmodern* society. For example, Stjepan Mestrovic describes postemotional society as one without oppression, yet as one wherein members are distinguished primarily by their incapacity for emotional commitment and empathy.[2]

The rising swell of rage in the modern era may seem to contradict the general demise of emotion, but it is more likely that rage is what remains once authentic emotion has ceased. The possible extinction of emotion has far-reaching ramifications for individual mental health, as well as the health of organizations, groups, and society generally. One advantage of the concept of a postemotional society is that it helps to explain the recent upsurgence of psychological disorders that are characterized by a pathological absence of experienced emotion rather than suffering related to negative emotion.

Modernity can be approached from the ways in which it affects personality and social character traits. Increasing reference has been made to a *modern person syndrome* that involves detachment from the past and present, affectional allegiance to technology, material ambitions that take precedence over social and environmental concerns, and a commercial view of justice.[3] This syndrome has been associated with certain favorable traits, such as an increased openness to change and innovation, the ability to juggle opinions about multiple matters, and the view that others will uphold contracts and obligations.[4] No pattern of cultural evolution will be entirely negative for members. Even so, many observers have been impressed primarily with the psychologically corrosive effect of modernization, and the resultant psychopathology that finds its way into individual members.

VARIETIES OF MODERNITY

Modernization tends to be portrayed in close proximity to Westernization, the products of which include personal autonomy, self-reliance, future orientation, a strong appetite for change, capitalistic heroism, and success-mindedness. However, this combination of characteristics is representative of American-style modernization and does not reflect an inevitable outcome of modernity. In this regard, it has been demonstrated that societies can become modern without shaping themselves along the lines of Western (or American) culture. Furthermore, in the course of modernization, it is not requisite for a society to abandon itself fully to a materialistic orientation, to adopt an individualistic orientation, or even to relinquish traditional cultural frames of reference. It may be that other cultures possess traditions that can insulate them partially from the pathogenic properties of unabashed Americanization.

Recent decades have seen the modernization of some East Asian countries (e.g., Japan, Korea, Taiwan, Hong Kong, Singapore). But, to some extent, they have modernized in ways that reflect their own values, traditions, and cultural heritages. Unlike the trend in the West, Easternization has been able to retain a certain degree of collective identity, cooperative endeavor, and respect for authority.[5] It has also been able to keep alive various Eastern cultural themes, including harmony, resignation in the face of hardship, acceptance of duty and sacrifice, and an appreciation of history. This approach to modernization might enable certain Eastern cultures to avoid some of the common side effects of Westernization, such as the undermining of spirituality stemming from excessive commercialism, the collapse of community resulting from individualistic self-seeking, and the breakdown of relationships as a consequence of the eclipse of collective responsibility.

This suggests that some modernization strategies may be more conducive than others to mental health. In the case of Easternization, for instance, we see a pathway to modernity that has the potential to retain social and interpersonal ties. If we accept that human beings benefit from intact social relations and the coping advantages that those provide, our logic tells us that Easternization would not lead to the same degree of alienation-based distress that can be found under Western modernity. Furthermore, if one wishes to explain the current epidemic of some mental health problems in the West, it is necessary to examine the specific structures that exist within our Western mode of modernity.

Western modernity, by contrast to some patterns of non-Western modernity, has been described in relation to high degrees of structural-functional differentiation, as well as unprecedented social mobilization that operates in conjunction with liberal capitalism.[6] The working mechanics of this capitalistic system have resulted in the subordination of social, economic, and political values to the logic of the market. The values of personal autonomy have risen to ascendancy in an increasingly hyperglobalized environment that ushers in a type of consciousness that diminishes prospects for solidarity. This again differs from some non-Western styles of modernity, wherein traditional values and localisms are able to coexist with the workings of modernization.

A distinction has also been made between inner and outer modernity.[7] *Inner modernity* refers to a modernization process that can unfold with regard to meaning, purpose, values, and spirituality. Some of these can come into conflict with *outer modes of modernity* that are encapsulated in materialism, technology, and competition. The idea that one can be modern without the stereotypical external appearance of modernity forces one to stretch our definitions of modernity. For instance, if we judge modernity in terms of the present ecological crisis, it is tempting to conclude that a society in which members live in harmony with nature is more modern than a technologically advanced one wherein members contribute actively to the undoing of the physical environment. Tourists visit the Amish and Mennonite communities, finding their backward ways to be a source of curiosity and amusement. But their ecosensitive life-styles may be prototypes of modernity that can lead us toward a much safer future. So it is important not to frame our understandings of modernity solely in relation to Western meanings.

THE CULTURAL FOUNDATION OF MODERNITY

Rather than conceiving of modernity as a process that operates in a contextual vacuum, it is important to recognize that virtually all aspects of modernity are mediated by social and cultural mechanisms of various sorts. Similarly, the myriad changes that the progression into modern life comprises are inevitably associated with changes to cultural formats. Since we are creatures of culture, modernity's influence on mental health must be kept close to an analysis of the psychological and emotional repercussions of modern cultural designs. This assumes that the overall experience of reality, which includes mental health components, is determined to a large extent by motivations, goals, beliefs, attitudes, and general orientations that can be traced to the process of enculturation. Even the influences of modernity that involve changes to the physical environment can be seen to unfurl in relation to revised cultural strategies.

The problem for psychologists studying modernity by way of cultural structures is that the field of psychology is still rooted deeply in individualism, the flawed assumption that individuals operate largely as isolated units who themselves are the principal translators of reality. At the moment, individualism lies at the heart of most psychological theories of normal and abnormal behavior. This includes the voguish cognitive theories that see behavior and emotions as the result of cognitions that arise within, and are self-delivered by, the individual. This translates into therapies that locate much of the blame for mental disturbance within the individual.

Edward T. Hall, the renowned culture theorist, once commented that the most powerful of all human motivations is the drive to *learn one's culture*.[8] He understood that culture is synonymous with survival, and conversely that any individual's existence is jeopardized by a failure to achieve a necessary degree of unity with culture. The learning of one's culture remains the requisite motivation of people even in modern hyperindividualistic societies wherein the behavior of members seems to have considerable private input. Even the contemporary "do your own thing" or a "find your own way" orientation can be seen to have clear cultural roots.

Many formal definitions of culture make reference to the fact that culture is the sum total of learned *mental* constructs and behaviors that are transmitted by way of social learning."[9] Melford Spiro goes further in describing culture as a *cognitive system* that programs both descriptive and normative constructions about nature, human beings, and the social world in which we operate.[10] The close interface of culture and cognition lets us speak of cultural cognition, a concept that has the potential to bridge the current gap between cultural and cognitive processes.

One dimension of cultural cognition is the system of values and meanings that ultimately shape most aspects of human reality. Another is the accumulated pool of knowledge used by members to approach all types of situations, events, and problems. The structural organization of cognition also comes under the influence of culture. According to Robert Serpell and Wade Boykin, culture is involved in the construction of the cognitive architecture that results in certain patterns of mentation.[11] Rather than implying that culture is responsible for a completely predictable cognitive style, this means that culture determines the constraints, possibilities, and routines in which members are invited to operate. These routines refer to the subset of mental and behavioral regularities that, as a result of their collective acknowledgment, become the cultural basis for appropriate rules, contexts, and performances.

The process of enculturation is a conservative one that ensures a high degree of cognitive overlap between conventional forms of cultural life and the individual inhabitants of the culture.[12] But enculturation is not entirely monolithic since cultural texts are open to a certain degree of subjective interpretation. Modernity itself can introduce variables that can diminish the ability of culture to self-replicate in a reliable fashion, which has the effect of increasing variability within that culture. In fact, as will be seen, one of the main causal factors in modernity-related psychopathology is the growing inability of an overarching culture to organize and support individual members. This does not mean that these individuals desist in being culturally motivated, but rather that the final assemblage of their reality constructions will have a considerable amount of idiosyncratic contamination.

The argument that culture must be at the forefront of our understanding of human behavior, as well as modernity's mental health effects, does not rule out the existence of a fundamental human nature. In recent decades, many social scientists were shying away from any talk of a possible human nature. But fortunately the theoretical nihilism that spawned this sentiment has gradually succumbed to the stamina of common sense. It is once again acceptable to speak of cultural programs that interact with a host of natural human characteristics and proclivities.

One of these is the inherent drive of the human being to order stimuli and thereby be able to understand, describe, and predict the world.[13] The presence of a human nature is also revealed by the fact that all cultures share many common themes. The underlying sameness of cultural themes cannot be understood without some acknowledgment of inherent precultural tendencies that can be found in all human beings. It has been proposed by a number of thinkers that modernity has introduced cultural blueprints that distance members from aspects of their basic humanity, and that hypothesis leads them to frame the prospect of a modern mental health crisis in terms of certain dehumanizing effects of Western-type modernization.

MODERNITY AND THE PROBLEM OF HUMAN NATURE

Whether modernity is harmful or helpful to mental health depends on a number of factors. One concerns the way in which emerging cultural modernities interact with the essential constants that compose human nature. In theory, a healthy cultural structure would be one built around a *common humanity* shared by all human beings.[14] This type of enculturation format could thus be regarded as a process of humanization. But there is no guarantee that modernity's transformation of cultural structures will remain consonant with the elemental constitution of the members.

The well-known cultural disintegration hypothesis, as set out by Alexander Leighton, is a culture-based model of psychopathology that assumes that all human beings strive to achieve and maintain an "essential psychic condition."[15] This involves reaching an optimal tension level in relation to a range of basic human needs (emotional expression, satisfying interpersonal and sexual relations, physical safety, and so forth). But all of these needs, according to this hypothesis, are reliant on cultural conditions that enable members to satisfy these needs. This hydraulic formulation implies that cultural changes that make need satisfaction more difficult will translate into social and psychological problems. In other words, the human being has certain nonrelative need systems that, if ignored or infringed upon negatively, will promote a state of dehumanization.

The condition of dehumanization is considered by some thinkers to be the equivalent of madness, and the largest contributor to the current crisis of identity. Erich Fromm wrote about the modern mental health crisis in terms of the gap between culture and human nature. It was the dehumanization stemming from the human-nature gap that helped him to understand the deteriorating psychological health of the modern person and that led him to write that "we are a society of notoriously unhappy, lonely, anxious, depressed and dependent people who are glad when we have killed the time we are trying to save."[16]

Dehumanization and its undesirable mental health consequences have been linked to a number of transhistorical needs that have been neglected because modernity blocks access to need satisfaction. The following sections describe some of the specific needs that have been identified as essential ones that must survive cultural change if individual members are to remain psychologically healthy. As I describe them, I will argue their importance from a nonrelativistic position that implies a limit to people's tolerance for deprivation of these needs.

The Need for Social Connectedness

Aloneness and social alienation are intolerable states for the human being. We would whither and die, both psychologically and physically, if deprived entirely of the opportunity to relate meaningfully to other people. In the course of connecting with other people, we rise above puerile self-interest and trivial self-serving pursuits, with positive general benefits to the wider community. All functional cultures take heed of our inherently social nature. They operate in conjunction with this aspect of human nature and provide pathways whereby members can become united in satisfying ways. On the other hand, a hypothetical culture that for some reason does not allow for the satisfaction of our relatedness need will produce members who are prone to many types of psychological and emotional disorders. The motivational properties of modern consumer culture have been blamed many times for their tendency to dissolve social bonds, and to reduce for deprivation collective sources of coping.

The Need for Identity and Recognition

The need for identity overlaps with the need for relatedness because an identity cannot be forged unless a person has developed a significant relationship with the world of people, thereby making possible a distinction between the self and others. One comes to know oneself as a unique identity only through a process of merging meaningfully with the wider social context in which one must live and survive. The search for identity was not much of an issue in previous ages. The individual and the group were closely interwoven, and one's personal identity was determined predominantly by the role one assumed within the culture.

Most intact cultures, both past and present, have embedded within them systems that promote a distinct personal identity, while ensuring that the individual becomes fused with the group. Many non-Western cultures still have highly important rites of initiation whereby the young person is ushered officially into the broader culture. Although this process establishes the initiate's identity as part of the group, such practices almost always involve another component in which the young person is identified as a valuable entity in his or her own right. Very often, as part of these initiation ceremonies, special names, reflective of certain unique traits, are given to the person. This might involve the physical marking of the person in order to establish his or her uniqueness, or even the formal bestowal of a role within the group that is based on the person's special abilities. On the other hand, only the most dysfunctional of cultures would be devoid of practices that satisfy the crucial need concerning identity formation. The often cited failure of moderns to "find" themselves and to achieve a convincing sense of self has been traced to the absence of such official practices in modern society. It has been said that, in several respects, the modern self has become alien to itself.

The Need for Transcendence, Ritual, and Drama

Amplified awareness, which is the crowning evolutionary endowment of our species, becomes problematic if superimposed against a chaotic and apparently meaningless world. As hyperawareness collides with the unnerving complexity and senselessness of existence, we naturally seek explanatory frameworks that can orient us while providing satisfactory answers about the world and our place in it. Historically, culture played the central role in affording people the means to meet their transcendence needs. Since only more chaos would ensue if each and every individual set about the task of orienting him/herself, it is useful for people to become devoted in coordinated ways that do not cause excessive spiritual friction. Functional cultures have always done this by propagating belief systems and related practices that can be loosely defined as religion. In actuality, religion is a cultural universal that can be understood as the historical cornerstone of the human being's quest to meet its need for transcendence.

Nearly all cultures contain some socially sanctioned mechanisms (including beliefs, rituals, and dramas) whereby members can confront literal reality and achieve a satisfactory orientation to the world. A culture without this feature would contain many disoriented members, seeking a plethora of disjointed and uncoordinated ways to comprehend the world. Those who write about the modern mental health crisis refer regularly to the decline of the transcendental as a crucial factor.

The Need for Intellectual Stimulation and Personal Growth

The emerging patterns of intellectual life in the modern age have led critics to speak of cultural *dumbing* forces that have caused the intellect to become partially atrophied. Not everyone would concede that human beings have a deep-rooted need to use their brains. Yet some have argued that, by nature, we want to exercise our brains in meaningful ways and to remain mentally alive. As evidence for this, neurological and behavioral research indicates that the human brain wants to be engaged intellectually. We also know that nothing is more cruel than to deny a human being mental stimulation. If obstructed completely in this regard, such as in stimulus-deprivation research studies, the person will quickly deteriorate mentally, even to the extent of becoming psychotic. Among forms of punishment, one of the most dreaded is solitary confinement, again because it takes away all sources of stimulation. A culture that did not respond to our need for intellectual growth or, even worse, one that served to inhibit intellectual activity, would be expected to contain members who were frustrated as a result of stunted intellectual growth. Today social analysts are pointing to a worrying consensus of stupidity that is contributing to a number of contemporary emotional and existential ills.

The Need for Culture

Culture itself must be viewed as part of our deeper structure. We are naturally inclined to learn to follow, and participate meaningfully in, culture. Our very existence relies on our ability to act out successfully our cultural imperative. By design, human beings are not equipped to survive as unrelated units. We are reliant upon being part of a culture that not only can ensure physical survival, but also is aligned with the full range of our human needs. Under certain conditions, cultures can break down and lose some or all of the integrity that makes them viable and capable of successful transmission. Those who associate modernity with madness sometimes assert that moderns are forced to construct reality without adequate levels of cultural input. Their mental worlds become precarious as they improvise, and proceed on the basis of, reality configurations that are so idiosyncratic that social conflicts and dysfunctions are inevitable.

MODERNITY, UNNATURAL COMPROMISE, AND ASOCIAL FREEDOM

The concept of cultural fitness helps to explain how all types of cultural transformation and modernization may, or may not, translate into psychopathology. A leading thinker on this subject, the anthropologist Raoul Naroll, wrote about cultural fitness in relation to many categories of psychosocial pathology, demonstrating that entire cultures can be sick if the "moral net" deteriorates beyond a certain point. His book *The Moral Order* identifies the types of developments that can cause a culture, and its members, to develop pathological characteristics.[17] Like others who see that we have a human nature that remains constant, Naroll perceived that all viable cultures throughout history have succeeded by organizing themselves around the actual nature of the human being.

Naroll spoke of the human instinct for meaningful relationships to others, for official ceremonies that connect the individual to the group while fostering a sense of identity, for cooperative and shared activities that weave people into a community, and for convincing beliefs and rituals that allow members to find refuge in the spiritual world. Together, these constitute the moral net of culture. Members of a culture can expect mental health advantages if the moral net is intact, whereas endless ills emerge when a culture's moral net becomes weakened.

The inability of a culture to take adequate account of the core requirements of its members can sometimes trace to happenings that precipitate social change on a scale that exceeds the culture's ability to adjust to those changes. Included here are disasters of various sorts, widespread migration resulting from war, breakdowns in belief systems, and political calamities. The affected culture might experiment with short-term improvised strategies that prove to be misguided.

Sometimes, when cultures suddenly come into contact, one culture is overwhelmed and thrown out of equilibrium. Much of the actual research examining the relationship between modernization and mental health has focused on the issue of culture change. One consistent finding has been that rapid culture change from a non-Western to a Western orientation raises the level of mental illness. A cultural disintegration model would explain the escalating rates of psychopathology in terms of the affected culture's diminished capacity to accommodate the essential needs of its members. A similar type of interpretation could be made with regard to the research that has found strong correlations between modernization and specific types of mental disturbances, such as depression, psychosomatic disorders, anxiety disorders, and alcoholism.[18]

Hypercapitalistic cultural designs have also been imputed to be a primary source of dehumanization since they underpin a society in which impersonal economic forces have taken over from traditional social ones. They petition members to enter the commodity sphere and to entertain general life orientations that preclude the satisfaction of more important nonmaterialistic ones. America, as the fitful climax of material reality, has attracted many descriptions of its inhabitants as joyless and dispirited. In his book *The Unsettling of America*, Wendell Berry explores the maddening effects of modern capitalistic structures in America, which lead him to conclude that "an American is probably the most unhappy citizen in the history of the world."[19] Hypercapitalism, and the related thematics of discontent and unrestrained consumption, may be examples of cultural survival mechanisms that omit key human considerations from the overall life equation. Their dehumanizing effects may receive their energy from the negative freedom that is the foundation for capitalistic success.

When cultures are stable, and when they fall at the healthy end of the moral net continuum, we would expect in theory to find relatively pathology-free members. It may seem fantastic to speak in terms of entire societies that are free of psychopathology, but several reports can be found of societies that, when discovered, had no apparent indications of "neurotic" afflictions. Jean-Jacques Rousseau, whose writings in the eighteenth century are sometimes seen as the start of the modern study of culture and psychopathology, commented on the healthy mental constitution of "savages." The groups that he observed were, in his words, "without hardly any disorders save wounds and old age."[20] This led to his controversial assertion that civilization somehow proves toxic in terms of mental well-being.

Even in more recent times, one can find detailed accounts of cultures wherein members are immune to the types of mental disorders that are so common in the West. Some of these are described in the following chapters. Among other things, it will be shown that the so-called clinical mental disorders are not inevitable. Instead, the degree to which members suffer these disorders may be largely the result of psychic predispositions associated with recent cultural developments and the overall process of modernization. As a prelude to this, the next chapter examines the general fate of identity, as well as consciousness and psychological defense, under conditions of modernity.

CHAPTER 2

Megatrends in Identity, Consciousness, and Psychological Defense

The self refers to the executive organizing tendency that lets us come to know ourselves and the world.[1] It gives continuity to our experience, while creating consistent patterns of behavior and cognition that become the functional basis of the social environment. Throughout most of human history, the identity of people tended to be an experiential embodiment of traditional cultural representations and idioms. The texts and the resultant identity structures of different cultures vary in terms of their mental health implications and consequences. Francis L.K. Hsu writes about the self in cross-cultural perspective, observing that, among other goals, the modern Western self tends to seek psychosocial homeostasis through control of the physical environment. This expresses itself in a number of related behavior patterns: building business empires, exploring and exploiting new territories, acquiring and collecting, and so forth.[2]

A long list of labels has been used in recent years to convey the type of self that has surfaced in recent times. Among these are the *problematic self*, the *empty self*, the *California self*, the *maximal self*, the *isolated self*, the *lonely self*, the *depleted self*, the *mutable self*, the *endangered self*, the *fragmented self*, the *media self*, the *raging self*, the *marginal self*, and the *impulsive self*. Many of these have overlapping meanings, and the self that emerges from conditions of modernity is probably a complex composite of these and other portrayals.

THE FREE-FLOATING INDIVIDUALISTIC STRUCTURE OF IDENTITY

The trend toward individualism is the most frequently cited contributor to the modern health crisis, and in particular the diffuse emotional craving that derives when the private self becomes the locus of reality. The *individualistic self* refers to an identity that is centered within itself, motivated more by personal consideration than by social consideration. It is associated with traits and survival strategies such as self-dependence, private achievement, competition with others, and self-gratification.

The goals of the individualist take top priority, even when their quest is detrimental to the group. Loyalty is mostly self-directed, and emotional bonding to the wider group is diminished. The term *neoindividualism* is used to describe the extreme levels of individualism that have emerged in the United States and, increasingly, European countries. This contrasts to many non-Western cultures, where social relations are of primary importance and an individuated member would be regarded as socially pathological.[3]

Modern individualism involves a rearrangement of human relations in which social consensus is no longer the principal guiding force. With the waning of unanimity, and the subsequent arrival of the indeterminate other, moderns have been transported into an increasingly phenomenological consciousness style wherein truth and knowledge are accessed by private subjective interpretation. The modern self has become so constricted, and so far removed from a wider social context, that some people find themselves unable to share with others anything except consumption and leisure.[4]

Rather than interfacing with a stable cultural reality, the self has become a fluid vehicle for ongoing negotiation. Its open free-floating design allows it to accommodate itself to an environment that has lost a quality of permanence. Furthermore, it represents a type of self-investment, operating via internalized control, that is a realistic solution to new social circumstances that offer little reassurance in terms of deep security.

Although non-Western cultures usually have more collectivist social structures, some exceptions have been pointed out, such as the Mbuti Pygmies of Africa and the people of Bhutan in the Himalayas. But, upon closer inspection, the individualism that can sometimes be identified in non-Western settings turns out to be embedded in traditional cultural learning. For example, Bhutanese culture still rests on a monastic system that instills in its members an urge to acquire and live in accordance with Buddhist knowledge and wisdom.[5] At the heart of their belief system is the tenet that evil and the full range of this-world ills are the result of greed and ambition, and that enlightenment involves transcendence from the social sources of these contaminants. They learn about an interpretation of karma that inclines members to develop a conceptually bounded separate self that entails very few sociocentric themes or injunctions. In this way, members are free to accept the full karmic consequences of their actions. Yet this type of individualism differs considerably from its Western counterpart in that its motivations and manifestations are merely an extension of a long-standing cultural model of selfhood.

In modern Western settings, individualism involves independent self-construal strategies that require members to cope through personal control, direct action, and confrontation with others. By contrast, people from collectivist cultures make more use of interdependent self-construal techniques that achieve coping less directly, by way of cooperative effort and alignment with the group. If changes are necessary, collectivists tend to participate in the changes to the group, rather than making abrupt changes to the private self. If change is difficult or impossible, collectivists are more likely than individualists to accept the situation and modify their wishes accordingly. By contrast, individualists would be more inclined to persist independently at altering circumstances in order to achieve their personal preferences.

Some benefits have been associated with an individualistic identity structure. Among these are accelerated economic development, less likelihood of government corruption, increased creativity and innovation, and better responsiveness to situations that require change. Heightened creativity and greater flexibility are also possible when individuals are no longer bound by preordained cultural knowledge, goals, and routines. The cultural exile has greater freedom with which to magnify the number of opportunities that life offers. There is also a certain amount of romantic appeal to the prospect of a powerful individual prevailing over a dull fate of mindless following and spineless other-reliance. Several nineteenth-century philosophers fueled the notion that dumb society was the enemy of the noble individual, and that only cowards and weaklings allow themselves to be tyrannized by dreary convention. This attitude has given birth to more than a few ardent supporters of American-style individualism.

But the picture is not so bright when one considers the relationship between individualism and mental health. Of the reviews that have been carried out on this topic, most have concluded that individualism is associated with specific social and psychological ills, including clinical depression, suicide, crime, divorce, child abuse, stress, and anxiety-related disorders. Although collectivist cultural structures have certain potential drawbacks, research shows that they are more conducive to mental health.

One explanation is that collectivism emphasizes harmony within the group, which, in turn, reduces the stresses and conflicts of everyday life. The fact that collectivism is associated with lower levels of competition may lead to greater security and perceived coping ability. It seems that collective coping eases the person's task of dealing with difficult life experiences. The burdens of life are lightened when the group can absorb some of the responsibility. In a related way, members of collectivist cultures make internal attributions of failure less frequently than their counterparts in individualistic cultures.

Many traditional cultures have not even evolved lexical concepts to communicate the possibility of an autonomous self. The rituals and customs in such settings tend to revolve around sociocentric themes, with the aim of forging identity along the lines of group solidarity. One psychological advantage of such an arrangement is that members have ready access to well-established formulas that provide structure to their sense of self. They feel supported by historical templates that facilitate the interpretation and management of life events.

The utilization of socially sanctioned identity templates promotes an other-connected self in which the person is keenly aware of his or her place in the group. The self achieves depth and substance only when it has been defined in a broader social context. But modernity has brought about a situation wherein identity is forged within a partial social vacuum, thereby replacing official practices with discretionary techniques.[6] When the self begins to define itself in isolation, a subsequent loss of emotional flexibility and hardiness that limits coping ability results.

A variety of psychological disturbances became more likely once Western culture grew individualistic to such a degree that people lost membership with the group. This is reminiscent of Émile Durkheim's claim that Western culture has become a disorganized dust of individuals who have been freed too much from all genuine social bonds. Martin Seligman argues that, as hedonistic islands adrift from a larger social support network, increasingly we have come to function as market pawns who closely resemble the commodities we are being conditioned to consume.[7] The trend toward all-consuming individualism is accompanied by a loss of personal control, as well as the emergence of what Seligman calls the *maximal California self*.

This California self is the ultimate expression of modern individualism in its most inward, narcissistic, self-centered, and self-serving form. To the California self, the primary reason for living is to make the right choices and to consume the right things in order to maximize pleasure and minimize pain and, in general, to get the most from life. Yet this identity structure operates at a distance from the stabilizing effect of the wider community. The California self succumbs easily to states of psychic disruption due to its lack of emotional commitment to the commons and an identity that places inordinate emphasis on personal and product outcomes.

Generally speaking, it is not difficult to understand why collectivism might be more friendly to mental health than individualism. In the Cook Islands, for example, one is quickly struck by a profound sense of belongingness that derives from their collectivist orientation.[8] Despite acculturative forces that may eventually erode their collective identities, their traditional social organization structures still exert a dominant influence on selfhood formation. It is interesting to note that no cases of homelessness have ever been documented in the Cook Islands. Members of this culture speak with pride about the "Cook Island family" and the way in which one never feels alone there. The overarching social embrace experienced by members of such a culture are certain to impede the psychopathology-proneness that seems to exist in the West.

Whereas individualism tends to be associated with mental ill health, it has been argued that there are different types of individualism and that some types may be less harmful psychologically than others. For instance, one can distinguish between alienating individualism and reciprocal individualism.[9] Alienating individualism, which is rooted in Calvinistic theology, is regarded as the type that exists in contemporary Western culture. It is associated with anxiety, loneliness, existential isolation, powerlessness, and compensatory egocentric preoccupation.

By contrast, reciprocal individualism involves a form of independence and self-reliance that remains tied to the goal of group harmony and concern with the welfare of the collective. As we have seen, the individualistic activities found in some non-Western cultures are acted out in the wider perception that the person is fused to, as well as responsible to, the community. Individualism of the reciprocal variety entails self-differentiation that is associated with high affiliation and with a social distancing process that entails a simultaneous relatedness. The community remains the person's center, rather than the person's becoming centered in himself or herself. This permits the unfolding of the individual's potentialities while he or she enjoys the benefits of a symbiotic connection to the wider community.

In *Habits of the Heart*, Robert Bellah refers to the radical individualism that exists today in the West, noting how it yields a disorienting nihilism that leaves people with a disturbing compulsion somehow to overcome "the emptiness of purely arbitrary values."[10] However, in trying to understand Western individualism, one must be careful not to suggest that the individualistic self lacks a cultural conditioning framework. It is true that the modern self is an adaptable, improvising, and malleable one that has less psychological grounding than in previous ages. But there is a functional aspect to the cultural practice of constructing identity as a constituency of self-investments. It makes possible an unprecedented degree of pragmatism that is not diluted by ingrained histories related to obligation, duty, and morality. The self is free to profit, and that capacity is the underlying all-pervasive cultural motivation that is absorbed by members: I profit; therefore I am. As a bundle of desire requiring utmost maneuverability of identity, the interchangeable feature of the modern self enables the person to stay dissociated from an enduring core, and that dissociation in turn allows it to manipulate better, and profit from, fluid and novel circumstances.

The free-floating nature of the modern self is consistent with the growing impression that one's fate is determined at all levels by market forces, rather than sources of power that reside in the social domain. This situation does not mean, however, that individuals are doomed to doubt and uncertainty. Most members are able to superimpose cognitive biases on market unpredictability in order to extract hope of winning as a result of favorable market movements. Beyond that, a certain solace can be forthcoming from the knowledge that one can tip the market odds in one's direction through acquired expertise or clever manipulations. This carries with it the positive illusion that market success could be converted eventually into greater social visibility and reward. However, the emotional attachments that can be made with the market are less sustaining than those that develop from a sociocentric milieu. Likewise, market support lacks many of the mental health advantages of social support, a rapidly disappearing facet of contemporary life.

Gergen's concept of the *pastiche* personality captures the notion of a self that is constantly adrift from any stable core. He defines this new creature as "a social chameleon, constantly borrowing bits and pieces of identity from whatever sources are available and constructing them as useful or desirable in a given situation."[11] The identity of the pastiche person is a thoroughly managed one wherein success is actually dependent upon avoidance of a true self. This type of self is provisional and pragmatic, pieced together in order to extract the full potential from any presenting set of circumstances. The person is deposed sufficiently from a deep abiding self that shame is not experienced as a result of inauthenticity and self-serving manipulation. True character loses its value as the person becomes an exercise in false advertising, and as life becomes a kaleidoscope of fleeting and ever-changing choices that feed one's developing appetites.

In this vein, Robert Jay Lifton uses the label the *protean self* to describe a modern self that is preeminently adaptable, with few of the traditional psychological moorings.[12] The fountainhead of this identity is the current condition of rapid flux, confusion, and restlessness. It also traces to a cultural environment where beliefs, partners, jobs, and residences change on a regular basis. Like the modern world itself, the protean self is inconstant, unpredictable, and unattached. This self structure allows short-term allegiances, but, when the need arises, the person can just as easily discard these and move on to the next set of demands. Proteans are even reluctant to forge a relationship with thoughts and ideas since those too may need to be modified on short notice.

Modernity has been compared to a type of psychological exile wherein individuals become metaphorical strangers as a result of detachment from overarching cultural schemas.[13] The loss of these schemas makes it more difficult to operate within a world of certitude, conviction, and truth. In the absence of adequate boundaries, the self also lacks the ordering capabilities that establish the foundation for personal potency. Many types of psychopathology can emerge when the boundaries of the self collapse, and when the person is left with insufficient structural integrity to experience inner mastery.

EPHEMERAL IDENTITY AND SELF-ABSOLVING MORALITY

The modern person is largely free from tradition, community, and shared macrounderstandings of the world. This freedom impacts upon our moral relationships, and in turn upon some important determinants of psychological well-being. As modernity continues to liberate the self from time-honored sources of definition, individual members find themselves unable to discern moral reference points beyond themselves.[14] The conflicts that fuel moral anxiety have been relocated to the private realm, and moral participation has become more arbitrary as a result of a depletion of external conformity motivators.

Throughout much of human history, moral anxiety served to ensure an adequate adherence to social restraints, while also unifying members in relation to agreed-upon taboos and ethical improprieties. Collective morality played an integral role in regulating integration into the community and establishing the basis of difference and hierarchy.[15] The idea of a "good" person was charged with social meaning, and moral anxiety itself was motivated by a connectedness to the group. Similarly, moral codes were extensions of larger social institutions and represented guidelines that held communal value.

By contrast, the moral center of the modern age has shifted to the individual, with ever smaller amounts of moral order being coordinated at the level of culture. The good person of today is one who is good at something, or good in the respect of being well equipped to succeed.[16] The once heralded act of doing the right thing has been superseded by having achievements that entail the right solutions and techniques. Unlike that in many traditional cultures where success was defined primarily in social terms, the new success story is a tale about private glories that, if well promoted, enjoy the additional satisfaction of distant applause.

Contemporary society is characterized by moral individualism, and in particular an amoral immediacy that uses the principles of mass consumption as moral placebos that serve private interests.[17] To facilitate this mechanism, social taboos have been dismantled. It is becoming difficult to identify activities, beliefs, or inclinations that raise social eyebrows. Through the demotion of the social conscience, individuals are now free to invent their own moral commandments in relation to their own perceived wishes, and to absolve themselves for infractions arising outside them.

The ascendancy of the personal conscience reflects a new dynamic in which individuals form moral contracts with themselves. Without the social mediation of morality, defining aspects of morally appropriate behavior have been equated with the act of being good to oneself. This is reinforced by the breakdown of morally meaningful relationships. Friendships have become largely symbolic, with the myth of their genuineness maintained mostly by a series of impression management strategies.

Exploitation of others no longer registers as a taboo infraction, but rather as a creative and morally neutral strategy that contributes to effective engineering of the alien external world. Inhabitants of this cultural milieu of self-justification have a very weak sense of service to community, or even to those who are perceived as friends. They attach moral significance to instant gratification, while remaining largely oblivious to moral satisfactions involving selflessness and social sacrifice. With a dearth of genuine social interest, even the most advantaged moderns have a tendency to regard themselves as somehow deprived, and deserving to be considered their own charity cases.

Moral tension is now roused when the individual betrays himself or herself and participates in enterprises that contravene the self-contract. This usually means that the person diagnoses an internal process that could prevent a result of maximal personal gain. But moral codes have come to subsist in an ambience of nearly total freedom, which releases the person to construct any moral order that is within the scope of imagination. Increasingly, morality consists of the moral deals that individuals make with themselves. Social image remains important, but the goal of being celebrated has been substituted for the former pressures to be good. The most celebrated of us are nearly free of moral obligation and moral misgiving, with that freedom being both a gift and an invitation to self-destruction.

Socialite tendencies of the past have given way to tendencies that entail attempts to make a favorable impression on oneself. This is a simple extension of the perception that my only real friend, and my most dreaded potential enemy, is myself. Modern immorality communicates itself to the individual as a variety of guilt that stems from self-disappointment and the letting down of oneself. In some cases, this can escalate to an angry self-condemnation that spills over into aggression displaced onto others.

With self-satisfaction as the new basis for moral evaluations, moderns have become removed from traditional goodness opportunities that historically have served as the basis for self-regard. The case has been made a number of times that being a good cultural member may be a universal human need that fosters security and well-being by informing the person of a legitimate place in the group and its survival practices. The ancient Aristotelian claim that one must be good in order to be happy rests on the related premise that life satisfaction and healthy-mindedness are dependent upon modes of moral action that transcend mere self-interest. When autonomous individuals rely chiefly on self-goodness prescriptions, they can become predisposed to self-concept impairments and existential anxiety, as well as a variety of disturbances that are manifestations of stunted identity development.

The forms of moral development that are conducive to mental health are contingent upon a perceptible social identity. The departure of morality from the social arena is a partial reflection of the capitalistic structures of Western modernity that replace virtue with instrumental rationality, profit motivation, and power accumulation.[18] Whereas profit-oriented capitalism offers a poor foundation for a legitimized moral cosmology, it has been speculated that a second modernity is about to revolutionize moral sentiment and give way to individualistic modes of compassion that are not reliant on a moral society.[19] The current trends toward asocial morality, and morality without community, also echo noteworthy changes that have unfolded in terms of the broad relationships between the individual and society.

SOCIETY, THE INDIVIDUAL, AND NEW PSYCHOLOGICAL DEFENSES

In premodern times, there was very little separation between the self and society. The social self was experienced as largely synonymous with the personal self, and that assumption rendered useless the entire concept of conformity. Idiosyncrasy, creativity, and eccentricity were rationed carefully in order to preserve social connectedness. Most members felt no need to choose between their own perspectives and those of the society since their world was formed primarily by means of a shared cultural reality. Automatic rebellion was not a conspicuous aspect of premodern cultures, which typically reproduced themselves over many generations with only small revisions. Within this format, a high degree of social restraint was imposed upon private urges that lacked this shared quality. However, modernity has exerted new sets of influences that have reduced the extent of overlap between society and its individual members, a development that has major implications for psychological defense strategies and overall mental health.

The transition in modern times from communitarianism to individualism, and from social character to private personality, has seen the self become its own governor of psychological defense. The loss of cultural coping strategies has lifted the importance of intrapsychic defenses and restricted access to madness techniques that offer patterned guidance of symptom formation and conflict resolution. Socially sanctioned religion once assimilated, and to a large degree normalized, the person's participation in adaptive symptom deployment. However, the retreat of the social and the religious has required alienated individuals to improvise psychological defenses without clear cultural guidance.

Shrinkage of the Social Unconscious

Early last century, Freud described the psychic tension that is generated as society pressures the repression and/or sublimation of drives that reside within the individual. In many respects, his theory embodied the premodern relationship between individual and society wherein a social unconscious functioned to minimize conflict and to ensure homogeneity. The concept of the social unconscious was originally proposed by Erich Fromm in order to explain the way in which culture channels collective energies for the sake of cognitive and behavioral synchronization. It has been elaborated upon in conjunction with the notion of social character, which refers to the shared personality profile of a culture. According to Fromm, the social unconscious is the specific mechanism responsible for the manufacture of the social character, and the means by which the content of consciousness is determined.[20] To understand this, one must recognize that the unconscious is largely a cultural product, or more specifically the result of a dynamic interaction between culture and the individual.

The social unconscious is meaningful in terms of our present discussion since it is the cultural technique used to constrict consciousness and to identify which possibilities should be repressed by members. Once possibilities are filtered out and coded as cultural taboos, the individual is distanced from desires and drives that are related to these taboos. Prior to modern times, the social unconscious was a crucial part of culture's strategy for reducing differences, maintaining control, and coordinating the learning of culture. Traditional monocultural societies had a large investment in the processes of inhibition and prohibition since these were the basis for integration, as well as effective coping made possible by a shared reality.

In a sense, the premodern social unconscious was the repository of those individual wants, thoughts, impulses, and desires that were collectively repressed as culture tried to impose restrictions for the purpose of consolidating a cultural identity, but modernity has initiated an entirely different survival strategy in which active attempts are made to reduce the size of the social unconscious, and thus to minimize the number of restrictions that are experienced by members. Moderns, who dwell in a world of vanishing barriers, have increasing difficulty making sense of rules or sanctions. They have little awareness of an authoritative center that has more credibility than their own random fancies.

The global amalgamation in which moderns find themselves has little utility for values that are tied to regulating cultural systems, so it tends to exonerate all private aspirations and ambitions. There is no longer much validity to the psychoanalytic premise that the inner person is forced into a compromise with the restrictions of society. Gone is the superego that once formed as morally conflicted individuals relinquished id impulses and internalized limitations toward the condition of psychic homeostasis. Instead, the modern age has realigned itself in relation to a rapid expansion of heterogeneity, as well as economic operating principles that beckon autonomous individuals to fabricate themselves with abandon, and with oblivion in regard to rules other than those that make for a zealous consumer. In this climate, moderns are restrained only by the limits of their tolerance for their own superficiality and social indifference.

The End of Repression as a Psychological Defense

Modern society has very little use for repression. In fact, there is almost nothing any longer that requires repression. The one major exception is the social nature of the human being, which represents a threat to the level of consumer motivation. In this regard, one price of modernity is the way in which it interferes with affiliation and sociality needs. But rather than a situation in which the real self is doomed to conflict with an oppressing society, modernity has established a self that copes by way of impulsivity rather than institutionality. To be oneself now means that one experiments actively with oneself, rather than being held hostage to rehearsed cultural myths that define expectation and potential. Even though exposed to new forms of ontological insecurity and disability, moderns can now draw on endless alternatives as they cast and recast their identities. Any former social hints about self-renunciation have been silenced by new strategies of enculturation through entertainment and overindulgence.[21] These are an extension of the wider postintellectual trend toward enculturation by banality designed to enlarge even further the perceived size of the consumer cosmos.

As impulsive consumers of possibilities, moderns do not necessarily develop any genuine individuality since they are products of standardization, derealization, and linearity. Yet they are able to navigate the open consumer expanse without conscious awareness of limitations beyond those that are monetary and technical in nature. Some of these limitations are ameliorated by new modes of cultural magic, most notably eulogized credit, that take one always closer to the satisfaction of one's full range of consumer appetites.

With social repression mostly out of the way, we have seen an eclipse of most conflicts between self and society. Instead, moderns encounter a new self-self type of conflict in which they themselves come to represent their only potential source of repression. They operate according to the motto "I owe it to myself" and engage in an inner battle in order to get the most out of themselves. Traditionally, the social roles assigned to members helped to identify the will of society and to proscribe the upper limits of self-attention and self-gratification. However, moderns no longer face threats related to infringements of society's will, but rather to threats associated with a deep fear that they might not be able to respond completely to their own will.

This has coincided with the decline of repression disorders and hysterical symptoms that were related etiologically to social sinning, and with the concomitant ascendancy of impulsivity-related symptoms that communicate the demise of temperance.

Supplanting a coordinated social strategy that regulates attention to inner impulses is a marketplace that supports itself by perpetual indoctrinations that foster a sense of personal entitlement. An important secondary process is the cultural manufacture of unwarranted self-esteem that increases the amount of entitlement the person will seriously entertain. Psychologists are gradually coming to recognize entitlement as one of the central defining characteristics of the modern psyche, and as one of the new social traits around which psychological symptoms are constructed.

Dysfunctional entitlement is now regarded as a key explanatory factor in certain types of self-absorption psychopathologies that appear to be on the increase today. This includes consumption disorders, personality disorders of the narcissistic and borderline variety, and a range of interpersonal pathologies that relate to imbalances of personal gain. Even the recent upsurgence of kleptomania in Western culture can be interpreted in relation to short-term gain strategies that are motivated by exorbitant levels of experienced entitlement. The problematic feature of this arrangement is the considerable risk of dejection, self-disappointment, and depression that arises when expectations and entitlements go unrealized, or when dedicated self-servicing does not translate into positive emotional outcomes.

Psychological defense is now under the jurisdiction of intrapsychic, rather than sociopsychic, forces. Just as life has come to be construed as a process of self-creation and self-actualization, the individual relies more and more on symbolic anxiety reducers that do not transcend the self. In former ages, the social "other" was the principal avenue by which coping was enacted. However, the new line of psychological defense for moderns are anxiety reducers that symbolically enhance the perceived capacity to achieve all that to which we are entitled as individuals. If it is still correct to speak of repression, it has to do with the renunciation of social connectedness and basic relatedness needs. For this reason, the new patterns of psychic defense prevent the modern from being fully distracted, and adequately pacified.

The chronic agitation of the modern person attests to defense mechanisms that do not engage sufficiently the essentially social requirements of psychological immunity. They are inward systems that offer little salvation from the multiplicity of stressors that accompanies contemporary life, and that particular lack explains in part the rash of internalization disorders (e.g., depression) that have appeared in recent decades. The social alienation that lies at the heart of the modern psychic defense also helps to explain the current rise of externalization disorders, which tend to revolve around flawed social communication, attachment deficiencies, and gross underdevelopment of social facilitation skills.

The problem of accessing cultural coping mechanisms makes modernity better suited to regression than to repression. As a defense, regression fosters emotional estrangement from the inner self, as well as a greater capacity for psychological bonding to primitive distracting consumer heroics. This combination has significant economic advantages but has spawned a society of easily undone members who are forced to search constantly for defenses that can perform in the absence of collective coping. The self-as-customer phenomenon, as well as the cultural fixation on youthfulness, are manifestations of new regressive tendencies that are facilitated by economic motives.

MODERNITY, CONSCIOUSNESS, AND EMOTION

As part of the retreat of the social, moderns have been less guided by the *feeling rules* that were readily available in premodern cultural designs. These are the socially sanctioned prescriptions that are made available to people in order to guide the expression of emotion along clearly defined pathways.[22] They constitute the emotion work of culture, which reflects the traditionally interactive nature of human emotion, as well as the way in which culture once regulated subjective experience as a means of avoiding dilemmas of emotional expression.

The cultural management of emotion that existed in former times permitted spontaneity in a variety of emotion-generating situations. At the same time, constraints were imposed on the emotional world through the deployment of shame, embarrassment, and other conformity-encouraging emotional warning systems. However, modern culture is organized around artificiality and the sale of images. The mutable emotions of its members act in close alliance with commercial unreality, while promoting the self as a marketable commodity. The selling of oneself is a lonely exercise in which the individual works within a context of disorienting emotional freedom in order to validate him/herself through creative experimentation. Self-promoters scan the full range of emotional possibilities in order to package themselves appropriately for the demands of specific circumstances.

Instead of emotions that are societally determined, circumspection and improvisation characterize the emotional experience of the modern person. Each separate individual hatches feeling rules on an as-needed basis; that is possible because private emotion projects are no longer the threat they once were in order-seeking and conformity-dependent societies. As the responsibility for enculturation has switched from the group to the individual/media level, emotions have undergone a commodification process that has allowed them to play a central role in the maximization of personal profit.[23] They have become consumables that, although not directly relational in nature, can be worn and discarded in the course of establishing a strategic dialogue with the world of others.

The fact that modern emotions lack a deep sociality offers a flexibility that would not be possible if emotions were socially regulated. The deregulation of emotion has coincided with the lowering of shame and embarrassment thresholds, which has eliminated impediments to the use of emotion for self-management and self-gratification purposes. Even though moderns are free to enlist limitless emotional options, the gamut of truly motivating emotions has been condensed into the experience of desire. Self-serving hedonism is a logical life-style choice when desire replaces other emotions, and when distracting consumption becomes the foremost escape mechanism of cultural members.

These developments can be understood as aspects of postemotionalism in which culture has come to rely on surface quasi feelings designed to enable emotionally eviscerated members to pursue consuming self-interest without civil considerations.[24] Emotional exchanges, as they have evolved in the post-other-directed era, have been purged of honesty in order to expedite the tour of a pleasant personality through the complexities of socially unsupported capitalism. Commodified emotions may be undersocialized and thus prone to anarchic repercussions, but they are a response to the general emotional ambivalence of modernity in which the task of emotional coping has been assigned to the individual.[25]

With the loss of social modes of emotional discipline and direction, the emotionally deregulated world of the modern is one in which whim easily achieves dominance. The ongoing use of emotion as a means by which to administer one's social veneer can create undesired consequences as one's whims collide with those of others. This aspect of postemotional culture has contributed to the rising rates of psychopathology that involve interpersonal impairments due to an insufficiency of emotional regulation. Ultimately, the reliance on readily dispensable quasi emotion fails to deliver on the inescapable need for self-validation. Social anxiety is also generated as ad-libbed emotional communication renders unpredictable the impact of its action.

The cultural abandonment of emotion has paved the way for the deeper experiences of deadness and flatness that are frequently described as the most fundamental emotional realities of the modern person. Such a situation is certain to occur when emotional control has been removed from its historical social context, and when emotion itself lacks sustaining qualities beyond its immediate pragmatic usefulness. It is not surprising, as will be seen later, that psychic deadness and other related existential disorders have been increasing steadily as modernity has transformed our relationship to our emotions.

By contrast to the institutional self, the alienated whimsical self has the chronic problem of emotional habituation that drains vitality and enthusiasm. In this regard, the postemotional age has made pathological boredom, as well as boredom-relieving self-destructiveness, into very pressing mental health concerns. The following words are spoken by an adolescent with "borderline" traits, but they are a telling treatise on the general background tone of modern emotional experience.

> I'm getting bored a lot now. I wonder if anyone would understand a person wanting to hurt themselves just to relieve the boredom. When I'm feeling physical pain it somehow proves my own existence and eases the deadening sameness. When I'm hurt I'm feeling something other than time moving. There's a lot of restlessness inside of me. Good or bad I want something to happen. I'm even willing to do something bad to make it happen.[26]

The transfer of emotion from culture to the individual has led to a paradoxical dimming of awareness of the emotions, and to a decline of the emotional self. Once again this is because emotional experience must be patterned at the level of culture before it can become stable and authentic, and also because the emotions have become a transient patchwork display that merely facilitates manipulation of the outside world. Thus, even though emotion is now more interiorized, it is also more alien and more external to the self. One important mental health consequence has been that emotional self-awareness no longer functions effectively as a psychic defense mechanism. Without sufficient emotional consciousness or emotional intelligence, moderns are impelled to cope by means of identifications with externalities contained in the material world, and in particular the offerings, signals, and signs of consumer society.

The evolution of consumer consciousness has unfolded in the context of self-regulated emotions, which is one facet of the more general process whereby modernity has externalized consciousness itself. Externalized consciousness has been described as "a shift from an internal matrix of intrapersonal-interpersonal-impersonal consciousness to a predominantly impersonal consciousness as manifested by a preoccupation with the external world of material phenomena."[27] The essentially impersonal and asocial nature of externalized consciousness has seen moderns retreat from collaborative construals of the world.

As with emotion, consciousness has gravitated toward an internal locus of control that does not much avail itself of cultural guidance and sanctioning. But, again like emotion, consciousness has crystallized itself on extraneous vagaries that actually diminish consciousness of internal processes and that limit their potency as coping devices. Stephen DeBerry mentions some of the specific ways in which externalized consciousness expresses and locates itself in modern consumer society.[28] These include alignment with greed and acquisition motivations, superficial idealization of consumer heroes and celebrities, attention to externally manufactured needs and desires, precedence of physical appearance over inner values, commodified social relations, frenzied consumption, and the entertainment of unreality.

Among the mental health consequences of externalized consciousness are heightened propensities toward narcissism, alienation, intimacy problems, meaning-related disorientations, affective communication impairments, fetishistic attachments to material objects, reality confusion, and self-knowledge gaps. As individuals who have come to relate to emotion and consciousness as exchangeable commodities, moderns have become distanced from the communal operations that historically have immunized members from a range of psychopathologies. The next chapter explores what has happened to some age-old mental health prophylactics as a consequence of the commodification of culture and the launch of consumer consciousness.

CHAPTER 3

Materialism, Consumption, and Mental Health

Consumption has forged intimate links with modernity itself. Institutions, governments, and organizational bodies have come to operate in tandem with the operating principles of consumption. The experience of the modern is in many ways synonymous with the practice and experience of consumption. Human culture has been overtaken by economic forces that have become the central determinants of personality traits and madness techniques. It is becoming increasingly accurate to speak in terms of the *economic construction of reality*, rather than the cultural construction of reality.

One cannot overestimate the reach of consumerism as it penetrates all aspects of our lives. It has been synthesized into a macroscopic socioexistential orientation that plays a decisive role in shaping our values, meaning systems, relationships, political leanings, goals, life-style arrangements, and daily routines.[1] Consumerism has become a total way of life in the West, and the primary means by which members interpret the human and physical world. Unlike religion, which dominated consciousness in premodern times, consumerism now exists as the main mode of cultural reproduction.

As a cultural process, consumption has been described as an order of signification that exists in a world wherein objects are a primary means of symbolic communication.[2] Over time, consumer objects come to acquire social meanings, and to have certain cultural codes attached to them. They become social signifiers that are employed to differentiate cultural participants. Consumers participate in a host of symbolic actions in order to amplify the object meanings available to them. As this transpires, personal consumption becomes the new, albeit alienated, vehicle by which individuals find their place in public life.[3]

Modern consciousness is an undifferentiated kaleidoscope of consumer images and choices that must somehow be employed in order to establish a basis for identity and self-evaluation. In the "all-consuming society," as it has been termed, the general process of consumption has become for members a way of being themselves, but one that demands constant renewal since consumption-based modes are quickly spent.[4] Despite the general formlessness of consumption as a cognitive search engine for meaning and design, it has nonetheless been anointed with prodigious value for its preeminent role in cultural survival. This is so much the case that superfluity and banality have become legitimate components of modern understandings of the self and the world.[5]

The current triumph of the superfluous differs from the situation during early capitalism when selective consumers still maintained an identity that was circumscribed more widely than that of self-as-consumer. In more recent times, consumption has come under the control of prodigious industrial forces that manufacture, organize, and manipulate desires, as well as the consumption patterns that satisfy those desires.[6] The satisfactions associated with many types of consumption have deviated so far from real sources of need that they are best understood as a type of irrational sensuality that has been stripped of all profanity in the vague hope that it can continue to generate excitement.[7] Yet, even though needless consumption has been purified of its associations with repulsiveness and vulgarity, the use of consumption as society's primary organizing principle has a number of ramifications for mental health and general well-being.

CONSUMPTION AND UNHAPPY CONSCIOUSNESS

In his book *Escape from Evil*, Ernest Becker describes modern consumerism as a second-rate religion and adds that "today we are living with a grotesque spectacle of unrestrained material production, perhaps the greatest and most pervasive evil to have emerged in all of history."[8] He goes on to denigrate consumerism as an aberrant pathway to cultural heroism that is highly destructive to psychosocial well-being, yet there is little doubt that unbounded consumption is quickly becoming the basis for heroics in the whole of the global community.

No one would disagree that consumer culture has made essential goods more affordable and accessible to its members. Endless consumable objects and services of every description make tasks more convenient, while creating the potential to enjoy free time. Frequently, the time that is liberated by our many time-saving offerings is used for additional money earning. This tends to erase the life advantages offered by consumables, but at least the option exists to exploit the fruits of consumer culture, and to live more varyingly and leisurely than people of any former age.

Despite such benefits, there is a good deal of evidence that the evolution of consumer culture constitutes a development that is antagonistic to aspects of the human psyche. The cultural celebration of the object has imprinted members onto the material world and thereby distanced them from the deeper timeless plane of existence. Life can become an uninspiring search for solutions to one's artificial tensions and false needs, which is more likely to foster ennui and dullness rather than happiness. Style, rather than character development, becomes the end goal of personality. In the "dream factory of endless consumption," as Jerome Braun writes in relation to modern social pathology, character traits such as thoughtfulness, compassion, and wisdom receive little recognition since they do not contribute significantly to economic productivity.[9] Instead, modern economic and cultural structures are better suited to those who can maintain a supply of consumable escapism and titillation within a context of declining social continuity and hedonistic self-gratification.

Consumerism has substituted homogenous elements for all the important dimensions of life, including work, leisure, nature, and culture itself.[10] There is also an unreal and fleeting quality to the objects that populate our world. In the past, objects were considered desirable if they were well made and durable, and if they could be employed as a useful part of our everyday lives. But durability and quality have been superseded by fashionability, which sustains the overall cultural enterprise of unremitting craving and perpetual consumption.[11]

The concept of consumer confidence has become a core measure of economic well-being. At the level of the individual, consumer confidence is experienced as a generalized sensation that life, as a process of absorption, is going according to plan. But although consumption is promoted as the new pathway to redemption, there are few guidelines available to modern-day consumers. A disturbing gap has been created between the object of consumption and the images that have been promoted in relation to that object.[12] In the absence of meaningful guidelines, consumers can fall prey to disappointment, disillusionment, and insecurity.

Institutionalized overconsumption has been blamed for an "unhappy consciousness" that has emerged in modern consumer culture.[13] One reason for this is that the goods and services that dominate our cognitive worlds have become loose abstractions that are uncoupled from their original intentions. The free-market consumer is psychologically manufactured in order to abandon tradition in favor of a contest with discontent. Other psychological and spiritual coordinates fade into the background, leaving the person vulnerable to distortion and unreality.

Immersion into the realm of consumer symbols fuses people to a relentless series of externalities that cause a self-estrangement that cannot be remedied with a prescription for continued self-indulgence. The outcome is a type of "consumer vertigo" wherein a disintegrated social reality has been replaced by an intense inquisitiveness about the offerings of the consumer world.[14] In the end, we no longer possess the ability to recognize ourselves except as a fluid identity that forms and reforms over the course of endless consumer trials.

Consumer consciousness has made identity formation part of an agreement in which culture endorses a type of free trade within the self. One can experiment in a random way with transient personalities that can be gleaned from the pool of consumer symbols. This has had the effect of legitimizing cyclothymic traits wherein the person alternates erratically between differing mood states and presentation styles. Extravagant degrees of caprice can now be rationalized in terms of creative exploitation of consumer potential. The fact that consumer identities do not congeal into a meaningful totality causes the experimental personality to seek integrity by way of external definitions related to consumer reality. As identity becomes another object of consumption, consumer themes such as quantity and excess come to play a bigger role in maintaining adequate identity structure.

EXCESS, BORROWED HEROICS, AND NEGATIVE OUTER MODERNITY

Homo consumens attaches considerable meaning to the sheer volume of consumption. The actual concept of excess has taken on new and refined meanings. It used to convey the notion of redundancy and uselessness with regard to the elements that exceeded some measure of requirement. The active pursuit of excess was once framed as a moral decision that was potentially offensive on the basis of waste, indirect deprivation of others, or social codes about the virtuous nature of conservation. But consumer culture has introduced a revised social dynamics that sanctions insatiability and honors the unappeasable person as an ideal citizen.[15] At the same time, the prospect of excess rekindles the hopes that were once derivable from commitments to the human world.

This new ideal citizen can compensate for inner vacuity with high degrees of excess that signal successful cultural participation. The social message that one has attained comfort and contentment has lost its potency and has been supplanted by the need to surround oneself with consumer trophies that blazon one's achievement of excess. The trophies that disclose consumer mastery increasingly are ones that convey technological chic and modishness. The consumption of new technology is quickly becoming the primary stage upon which consumers champion themselves.

No moral condemnations are forthcoming even if the quest for excess has only the effect of further amplifying greed and avarice. The brief reign of conservation mindedness has been silenced by cultural motives that have banished almost entirely the dated idea of "too much." In order to facilitate the mentality of excess, members have had to be conditioned in order to want, but not to pause when wants are threatened by satisfaction. Some early theories of personality espoused the view that human beings, by their nature, go on to satisfy the full range of their higher needs once they have met their basic ones. But current enculturation plans allow members to remain needy regardless of the amount of consumption and accumulation that has taken place. Modern modes of consumption are almost entirely unrelated to a sense of satisfaction; that means that members are never liberated from low-level discontents.

The perceived need for excess interacts with constant frustration in order to elevate the demand for financial resources. It has been estimated that the life-style to which people aspire has become twice as expensive as it was less than two decades ago.[16] The cost of this dream has now risen to more than double the average income of American households. This means that a large and widening gulf is developing between actual income and consumer aspirations. This is reflected in the dissatisfaction that is experienced with regard to people's incomes.

In a 1998 American survey, 85 percent of respondents reported that a "six-figure" income would be required in order to service their yearned-for life-style.[17] Only 15 percent of those surveyed stated that they would be contented with "living a comfortable life." Even high-income earners felt that their material needs were unmet. Of those earning between $50,000 and $100,000, over 40 percent reported, "I cannot afford to buy everything I really need." At incomes above $100,000, there were still 27 percent who felt themselves financially incapable of funding their basic needs.

In the United States, the saving rate has dropped to below zero, demonstrating the determination of consumers to procure unaffordable life-styles. The discrepancy between income and consumer desire has smoothed the way for an all-pervasive credit industry that enables members to entertain the illusion that they have greater consumer potency than their finances would otherwise dictate.

Media socialization has jollified indebtedness, and consumer consciousness has been endowed with a magical thinking format that gives a mystical feel to the act of exercising credit. The magical properties of new age indoctrinations of credit are easily revealed during interviews with heavily indebted credit users. Many of them report that it never occurred to them that the exercise of credit involved any sort of repayment requirements. The psychodynamics of credit entails an irrational *hyperbolic discounting*, a term used by economists to describe how future consequences are disregarded in favor of immediate gratification.

Rather than an announcement of financial ineptitude, credit has become to the hyperbolic consumer an intrapsychic currency that reassures people that they are worthwhile members of society. It symbolizes choice, opportunity, power, and solvency. A lack of credit has become a recently circumscribed infirmity that diminishes self-respect and fuels a sense of social abandonment. In trying to rebuild lost credit, people are aiming to restore their credibility as consumers who have at least some capability of enjoying excess, and thus of being somebody. It is therefore not surprising that economic prosperity and rising wages only serve to increase consumer debt.

Consumer debt in America continues to set new records, as nearly 20 percent of household income currently goes toward the servicing of debt. At the end of 1997, total household debt in the United States stood at $5.5 trillion, and it has been on the rise since then. Credit card debt more than doubled in the past 1990s. This general situation would be perceived as a sign of serious social pathology were it not for the positive cultural connotations that have been attached to credit. The enhanced social status of credit-mindedness has masked the emotional stress and interpersonal turmoil that are often the result of debt life-styles.

Excess that is achieved by way of credit differs from a real circumstance of excess. In fact, credit consumption has the opposite result since regular interest payments siphon off part of the person's spending power. Debt also makes the person more vulnerable to total financial insolvency. Bankruptcies are running at nearly 1.5 million annually in the United States. Yet a credit mentality engages a type of psychology in which the individual experiences credit as an honorable methodology for alleviating the pain that is imagined with regard to waiting. Consumer culture has transformed waiting into a shameful limbo that can only be escaped with sufficient quantities of credit. Therefore, credit transports consumers ahead in time and makes them acceptable *now*.

Thornton Wilder, in *The Bridge of San Luis Rey*, describes a detestable group of people who are "drunk with self-gazing and in dread of all appeals that might interrupt their long communion with their own desires."[18] This description captures quite well modern consumers' forsaken journey through unremitting longing and petition. One way in which this might contribute to unhappy consciousness is related to the physical and emotional demands of greed. Another has to do with the stunting of motivations that could promote growth, creativity, and elevated awareness. Still another potential pitfall comes to light in terms of the old adage "After intercourse the animal is sad," which refers to the existential deflation that derives from the loss of anticipation as the basis for motivation. Continual realization of targeted objects of desire results in an emotional void that is experienced as failure because of the persistence of emptiness that mocks all attempts at satisfaction.

In a classic essay, Philip Cushman wrote about the "empty self" as the identity structure that is fostered by prevailing cultural dispositions.[19] That is, people tend to have a view of themselves as empty entities that require filling. The growing profusion of services, possessions, comforts, and extravagances that are becoming available to the middle-class majority do not mitigàte people's experience of themselves as empty. Consequently, their behavior is geared toward actions that involve consumption, or taking in, so this empty self can be filled. But people become more and more desperate as they seek to resolve their emptiness. This empty identity is permanent; therefore, the person never experiences the self as full, or fulfilled. Thus an ongoing life-style develops whereby the person feels compelled on a continuous basis to nourish the self.

A negative outer modernity has been described in relation to the exaltation of consumption and materialistic motivations.[20] This refers to a mode of modernity in which cultural members restrict themselves to the realm of *materially purposeful* thought and action that is, in turn, tied to the economic aspirations of infinite productivity and unfettered consumption. Such cognitive shaping is at the other end of the continuum from that envisioned by the Buddha in his enlightened society. There, great emphasis was placed on all sorts of materially useless pursuits, including peacefulness, social harmony, understanding, freedom through selflessness, reflection on the essential nature of reality, the cultivation of positive emotion, and liberation from artificial worldly desire.

In some ways, Buddha's enlightened society was considerably more modern than today's society in that it recognized a need for *being*, which was far more advantageous to psychological well-being than desire and material imploration. To achieve a state of being is to become fully alive and to experience a genuine relatedness to oneself and the world. As the modern world gravitates increasingly toward materialistic ways of comprehending reality, one sees fewer and fewer signs of joyous living that is achieved by way of being.

It is interesting to hear about people who have enjoyed deeply satisfying lives by enabling themselves simply to be. For example, Robert Thurman writes about his years of training to be a Buddhist monk.[21] By his account, he owned nothing at that point in his life, other than the modest clothes on his back. He spent no money on consumer goods, watched no television, and never listened to music. Thurman gave not a thought to cars, houses, career, competition, money, or fashion. Yet he recalls existing in a rich orgasmiclike state of being that was suffused with inner well-being and enormous excitement. By making himself poor and small, he had made possible the greatest contentment he had ever experienced. Eastern thinkers have long known the inner peace that is made possible by overcoming the ego. In an opposite way, the outer modernity of Western culture has the effect of maximizing ego in order to lead people down the path of consumption more easily.

Contemporary modes of capitalism flourish on ego inflation that is activated by consumer involvement in response to need vexation. Consumption has been so accepted as a remedy and guide for living that we no longer even flinch when we are referred to, both individually and collectively, as consumers. Little skepticism is generated by politicians who designate *consumption growth* as a measure of social and economic prosperity. The traits of materialism, greed, and unbridled consumption are so ingrained that it is impossible for us to comprehend cultures that are not structured in this way, yet some governments, in a preemptive strike against the commercialization of children, have begun to enlist regulatory legislation. For instance, in Sweden and Quebec, advertising aimed at children under the age of 12 has been banned. It will be enlightening to follow the results of such measures to see whether they can prevent consumption from becoming an illness.

PSYCHOLOGICAL EFFECTS OF MATERIALISM

Materialism has been defined as "a cultural system in which material interests are not made subservient to other social goals and in which material self-interest is preeminent."[22] It refers to the degree of importance that a person attaches to possessions, and the extent to which consumption becomes the primary source of satisfaction, as well as the dominant mode of motivation. One reason to suspect that materialism may not be entirely conducive to psychological well-being concerns the relationship between materialistic consumption and discontent.

Whereas initial consumption can create the experience of pleasure, the phenomenon of adaptation soon ensures that the pleasurable sensations become neutralized.[23] Satisfied desires are automatically replaced by new ones that demand attention, but it does not take long before the object of consumption fails to offer any sort of thrill, and that again speaks of the "sadness after intercourse" effect. The consumer encounters confusion when the act of consumption does not deliver the expected pleasure and happiness. Even young children can be affected by an agitated bewilderment that stems from this breach between heightened anticipation and actual experience as it relates to consumption.

A different situation exists among the poor, who lack the means to act upon much of their consumer desire. They often experience the frustrating awareness that their extreme financial constraints are somehow blocking access to socially defined pathways to happiness. This idea often combines with feelings of inadequacy related to their knowledge that they have fallen short with regard to the definitions of success acknowledged in consumer society. Consumption sometimes becomes an obsession for such people, and it is not uncommon to see them neglect basics and essentials in order to squander money on highly visible objects loaded with consumer prestige. Debilitating debt can be one of several negative effects of this form of compensatory consumption.

The interworkings of materialism, desire, and discontent constitute the backbone of the current system of capitalistic economics.[24] Economic growth is stimulated as powerful cultural suggestions are disseminated, via the media, in order to lock in motivation toward impossible ideals and images. With further consumption as the solution to the inevitable discontent stemming from the overall process, the economic system grows and becomes more robust. The malcontents who function as the cogs usually continue to cooperate even if they perceive the ways in which they are being manipulated, or the many other costs that are involved, including environmental degradation and impaired relationships.

On the subject of interpersonal relationships, research has demonstrated that materialism is associated with self-centeredness and a loss of concern for others.[25] In one study, participants were presented with a hypothetical situation in which they had been unexpectedly given $20,000. Then they were asked a series of questions with regard to how they would use that money. Those high on materialism reported that they would spend three times more on themselves than the low-materialism respondents reported. They also said that they would contribute significantly less to charitable organizations and give less to family and friends than their low materialism counterparts. Also administered was a Nongenerosity Scale, which measured lack of generosity with possessions and nonmonetary resources. Similarly to other aspects of their study, a strong correlation was found between materialism and nongenerosity.

Another feature of this study is worth mentioning here. When questioned about their values, those high on materialism were far less likely than low-materialism respondents to say that they valued "warm relationships with others." Curiously, although more self-centered in general, those high on materialism placed less value on self-respect than low- materialism respondents. Maybe materialistic pursuits are facilitated when one ignores not only other people, but key aspects of oneself as well.

For some time, social analysts have been aware that materialistic cravings have the effect of creating life-style complications and imbalances that interfere with the quality of relationships. A number of them have recommended measures to turn our attention away from distracting materialistic cravings and to reacquaint us with our fellow human beings. For example, the notion of "voluntary simplicity" has been proposed as a chosen life-style orientation aimed at enhancing the quality of life by reducing the complexities that are invited by acquisitive materialism.[26]

A significant proportion of people today seem to be conscious of the superfluous nature of their consumption activities, as well as the unnecessary stresses they suffer in order to pursue materialistic objectives. A variety of surveys confirm that upward of 50 percent of people would, in principle, be willing to reduce material possessions, as well as income, in exchange for reduced stress and better relationships with family and friends. The fact that they do not act upon these feelings may be related to the therapeutic role that consumption has adopted. Nearly two-thirds of Americans report that they use shopping as a stress reliever. Only television watching and telephone talking rate as more effective in terms of stress reduction. Consumption has also acquired a social dimension that is the source of positive emotion and mutual support, however meager, for many people. Thus life-style simplifications that curtail consumption may represent a perceived threat to coping ability.

Originally, voluntary simplicity was conceptualized as a means by which to increase spiritual fulfillment by challenging clutter as the chief purpose of life. As a method of deliberate simplification, it involved a partial restraint of some superficial aspects of daily life in order that greater abundance could be achieved in more meaningful areas, including that of interpersonal relationships. More recently, the concept of voluntary simplicity has been approached more generically, defined as "a lifestyle intended to maximize direct control over daily activities and to minimize consumption and dependency."[27]

A similar orientation was preached by E. F. Schumacher, who celebrated voluntary simplcity as "a lifestyle which accords to material things their proper and legitimate place which is secondary and not primary."[28] Since this is a voluntary life-style, it does not apply to individuals who, out of necessity, live simply. Rather, the person has the means to live more luxuriously but for some reason has decided to reduce complexity.

One of the latest countertrends to materialism is the "simplicity circle," which consists of a small group of concerned people who support each other in the deliberate attempt to control consumption and to refocus life in terms of community, connection, and creativity. The Center for a New American Dream has an Internet website (www.newdream.org) that assists in the formation of simplicity circles and puts interested parties in touch with one another. Since the first simplicity circle appeared in Seattle in 1992, more than a thousand such groups have been formed in the United States, Canada, Europe, Australia, and New Zealand.

Yet, despite these and other attempts to encourage people to curb materialism, modernity has seen an ongoing escalation of this motivational orientation. As a reflection of this, the amount that people consume continues to increase at a rapid rate, even in the face of warnings about ecological destruction, resource depletion, waste management quandaries, and so forth. The amount we want has far outgrown the amount we need, and the size of the gap between want and need continues to grow. The persuasive associations that have been established among consumption, progress, and happiness will accelerate even further the release of consumption from the psychological constraints of need and necessity.

Although the trend toward consumption as an end in itself has many species-level implications, we must also comprehend this trend in terms of its mental health consequences. Some have argued that not all types of consumption are the same with regard to their impact on psychological well-being. For example, distinction has been made between instrumental consumption and terminal consumption.[29] The more benign of these is thought to be instrumental materialism, since this type serves a higher purpose, such as self-discovery, personal growth, attainment of higher goals, or furthering of human life. In the more dangerous terminal materialism, the ultimate goal of consumption is possession itself. Unfortunately, from a research standpoint, it has been very difficult to agree on criteria that can separate good and bad forms of materialism. Thus most studies in this area have approached materialism as a more general construct, without a simplistic imposition of value judgments.

Marsha Richins summarizes research showing that materialism is increasing at a rather sharp rate. For example, one study of high school seniors assessed the importance of having "at least two cars." In 1976, 40 percent said that this was very important; by 1986, this percentage had risen to 63 percent.[30] This study found similar increases when students were asked about the importance of having the latest fashion in clothes, a top-of-the line stereo, a summer house, and so forth. A different study asked adults whether or not having "a lot of money" was one of the main things they wanted out of life. In 1975, 38 percent wanted a lot of money; by 1988 this had risen to 62 percent. This pattern explains in part why psychologists and psychiatrists are encountering an increasing number of patients who are best diagnosed as suffering from money fetishes.

Some recent studies paint a fairly clear picture of the relationship between materialism and happiness. Russell Belk looked specifically at the relationship while measuring both variables in 338 subjects from five different pools (business students, secretaries in an insurance office, fraternity members, machine shop workers, and students at a religious institute). A significant negative correlation was found between materialism and happiness, leading Belk to conclude that "more materialistic people tend to be less happy in life."[31] But one cannot assume automatically that materialism per se is causing people to become unhappy. Another possibility is that already unhappy people turn to materialism in an attempt to achieve happiness. After all, materialism is the most prominent cultural suggestion, so it follows that some unhappy people would attribute their unhappiness to a deficiency of material success.

Other revealing research by Marsha Richins and Scott Dawson highlights the relationship between materialism and various aspects of life satisfaction.[32] They found that, as the degree of materialism increased, the amount of satisfaction with "life as a whole" decreased. They also found that higher levels of materialism result in reduced satisfaction with friendships and with leisure activities. Materialism was also associated with increased amounts of envy, a greater dissatisfaction with one's overall lot in life, and impaired self-esteem.

Taken together, the available research in this area indicates that a materialistic orientation has primarily negative effects on mental health. If this cultural theme is to be on the agenda of future mental health workers, it would be useful to study variations with regard to this trait. Of special interest should be those members who appear to be partially resistant to the cultural cognitions that underlie materialistic yearning and consumption-driven life-styles. It is still possible to locate individuals and families who organize their lives in noneconomic ways. They are worthy of our attention and study since they may hold the key for future social change. At the moment, however, we should not underestimate the hold that materialism has on members of our consumption-driven culture. Especially worrying is the rash of new pathologies that can be traced to consciousness patterns and general ontologies that are organized around consumption.

CONSUMPTION DISORDERS

The past two decades have seen a sharp increase in what has come to be known as *consumption disorders*. This category of psychopathology is still poorly understood, and investigators are just beginning to conduct research aimed at illuminating the causes. In fact, the literature on this subject dates back only to the late 1980s. In 1989, compulsive buying was identified as a type of consumption disorder that was becoming more prevalent in contemporary culture.[33] At that time, it was pointed out that numerous negative consequences stem from this type of disturbance, such as crippling debt, self-hate, and family disruption. Various research studies show that between 2 percent and 6 percent of Americans are beset by compulsive buying/spending.[34] This equates to between 6 and 15 million people. Research has found that upward of 15 percent of university-aged individuals either have this disorder or are at high risk of developing it.

Not all of the consumption pathologies involve symptoms that are directly related to material objects or money. For example, compulsive sexuality, binge eating, pathological gambling, and kleptomania have also been described as consumption disorders. There are commonalities in these various patterns of disturbance that are becoming the basis for a general theory of compulsive consumption.[35]

In defining compulsive consumption, reference is usually made to the uncontrollable drive to acquire, use, or experience an object, activity, or substance. Mention is also made of the highly repetitive nature of this symptom pattern, which has the eventual consequence of creating problems of varying degrees for the person and/or other people. It is generally accepted that the primary incentive does not lie in the practical or economic value of whatever is being consumed. Research confirms that possessiveness is not the foremost motive for compulsive consumption, and also that compulsive buyers experience no more desire to own things than other consumers.[36] In fact, many compulsive buyers pay very little attention to the object that is being purchased, and some cannot even remember what they bought. It is not uncommon to hear compulsive buyers describe their behavior as automatic and trancelike.

Factors that are more closely related to the genesis of this disorder include an impaired sense of self, personal powerlessness, social alienation, and feelings of cultural inadequacy. In many cases, this is magnified by a deficit in the ability to delay gratification and/or by high levels of cultural and media suggestibility that culminate in a stronger materialistic orientation. The rise of consumption disorders can also be understood as a consequence of diminished social continuity, and of the new place of consumption in the identity formation process. As the locus of need departs the human sphere and reemerges as idiosyncratic wish and fantasy, sometimes the person's only recourse for emotional reattachment is repetitive enactment of the consumer actions that have a superstitious link to wish and fantasy fulfillment.

Special attention has been paid to the integrity of the family as a factor that might help to explain the dramatic upsurgence of compulsive consumption. Research has found, for example, that children in disrupted families are more materialistic and more likely to develop disorders involving compulsive consumption.[37] The fact that upward of half of today's children are growing up in varying types of family disruption speaks in support of this factor as one important determinant of compulsive consumption.

Family disruption may contribute to the development of compulsive consumption in a number of ways. As families lose cohesion, they begin to fail as socialization mechanisms. The disorientation that this produces can increase the importance of consumer socialization, which in turn exaggerates the salience of one's relationship to consumables. Disruptions in family life can also cause members to employ possessions as surrogates for unsatisfying relationships, to the extent that these become the dominant "other." The ritualistic benefits of repetitive consumption can also assuage temporarily the stress that is propagated by family disharmony. When parental conflicts and inadequacies are at the heart of the disruptions, parents sometimes encourage consumer-mindedness in their children by arranging greater consumption opportunities for them. This practice fosters an outlook that equates affection, and emotional coping generally, with consumption.

The previously mentioned concept of the empty self helps us to comprehend the rise of all types of consumption disorders. As the self becomes empty, people try to fill the void with any means available to them. In this regard, consumption has become the preconscious mechanism whereby we compensate for a self that has been depleted. Since buying is such an all-pervasive cultural theme, it is to be expected that many members would turn to buying in order to remedy the experience of self-emptiness. But we could also expect that many types of consumption could be used in the futile attempt to fill the empty self.

In the course of outlining the evolution of the empty self, Cushman wrote that contemporary culture has configured the self in a way that makes members excessively vulnerable to the negative aspects of consumerism. His concern even led him to call for cultural and sociopolitical changes that could reconfigure the self in order to bring about less emptiness. Unless that happens, we will continue to see pathological utilizations of consumption. Cushman was especially worried about the consumption of drugs as a solution to the empty self. He saw how consumer culture communicates, especially by way of the media, the message that consumption is the ideal method by which to fill the empty self. People come to believe that consumption has the power to transform them and make them complete. Unfortunately, an increasing number have become convinced that the consumption of drugs has the same restorative ability. Drugs are also a commodity that can be employed as a passive means by which to consume one's way out of conflict, worry, insecurity, and emotional pain. More will be said later about substance abuse when we examine the inability of modern consumer culture to provide the necessary type and degree of reality regulation.

Time magazine declared 1980 the "Year of the Binge and Purge." Without question, binge eating has become another popular technique by which to contend with the problem of the empty self. A high degree of overlap has been reported between compulsive buying and binge eating, as compulsive buyers are more likely than other consumers to engage in binge eating.[38] Research also shows that women with binge eating disorders have greater inclinations toward compulsive buying than normal eaters. The fact that both of these problems are more common in women has been explained in terms of current socialization practices: women are rewarded, praised, and taught to derive pleasure from shopping and from activities related to food and body size regulation. However, growing numbers of men are also resorting to binge eating and compulsive buying.

A number of other consumption disorders have come to revolve around the body, which has taken on a large amount of symbolic significance in consumer society. In addition to those entailing food intake, disorders that involve compulsive efforts to achieve the hard body have arisen. It appears that during times of social crisis and disintegration the body has a tendency to emerge as a metaphor for cohesion, harmony, and control.[39] The body can be used as a vehicle by which to rejuvenate a sense of self when identity is threatened. Recently the hard body has come to represent not only a means to control, but a psychic shield that defends against the maladies and strictures of modern life.[40] Aspirations toward physical perfection in general have the additional function of gesticulating to a public world that is experienced by the aspirant as inaccessible and unresponsive.

MODERN ECONOMICS, UNREALITY, AND MENTAL HEALTH

Economic motives have become a dominant force in the shaping of the modern personality. Those that prevail today are continual growth, expansion, greed, and mass-produced desire. The traits promoted by different economic systems depend on the specific design and content of the economic models themselves. It follows that some economic arrangements will be more conducive than others to emotional and psychological well-being.

In assigning the social with an inferior status, the current economic era has promoted the lone, greedy, profitable, and economically rational being.[41] Profit is such a central theme in the modern economy that it has become the primary criterion for business competence. Indeed, profit has overshadowed all other economic motives. Enormously powerful lobby groups have emerged in all major segments of the economy to ensure that profits remain at a maximum. Even when the product is conspicuously harmful to human beings, such groups continue to concentrate on profits and almost nothing else. From time to time, we hear talk of ethical and moral considerations that guide some activities, but these too can usually be traced to a profit motive.

Throughout human history, the economy of a culture was much more closely linked to the human domain. It bore hallmarks of the full gamut of human needs, in addition to the short-term gain of a small number of providers. In premodern times, economies entailed a great deal more than profitable financial transactions since they blended intimately with the total way of life. However, there has been a dramatic breakdown in the human side of economics. The emotional ties between buyer and seller have disappeared, leaving only utilitarian niceties. The indifferent and calculating quality of the modern economic system is historically atypical, not only from the perspectives of human beings but also in terms of the economy itself.

Contemporary economic strategies sever attachments to self, community, and earth, with fragmentation and alienation as predictable consequences.[42] Economically generated detachments often take the form of unreality scripts that have considerable emotive appeal and unconscious credibility. A recent television advertisement for men's underwear boasted, "I've got something for your mind, your body, and your soul." Although we can readily see how underwear is for the body, what does it have to do with our minds and souls? This advertisement is one of an endless number of ways that the manufacture of unreality is being cultivated in order to manipulate perceptions, tastes, and consumption patterns.

The propaganda that manipulates our tastes leaves its audience with a subtle fear of rejection. With enough exposures, they come to feel that they as people are inadequate if their tastes do not correspond to those being celebrated for sale. In order to quell an irrational fear of abandonment, the people targeted in this way fall into line, convincing themselves that these marketed tastes are their own.

Another way that the modern economic system sustains itself is by concocting the erroneous experience of material deprivation. Advertising is a crucial aspect of the cognitive socialization that generates illusory deprivation. Many advertisements are designed with the specific goal of fostering an experience of inadequacy that can only be solved through the purchase of the specified product. Children as young as 2 and 3 years of age have begun to feel deprived if they do not have certain brands of clothing or toys. By 6 or 7 years of age, children's sense of deprivation is so intense that their entire reality becomes commercialized and commodified as a solution to their counterfeit impoverishment.

Certain defenders of the advertising industry have claimed that critics of advertising are guilty of elitism and the false assumption that consumers are basically irrational and easily guided by external forces.[43] The reasoning is that human beings are more thinking and more volitional than they are usually given credit for. Thus, if people abandon themselves wholeheartedly to the consumption of advertised objects, they have made a rational decision to do this. At the center of this defense of advertising is the philosophical assumption of human freedom, which means that advertising is unable to implant artificial tastes and desires since people are inherently critical in their exercise of freedom.

Some research supports the notion that people are not mindless pawns of media advertising. In one study, for example, it was found that only a small percentage of consumers believed that advertisements were completely truthful.[44] Granted, the majority of participants in that study felt that advertisements were a useful source of information, but most of them displayed a baseline skepticism that enabled them to question the intention of the advertisements. This ability usually emerges by 10 or 12 years of age. In addition, a distrust of advertising appeared to increase with age, as a result of increasingly sophisticated cognitions that permitted individuals to grasp the persuasive intent of the advertisements.

In another study, it was found that, by 6 years of age, 50 percent of children were able to recognize the persuasive intent of advertisements, and this percentage rose to 99 percent by 10 years of age.[45] This research also found that 65 percent of 6–year olds trusted all commercials, whereas this figure dropped to only 8 percent by 10 years of age. Other studies also show that consumers are able to exercise their critical thinking faculties in the face of commercial advertisement. One study found that 95 percent of adolescents were not only skeptical of advertisements, but able to identify the specific misleading aspects of advertisements and misleading product tests.[46] Another demonstrated that 80 percent of 10-and 11-year-olds were able to recognize that cigarette advertisements were designed to induce people to take up smoking.[47] There exists considerable evidence that, by adolescence, a fairly negative attitude develops toward advertising. As a result, it has been suggested that people's general distaste and skepticism concerning advertising lead them to tune out, or at least be highly vigilant, when exposed to advertising.[48]

It may be heartening to think that most consumers are critical, vigilant, and able to resist the influence of persuasive advertising, but the research discussed previously is not sufficient to establish that this is the case. Most of those studies showed only that consumers employ critical analysis when they are asked to do so consciously. It is quite easy to take a single advertisement and, with the guiding hand of an experimenter, figure out its intention and then express skepticism. But what about the thousands of advertisements with which we come into contact? The vast majority of those are never processed at a conscious intellectual level, so the question remains concerning the extent to which people are able to scrutinize critically and then reject the subliminal category of advertisements.

There is also no proof that the ability to perceive intention will make a person impervious to the advertisement as a mechanism of persuasion. For instance, of the 80 percent of adolescents who can see through cigarette commercials, not all of those will be nonsmokers. If such commercials were not effective, the industries involved would not be spending millions of dollars in this way. An additional cause for concern is that advertising is being aimed increasingly at children of younger and younger ages.

Dominique Bouchet refers to modern patterns of want and desire in the context of consumer demands.[49] In former ages, demand was influenced far more by the values and norms that were transmitted through tradition and education. Prior to the advent of consumer culture, people had lots of time to relate to available goods. The choices made were usually those that were connected to existing reality-based local demands. Since the emergence of the consumer revolution, demand has been transformed into whatever is conceivable in order to maintain novelty, which in turn stimulates production and consumption. Marketing and advertising are the primary tools for making consumer demand as elastic and insatiable as possible, but Bouchet sees a high degree of disorientation with regard to consumer demand because the multiplicity of consumer possibilities is now so large and so vacillating that people cannot possibly contemplate all options. We have reached a stage at which culture itself is no longer able to interpret the value and meaning of the options that come and go with such speed. Even marketers struggle to inform consumers about the new possibilities that compete for their attention. Members ultimately participate in a cultural forum that has no more pith or direction than its own products and consumption prescriptions.

Economic manipulations that rely on unreality consumption have a tendency to decenter the person, while promoting values that can be unhealthy and self-destructive. Successful marketing is increasingly the result of a calculative implantation of distorted values that sell an image by way of subject-object confusion.[50] Much of the contamination of values concerns the body, which is the first thing moderns encounter as the self turns inward. Once the body becomes an extension of the consumer market, individuals scrutinize it from a greater and greater distance and evaluate it in relation to fragmented images they have of themselves. This process can become so complete that they begin to experience their own bodies from the perspective of the other, and in particular the media "other." It is at this point that people relate to their bodies in terms of internalized cultural expectations.[51]

In general, modernity has seen the general development of economic methods that incline people to prefer the lesser to the higher, and the inferior to the superior.[52] There is more economic benefit if people can become desensitized to the higher values of beauty, truth, and goodness, while acting out debased media messages without critical reflection. This is only a small part of the way in which moderns are succumbing to the corporate domination of culture, a force that is defining the emerging global economy.[53]

GLOBALIZATION, PANCAPITALISM, AND WELL-BEING

Globalization is a revolutionary development that affects all areas of our lives and requires that we rethink our current understandings of society and culture. We have come to the end of the era in which discrete societies function within their own confines. Rather, we have an emerging global society that lacks unifying principles or the means by which to be internalized in concrete ways.

The global complex presents itself to us as an abstraction that is completely unlike the designs of the singular societies of the past.[54] With every technological advance throughout history, human beings have been put closer in touch with each other, but the pace of this process has increased exponentially in recent decades, and its effects are being felt as never before. However, mental health professionals have yet to ascertain possible repercussions of globalization. Without doubt, this will be one of the most important topics in future years.

Globalization is a geographical constriction that causes cultural and social organization patterns to recede. Theoretical analyses of globalization have focused on many diverse factors, including the economy, consumption, social power, institutional authority, and cultural structures.[55] Attempts to isolate the notion of globalization can become bogged down in overlapping topics such as industrialization, modernization, Westernization, technological change, and economic development.

Globalization touches on issues involving the increasing integration of international financial markets, the transnational direction of industrial production, and the growing mobility of information, goods, and capital. It is not a smooth or unilateral process; nor is there any assurance that global elements will be integrated in ways that are meaningful and useful. It affects various groups in different ways, and it would be unreasonable to describe singular consequences that applied to all populations. Also, in most instances, the effects are not simply positive or negative, but a blend of the two. The same undoubtedly pertains to the mental health consequences of globalization.

Several potentially positive outcomes of globalization have been mentioned.[56] These include increased standard of living; contact with alternative values, attitudes, and beliefs; novelty; enhanced social awareness; social mobility; wider basis for meaning and purpose; openness to new experience; and renewed optimism in the future. Among the negative outcomes that have been associated with globalization are fear and anxiety; distrust and paranoia; demoralization and hopelessness; identity confusion; culture shock; future shock; homelessness; cultural disintegration; acculturative stress; ennui, boredom, and meaninglessness; and crime and violence. From this, it is quite clear that globalization is a crucial topic of inquiry for health professionals in a wide range of disciplines.

The concept of globalization has also been seen as an explanatory factor in several other recent developments, including the homogenization of cultures, collapse of tradition, breakdown of local support systems, spread of Western values and life-styles, urbanization, migration, erosion of national sovereignty, conflicts between nations and multinational conglomerates, growing gap between rich and poor, exploitation of developing countries, environmental degradation, rise of anti-globalization forces (e.g., fundamentalism, racism), and conflict among secular, religious, and technological bodies.[57]

With globalization, individuals and entire societies become interdependent, and personal well-being is made reliant on events that are remote and poorly understood. Global culture causes members to struggle for a sense of control as they try to bridge the widening gap between local and distant spheres of influence. It entails a growing amount of differentiation that creates problems of integration, at the levels of both the individual and the society. The segmentation and pluralization of the new global world contribute to many contradictions that inhabit the global community. A massive quantity of poorly understood inputs can generate tension, anxiety, and disorientation. Consciousness itself is strained by a multidimensional and multirelational world that imposes new complexities on all forms of human endeavor.[58]

The fact that globalization removes us from the source of the event has implications for many people. Throughout much of human history, there has been some degree of continuity in the course of daily life. Workers had some grasp of the reasons for their work and some knowledge of those for whom the work was being performed. Even if they had little or no real power to alter their circumstances, their familiarity with their situation probably gave them the sense of having some control.

Globalization has the effect of drawing the outside world closer to us and giving us a sense of unity at a higher level. In this way, it tantalizes us through exposure to new differences, possibilities, and ways of understanding things. But globalization also generates stress and helplessness in some people because it operates at a level that is not perceived as manageable. Alienation is increased through globalization as people are enveloped by elaborate bureaucratic processes that do not intersect personal identity structures. They are immersed in other identities (both group and individual) that otherwise would not have gained their attention. Differing and conflicting values, morals, and perceptions are encountered as people come to inhabit the global world.

The abstract and dispersed systems that global culture comprises offer many new opportunities, while exposing members to greater risks. According to Anthony Giddens, the security crisis that lies at the heart of the modern identity prompts individuals constantly to construct and reconstruct their sense of self. To remain the same amid perpetually changing unknown systems is to put oneself at psychological risk and to activate the ongoing threat of the *problematic future*.[59]

Globalization sometimes generates stress at the national level since it can pose a threat to group identities. If leaders sense that exposure to outside information and influences can weaken their hold over people, action might be taken to restrict the input from distant global sources. Generally speaking, globalization has the power to weaken one's allegiance to national bodies, just as it does to one's own foundations of the self. The amount of stress that will be experienced depends on a variety of factors, including the degree of tolerance for differences and ambiguities that is possessed by the person or the state.

The consequences of globalization are shaped by the new type of pancapitalism that subordinates all sociocultural needs to the demands of capital.[60] Global capitalism commodifies culture and grows so powerful that it becomes impervious to regulation. Not even the threat of ecological disasters can diminish the momentum of pancapitalist enterprises. Global corporations have usurped the power held traditionally by political bodies. The transformation of people from active participants to pliant spectators has promoted a global passivity that safeguards the unprecedented freedom of the unseen workings of pancapitalism.[61]

Globalization and pancapitalism have a worse effect on some populations than others. Africa is one region that has been affected more than others by the negative consequences of globalization. Regardless of their location, the poor are once again the most victimized. Despite the opportunities created by global capitalism, its fruits are distributed with little justice in mind. Increasing numbers of people around the world are becoming poorer in relative terms. This is true in industrialized Western countries as well as developing nations that are striving for economic advancement.

This problem has become so acute that some people prefer to speak of the social and psychological violence that is a feature of the modern global economics, especially as it is acted out against those who populate the lower end of the socioeconomic continuum.[62] Not only does this system disadvantage the poor in material ways, but it also has potent cognitive consequences. Among other things, it breeds self-loathing and self-destructiveness in its victims by blaming them for their own poverty.

The solution to inequality remains unclear, however, as a result of the disputed ownership of this problem. In this regard, globalization and pancapitalism have led to a diffusion and externalization of responsibility for the psychosocial toxins that they produce. As the source of economic operations is perceived increasingly as being somewhere else, ignoring the entire issue becomes easier. Despite all the hazards of globalization, we should not lose sight of the many positive results that transpire when collisions take place between disparate cultures, societies, and viewpoints. It is not possible to turn back the clocks and retreat into a cultural cloister reminiscent of earlier times. Globalization is here to stay and to be a dimension of our lives with which we must cope. Such coping will depend upon an intelligent plan by governments and mental health professionals to increase the flexibility and tolerance of people to enable them to deal with diversity, change, and ambiguity.

CHAPTER 4

The Cultural Dynamics of Western Depression

The modern era has witnessed a sharp rise in the prevalence of depression in Western cultures. In fact, this phenomenon is so conspicuous that the present historical period is frequently labeled the Age of Depression. Until the late 1970s, scholars often used the phrase the Age of Anxiety to depict the general psychological zeitgeist. But increasingly certain structures that have a powerful depressing effect on large segments of the population have emerged. Special concern has been raised about the worsening problem of depression among adolescents and children, but the factors at work do not discriminate on the basis of age, sex, or socioeconomic class. Instead they represent a group of cultural pathogens that predispose the full range of participating members to the experience of depression.

The actual statistics concerning depression in Western culture are quite sobering. Clinical depression has become the most common presenting problem for those seeking psychotherapy. This phenomenon reflects the research findings that indicate a steady and rapid increase in the frequency of depression; in recent decades. Martin Seligman has summarized the existing research on the rates of occurrence of clinical depression; after analyzing different lines of evidence, among them several well-controlled longitudinal studies, Seligman concludes that depression is approximately ten times as common as it was only 50 years ago. He also considered all potential factors that could distort the available statistics, but the same pattern remained, drawing him to the unmistakable conclusion that there is an epidemic of depression today and also that there seems to be something about modern life that creates fertile soil for depression.[1]

An almost identical conclusion is reached by Olle Hagnell and his colleagues after reviewing the literature on depression, including the famous Lundy Study in Sweden, which spanned 25 years. They also found an alarming phenomenon: a tenfold increase in depression over recent decades, which led them to conclude that "it now appears as if the prevalence of depression is reaching epidemic proportions."[2]

Claims of rising rates of depression are supported by some suicide research. It is well documented that suicide rates, especially among the young, increased dramatically in recent decades. Just looking at American data from the years 1960 to 1973, one sees that suicide rates doubled during this period in the 15–24 age group. The suicide rate for young blacks nearly tripled during this same short span of time. We now hear regular reports of successful and unsuccessful suicide attempts by children as young as 10 years of age, and sometimes even younger.

Historical evidence suggests that suicide was extremely rare in premodern times, as it is today in many non-Western societies. Some exceptions can be found to the general rule that suicide is a product of industrialization and Westernization, for instance, the "preliterate" people of southwest New Britain in New Guinea have a reported suicide rate of 23 per 100,000, nearly twice as high as the American suicide rate. Explanations for this particular exception revolve around the way in which suicide in New Britain society became institutionalized and ritualized as a solution to life's difficulties, similar in some respects to ritualized suicide in traditional Japanese society. Yet, in considering the whole cross-cultural and historical picture, one sees clearly that degree of Westernization is predictive of suicide.

DEPRESSION IN THEORETICAL PERSPECTIVE

The ongoing upsurgence of depression in Western settings can only be understood in relation to historical developments that put members at increased risk. If depression were a universal phenomenon whose cause could be traced to organic factors, one would not see the high degree of cross-cultural variation that exists with regard to the prevalence of depression. As we will see, some non-Western cultures appear to have no indications whatsoever of clinical depression. If biological characteristics were the primary determinant of depression, they would also not explain the striking rise in depression in the West over recent decades. At the same time, one must somehow reconcile a culture-based formulation with the sizable body of research indicating a biological basis for the disorder.

For example, the evidence for a genetic component of depression is quite compelling. The results of a 1996 study of identical and nonidentical twins were typical of research in this area. It found a concordance rate for depression of 46 percent in identical twins. In nonidentical twins, however, the concordance rate was only 20 percent.[3] This seems to suggest that there is a heritability component with regard to the cause of depression. It has been proposed that this genetic proclivity translates into neurological irregularities, and some researchers point to low levels of serotonin as a possible precipitator of depression. Others have offered evidence that dysfunctional structures and processes within the neuroendocrine system, and in particular the hypothalamic-pituitary-adrenocortical axis, may lead to the experience of depression. For instance, an oversecretion of cortisol, an adrenocortical hormone, has been linked to the experience of depression.

Antidepressant medications, which are often effective in reducing the symptoms of depression, have reinforced the notion that this disorder has a biological basis, despite the fact that symptom relief does not imply an automatic causal link between depression and biological characteristics. Moreover, because even the latest generation of antidepressant medication is ineffective in treating depression, we are required to look beyond medical models for a comprehensive understanding.

Very few mental health professionals would argue that biochemical irregularities are solely responsible for depression. A host of other psychological, cognitive, and situational factors have also been implicated as etiological factors, but nearly all of these theories have been influenced strongly by the assumption of psychological individualism. For instance, the popular cognitive theories of depression revolve around cognitive distortions and irrational beliefs. Briefly, this popular theoretical stance maintains that depression is the result of a process whereby individuals self-deliver cognitions that foster a negative worldview, erode self-esteem, promote feelings of inadequacy, drain motivation, engender guilt, dampen social interest, and so forth.

Cognitive therapists have tried to pinpoint some of the problematic patterns of cognitions and "self-talk" that underlie depression. An example might be an overweight woman who falls prey to depression because of the belief "I am worthless and unappealing because I am so fat." Obviously, such a belief, or cognition, is clearly an extension of the enculturation patterns in contemporary Western culture. By contrast, cultures can still be found in which body fat signifies beauty, success, and status. Members of such cultures do not harangue themselves about being fat, nor does their size precipitate depression. Yet most cognitive therapists still persist in locating depression-generating cognitions within the individual, simultaneously overlooking culture as the source of most cognition.

Another popular psychological theory of depression revolves around the concept of helplessness. According to learned helplessness theory, depression derives from passivity and the experience of oneself as incapable of action and personal volition.[4] The person lacks a sense of potency and of

control. As such, these individuals are easily overwhelmed and even traumatized by life events. Helplessness can be learned to the extent that paralyzing stress, and concomitant depression, are experienced even in the face
of situations that are potentially manageable. A failure to cope becomes inevitable as the helpless person recoils from ordinary challenges, thereby
setting in motion a vicious cycle that maintains the depression. It is thought
that the condition is worsened when the sufferer attributes coping failures
to permanent and unchanging flaws in character and personality, rather
than transitory or external factors.

Like other theories of depression, however, the learned helplessness approach takes very little account of the broader cultural patterns and trends
that contribute to the *general* increase in the risk of developing depression.
If the experience of personal helplessness does contribute to depression,
the increasing prevalence of this disorder suggests that wider culture-level
processes are operating to predispose members toward helplessness and,
in turn, depression.

In a related formulation, hopelessness theory maintains that some types
of depression are brought about by the experience of hopelessness.[5] It also
argues that depression is fostered by expectations that "desirable outcomes" will not be forthcoming, or it can come about when the person has
expectations of undesirable outcomes that are combined with perceptions
of the self as incapable of rectifying the undesirable situation. This latter aspect of the theory overlaps with the theory that helplessness is a central
causal factor, but again it tends to locate the hopelessness solely at the level
of the individual, rather than considering the cognitive precursors that result from cultural shaping.

Although not often stated formally, another theory of depression holds
that the internalization of negative emotion can result in the experience of
depression. In this regard, it is sometimes said that depression is the opposite of expression. The prolonged inhibition of any emotion may lay the
groundwork for depression, but internalization models have paid special
attention to anger. Among other things, they gave birth to assertiveness
training as a popular therapeutic technique for depressed people. The simple logic behind assertiveness training is that outward expression is negative emotion essential for positive mental health. Training the person to
develop greater ability to externalize negative emotion, it is reasoned,
lessens the risk of depression.

For the most part, internalization models regard the emotionally constrained individual as the source of the problem, and little heed has been
paid to wider socialization practices that mediate the generation and release of emotion. Cultural dynamics play a key part in determining the
magnitude of negative emotional responses, as well as the availability or
nonavailability of cathartic pathways. Modernity itself has complicated the
emotion regulation process by introducing new forms of frustration, depri-

vation, and exploitation that cultivate negative emotion. The relevance of this trend to depression becomes apparent when we consider the simultaneous erosion of ritualized and socially sanctioned modes of emotional discharge.

Contemporary conceptions of depression also frequently involve the notion of loss. It may be the devastating type of loss associated with the death of loved ones, the breakup of marriages, and so forth. But we have also come to accept the prospect that material losses, even of a nonessential nature, can precipitate a retreat into a depressed state. The losses that culminate in depression are generally understood in terms of loss-related perceptions, expectations, and attributions that are thought to reside largely within the individual. What we tend to forget, however, is that all mental constructions about loss are intimately tied to cognitive socialization processes, and that people's responses to loss vary greatly from one cultural setting to another.

One can even find cultures that have little or no concept of ownership; in such cultures, no etiological connection between depression and material losses can be postulated. Across cultures there is also considerable variation in the response of members to the loss of loved ones. Sometimes this is experienced as part of a communal response that does not require a large degree of additional individualized reaction, so still again our task is to broaden the scope of our models in order to recognize the cultural underpinnings of depression.

CULTURAL PERSPECTIVES ON DEPRESSION

The best way to put depression into perspective is to begin by analyzing its prevalence and mode of expression across cultures. A broad generalization can be made about so-called clinical depression when it is examined in a wide cross-cultural context. In its full form, which entails an extensive psychological and cognitive component (e.g., sadness, self-doubt, self-denigration, guilt, personal worthlessness and low self-esteem, social withdrawal, loss of interest in life), clinical depression appears to be limited to Western culture. In non-Westernized cultures, there is little or no evidence for clinical depression as it is described in our diagnostic manuals. A great many of them have no words that describe depression as we know it. This alone, it has been argued, does not mean that members of such cultures do not experience depression. In fact, some investigators stop short of concluding that depression is a Western culture-bound disorder.

Instead, some prefer to assume that depression is universal, and that it is only the symptom patterns that vary from one culture to another. This has involved the creation of an artificial subtype of depression that has only somatic (i. e., physical) symptoms such as headaches, sleep problems, and digestive problems. Since these are known to accompany Western depression, the temptation is to speculate that somatic symptoms that appear in non-Western cultures actually reflect depression that is expressed in a purely somatic manner. But this entails the unwarranted assumption that all cultures must display depression since it is a feature of Western culture. Once this assumption is made, all that is required is to identify something that seems to overlap with depression (e.g., some somatic complaints) and to call that depression.

The claim that clinical depression is universal or inevitable does not stand up well to anthropological research that demonstrates that entire societies can be found that do not suffer from this type of psychopathology. An examination of their cultural structures can tell us a great deal about the nature of depression, as well as the viability of our current theoretical formulations. The next section examines briefly a well-documented instance of a society that appears to make its members resistant to depression. After that, I give some details about one of the many non-Western societies that lack entirely what we have labeled *postnatal depression*. This will provide some useful points of contrast as we seek to uncover the cultural structures that account for the worsening problem of depression in the West.

Example of Cultural Immunity to Clinical Depression

The Kaluli of New Guinea have been studied for decades by medical anthropologists, yet not a single case of clinical depression has ever been documented among any of these people.[6] When you outline the actual symptoms to them, they have no idea what you are trying to describe. To them, it sounds like an exotic affliction that falls well beyond the limits of their culture and their own personal experience. Additionally, it is not even accurate to surmise that these people experience the depression but simply express it differently or do not express it at all. There is no evidence of that either.

A few distinctive features of Kaluli culture should be mentioned here as we try to understand why Kaluli people do not become depressed. One of these has to do with their ability to avoid loss; in Kaluli culture, instances of major loss or other misfortune are followed by ritualized ceremonies whereby the victim is allowed to get revenge and compensation for the losses incurred. In all cases, the people involved are encouraged to externalize their emotional pain. The external target for one's negative emotion may be another person who has been identified as the source of the problem. If so, the offending party would be required to compensate the victim in exact measure for the loss suffered. This particular system of conflict resolution and emotion dissipation is based on the cultural tradition of reciprocity. It rests on the belief that each person has the right and even the obligation to seek reciprocity, or revenge, whenever an injustice has been done. The reciprocity is typically sought in a group setting, and the victim is expected to make, even praised for making, emphatic displays of anger in the course of eliciting compensation.

Even Kaluli religious practices embody the principle of reciprocity. They enable members to fend off losses that, are seemingly beyond their control, such as the death of a loved one. In Kaluli society death is not followed by the inward and sombre sort of funeral services that we typically observe in Western culture. Instead, the Kaluli are able to get revenge against the deities and evil spirits that were responsible for the death. Funeral ceremonies there revolve around this belief that, even in the case of death, the victims are powerful enough to fight back and get even. As part of the ritual process, the grieving victims act out the vengeance on other participants, who dress up and play out a role in order to symbolize the spiritual forces that are at fault in the death. The large group in attendance also gets involved and benefits vicariously.

The manner in which Kaluli culture protects its people from pathological states such as depression can even be seen in otherwise happy ceremonies, such as weddings, harvest celebrations, and the formal presentation of pigs. At these events, which are usually held at night, male performers dance and sing, while light comes from torches held by the audience. What makes these Kaluli ceremonies of special interest from a mental health vantage point is the way in which these ceremonies shift their emotional emphasis from light-hearted joy to rage, anger, and revenge.

For example, a wedding may begin as a jovial celebration of mutual love and the promise of new life, but, as the night goes on, the mood becomes more and more reflective and nostalgic as people are reminded of former marriages that were terminated by death and of cherished children who died. The ceremonial songs change as well, while drawing attention to departed ancestors and friends lost to death. Eventually, the wedding audience is reduced to tears and wails of anguish. Then the emotional ethos slides into anger and rage directed at the evil spirits who delivered death unto them.

Since the dancers are meant to represent these spirit forces, the Kaluli ceremony allows the emotionally charged audience to get symbolic revenge. This is achieved as members of the audience rush toward the dancers and extinguish their lit torches against the bare skin of these "evil spirits." Other members of the audience may take up weapons, such as spears and clubs, and make fearsome threatening gestures at the dancers. While this dramatic scene unfolds, the punished dancers continue to dance and sing, thereby offering themselves as official scapegoats for the collective emotional pain of the Kaluli people. Fresh dancers are brought in as needed, and the ceremony usually lasts the entire night. It should be noted that the burns inflicted on the evil dancers tend to be superficial ones because of the rather low combustion temperature of the torch resin. The ceremony concludes at dawn after a final ritual wherein the spirit world, in the form of the dancers, pays symbolic compensation to everyone whom they caused suffering, pain, and loss. With that, the participants become successful avengers and the ceremonial process culminates in feelings of euphoria, ecstasy, and rejuvenation.

It is intriguing to speculate about the absence of depression that seems to characterize certain non-Western groups. In the case of Kaluli culture, we see people who can fall back on beliefs and rituals that may serve to immunize them from depression. Their cultural practices are so potent that they are able to override any biological predispositions toward depression. All human beings need some mechanism whereby to achieve catharsis in relation to negative emotion. Kaluli culture displays wisdom and intelligence as it provides cathartic releases that are socially sanctioned.

If there is validity to the internalization model, we would in fact expect to find less depression in Kaluli culture than in one that provided no obvious and socially approved means for the release of negative emotion. Loss, as a potential precursor of depression, is virtually eliminated by Kaluli cultural practices. A learned helplessness model would also lead us to predict that people in Kaluli culture would be less at risk of depression. The cognitions utilized by members reflect the feelings of potency that are generated in them. Thus one would not expect to find the types of cognitions that we associate with depression in Western culture. The self that emerges in Kaluli culture is experienced by members as a highly effective one that inclines members toward a proud and uninhibited externalization of negative emotion.

Cultural Immunity from Postnatal Depression

Usually postnatal depression is explained as a reaction to hormonal disequilibrium stemming from childbirth. This biological hypothesis can be tested by asking whether postnatal depression exists in all cultures. If it does not, then one must question the hormonal explanation while exploring cultural factors that could account for the presence in or absence from a culture of this type of disorder; or, as with clinical depression, it could be that certain cultures are competent to the extent that their social systems can function to override biological predispositions, in this case the biological aftermath of childbirth.

Different research studies show that, after childbirth, between 50 percent and 80 percent of Western women experience the so-called maternity blues, and approximately 20 percent go on to develop postnatal depression. The severity varies considerably but usually ranges from mild to moderate clinical depression. Aside from the hormonal explanation, there are a number of psychological theories of postpartum depression. All of these focus on certain defects in the individual woman. The woman who develops postnatal depression is sometimes thought to be rejecting her womanhood and embarking on a sort of personal regression.

Other psychological theories have depicted women who develop postnatal depression as being emotionally immature, or lacking in social skills, or having anxiety problems that become exacerbated as a result of having a child. Still others have suggested that childbirth is a highly stressful event and that postnatal depression appears in women who are excessively prone to stress and lacking in coping skills. None of these theories entertains the possibility that the woman's culture, rather than she as an individual, might be responsible to a great extent. Yet this is unambiguously the case as one looks at the matter globally and discovers that many cultures have no postnatal depression, nor any equivalent of it. Equally striking is the finding that, as with clinical depression generally, postnatal depression is a psychiatric phenomenon bound largely to Western culture.

The cross-cultural research literature indicates a notable absence of postnatal depression in the vast majority of non-Western cultures, a result that could not be explained in terms of irregular data gathering methods or simple omissions from the literature on this subject.[7] There can be found a predictable pattern of practices that follow childbirth in most non-Western cultures, with the effect that women do not succumb to postnatal depression.

These practices often entail a series of rituals that serve to magnify the importance of the mother and her act of giving birth. Precisely defined social guidelines specify the behaviors that take place during the postpartum period, both for the mother and for the others in the community. There is usually a distinct culturally acknowledged postnatal period during which protective measures that dramatize the new mother's acute vulnerability are enacted. The woman's new status is made official with gifts and additional rituals that confirm symbolically her elevated standing. Often this coincides with pampered social seclusion and mandated rest as members of the community take over the new mother's responsibilities.

In order to appreciate the protective qualities of such cultural practices, it is worthwhile to describe the workings of a culture that enjoys a complete absence of postnatal depression. Since the early 1970s, anthropologists have studied the Kipsigis people of Kenya with regard to childbirth practices and their effects on the risk of subsequent emotional disorders. During this period, researchers were unable to document any cases of postnatal depression.[8] The reasons start to become clear as one uncovers the social arrangements that function to insulate new mothers from the potential emotional fallout of childbirth.

In Kipsigis culture, the *Saloita*, or new mother, is given many special attentions while also being expected to observe traditional restrictions. She is protected from public view for a 7-day postnatal rest period, and this protection pertains especially to men and strangers, even the child's father.

During this time, female relatives and close friends assume all her duties and look after her other children. Special cleaning rituals are enacted during the postpartum rest period. Behind the scenes, the woman's husband offers indirect support by acquiring needed objects and supplies for the newborn child, as well as securing special strength-restoring foods for his wife.

The special treatment afforded to the *Saloita* may last up to a full month and she frequently carries the title *new mother* for as much as 12 months. When the child is several months old, an important greeting ceremony is held wherein the new mother makes a transition to her usual role in the community. These occasions have nearly the significance of formal initiation ceremonies, and they are marked by gifts and happy greetings for the child. Once the new mother relinquishes that title, Kipsigis society recognizes her as a *Kwondo*, or "woman," a position that commands considerable respect, especially for a *Kwondo* who has had several children. This is in accordance with the Kipsigis tradition of assigning status to women partially on the basis of childbearing, a common method in the non-Western world.

Strong social support, combined with official rituals and ceremonies that interpret childbirth in highly positive ways, act to buffer any possible negative aspects of childbirth, while eliminating the risk of depression. It is interesting that among the Kipsigis, all this culturally based recognition and support is only forthcoming after the child is born. In the West, the opposite tends to be true, as considerable attention is given to expectant mothers, usually in the form of questions about their well-being and the number of months or weeks to the big day.

Some Western rituals are still alive to some extent, such as the baby shower, but this is again part of the practice of concentrating on the prebirth stage. When the big day comes, the Western woman begins her embarkation into the unsupported and uncertain world of motherhood. Many carry with them a disturbing sense of aloneness. Some resort to one or more of the hundreds of "how to" books about methods for handling and caring for infants, but many times these offer conflicting views. Other mothers simply improvise and learn as they go. In either case, most Western women no longer have the direct contact with experienced elders who serve as role models, that the Kipsigis and many other non-Westernized groups have.

The Western childbirth process frequently overwhelms the woman with the dual sense that she is basically unsupported except at the most superficial level and that the newborn is dependent upon her. This result is exactly opposite to that found in Kipsigis culture, which encourages feelings of dependency in the mother and enables her to draw on support as she indulges in this healthy form of dependency. Whereas depression and anxiety are common offshoots of the Western childbirth process, a culture such as the Kipsigis converts it into positive experience and simultaneously strengthens bonds among people.

DEPRESSION, CULTURAL CATHARSIS, AND MODERN RAGE

The absence of depression among the Kaluli seems to make sense in terms of internalization models of depression. In depression-prone Western society, members are forced into emotional constriction by a lack of culturally defined and sanctioned pathways for emotional expression. There is also the fact that many recent social developments increase the likelihood of negative emotions such as anger and frustration. It is easy to see the inner rage that is generated as a direct consequence of modern life. One source of this rage is the general dwindling of pathways to pride and self-respect. Traditionally, one derived pride from one's involvements in family, community, work, and religion, but all of these have been undermined as sources of self-worth. Rage also flows from a new type of deprivation that is fueled by our inevitable failure to find meaning and deep satisfaction with materialism and consumption as the basic assumptions of our cultural conditioning.[9]

The disappearance of cultural prescriptions for emotional catharsis is exacerbated by a higher degree of negative emotion that somehow must be managed. There is a resultant accumulation of impounded emotion that, if acted upon without cultural direction, can culminate in irrational displays of anger and rage. In this regard, the term *raging self* is sometimes used to describe the conditions of modernity that culminate in infantile psychic tantrums that emerge when the fueling of grandiosity and narcissism is followed by frustration.[10] As a result of frustrated desire and thwarted narcissism, an excess of unresolved emotion may increase the risk of depression. Even if some discharge can be accomplished by way of cathartic consumer strategies, these tend not to be effective enough to fend off eventful depression. Although internalized negative emotion may set some of the groundwork for depression, it is important to consider cultural mediation processes that serve to regulate emotion. For example, it is often possible to detect cognitive schemas that are employed in order to compensate for cultural templates that are potentially troubling from the standpoint of emotion.

A good illustration of this type of emotion work can be seen in Toraja culture of Indonesia, whose members are enculturated to deal with negative emotion in an almost opposite way from that used by the Kaluli.[11] Anger in Toraja culture is considered a taboo emotion, and displays of anger are actively discouraged. Toraja culture evolved as a nonviolent one that attaches primary importance to order, harmony, and group consensus. It cultivates and transmits the belief that displays of hostility and anger are not only shameful, but dangerous as well. This idea even penetrates their religious ideas, which teach that supernatural beings will punish those who give vent to anger. The Toraja also believe that the release of anger can result in mental and physical ill health. This pattern of cultural learning leads most members to absorb the taboo against anger and to disallow themselves the experience and expression of anger.

On the basis of a simplistic internalization model, we would expect to find a high rate of depressive disorders among the Toraja. But, like the Kaluli, they do not experience the type of clinical depression that afflicts modern Western culture. There are culture-based cognitions in Toraja culture that function to insulate members from depression in the face of ongoing emotional suppression. These protective cognitions emerge when a culture recognizes and responds to potentially toxic modes of conditioning. Rather than requiring members to repress anger, this method of cognitive enculturation invites them to keep alive this important issue. Anger comes to be seen as emotion that needs to be managed on a continual basis. As members grow into Toraja culture, they are prepared for anger control through clearly identified cognitions that enable them to deal with anger and other negative emotions as they arise. By contrast, it may be that modern culture is no longer capable of equipping members with compensatory cognitive scripts that can fend off the depressing effects of current cultural demands.

In general, we are more inclined to engage in emotional catharsis when we can participate automatically in predefined cultural steering processes regarding emotional discharge. Traditionally, the emotions of members were regulated with the guidance of clearly defined cultural maps. These communicated the information that enabled people to organize cognitive and behavioral strategies that were effective as catharsis devices, but cultural maps have given way to *self-steering* emotion regulation maneuvers that require a considerable degree of self-conscious improvisation.[12]

In the relative absence of cultural direction, individuals become their own emotional therapists, relying on their own maps for catharsis. But they are constantly confronted with information deficits that translate into uncertainty with regard to emotional expression. The result of privatized attempts to achieve emotional homeostasis is that individuals often resolve their emotional ambivalence by denying and/or inhibiting emotion that would otherwise be discharged if they had clear access to cultural maps. This is part of the general situation of social atomism that requires individual members to self-regulate without the advantage of culturally maintained master narratives. The eclipse of the cultural self, and the subsequent unavailability of the work of culture, have numerous implications for not only depression but many other psychopathologies as well.

INDIVIDUALISM, SUPPORT DEFICITS, AND DEPRESSION

Depression is part of the psychic price we pay for an identity structure that operates in isolation and with a high degree of arbitrariness. In Western cultural contexts, the individuated self personalizes the inner states of emotion and is easily overwhelmed by adversity and difficult life events. The results are self-blame, isolation, loneliness, guilt, existential despair, and other symptoms that manifest themselves in the Western brand of depression. By contrast, an unindividuated self is better able to locate problems at a less personal level. It avoids the emotional brunt of these problems by coding stressful life events in external terms, or in the wider context of a collective identity. In a sense, the collective is able to absorb much of the emotional fallout.

The eclipse of social support is a variable mentioned frequently by those who try to explain the relationship between depression and modernity. In general, research tends to show that social support protects people from the experience of mental disturbance. On the other hand, it also reveals that people with high levels of social support are less vulnerable to mental illness, and more able to cope with the types of life stresses and events that can precipitate psychological disorders. The protective effects of social support are apparent with regard to depression.

Most studies in this area have found that depression is less likely and less severe in people who enjoy high levels of social support. Research has also shown that social support acts to lessen the likelihood of postnatal depression.[13] The general trend of these findings extends to other cultures. For example, social support was shown to insulate female Taiwanese homemakers from feelings of depression that stemmed from stressful life events.[14] Evidence suggests that, like depression, suicide and suicidal ideation are less likely in highly supportive social environments.

Little agreement exists about an actual definition of social support, even though most of us have a sense of what it means to be supported in our social environment. It can involve emotionally sustaining behavior, assistance with problem solving, aid in overcoming barriers to goals, or knowledge that increases coping ability. Often the concept of "social network" arises in discussions of social support, referring to the extent of interconnectedness of one's social ties. The potential advantage of a network, as contrasted to nonintegrated social ties, is that it better provides for shared values, norms, and beliefs. The collective consensual element associated with integrated social networks may prove more beneficial to mental health than social relationships that exist in relative isolation.

Social support has been found to act as a buffer against depression in a diverse range of populations in addition to members of the general public. These include the institutionalized elderly, psychiatric patients, people with disabilities, victims of abuse, new mothers, heart surgery patients, stroke victims, and acculturated individuals. The exact ways in which social support works in relation to depression are still a matter of speculation. A number of theories have been offered to explain why social support guards against depression. Some can be described as vulnerability models whereby social support is thought to offer coping assistance through the modification of stress. This may come in the form of emotional support, information assistance, and problem focused coping. Conversely, low levels of social support may create a resource deficit that leads to feelings of failure and diminished effectiveness. As a result, the person may become more vulnerable to stress and more likely to experience dejection, hopelessness, and depression when encountering difficulties.

The social integration model postulates that the overall level of integration of a culture is important in determining whether or not its members will be susceptible to depression and other forms of mental disturbance. Rather than depicting social support as a stress buffer, it sees it as an independent cultural outcome that operates on behalf of positive mental health. This is rooted in Durkheim's classic work showing that suicide is not so much an individual act, as one that is intimately related to the cohesiveness and degree of integration of the wider culture. Well-integrated cultures were seen by Durkheim as having the beliefs, codes of action, and social control mechanisms that prevented at-risk members from committing suicide. They are able to insulate members from the full range of mental disorders by way of their capacity to provide moral support and by an exchange of ideas that offer strength in the face of adversity.[15] Cultures that lack cohesion place strain on individuals as they struggle with self-centered coping strategies. The social integration model predicts that depression and suicide will be more common in poorly integrated cultures since they fall short in terms of social and emotional support.

Symbolic interactionism provides still another perspective on the way in which social support prevents depression. Some of the pioneering theoretical work in this area was done by Margaret Mead, who saw the self as the result of *interactional* activities. Engagement in this social interaction process has the effect of forging self-identities and the methods whereby people evaluate themselves. However, the actual structure of identity depends on the quality and quantity of social relationships. Proponents of symbolic interactionism point out that certain cultural conditions can bring about deficiencies in social relationships, which, in turn, impinge on self-evaluations. This mechanism affects not only people's feelings of adequacy, but also their ability to extract a sense of life purpose.

The concept of alienation is often discussed in terms of declining social support and resultant increases in depression. Different definitions have been employed, but *alienation* usually refers to social disengagement, normlessness, powerlessness in relation to social affairs, impaired faith / trust in others, and perceived purposelessness. The experience of social isolation that accompanies alienation is opposite in many ways from the emotional concomitants of traditional modes of social support. One notable research study assessed both alienation and level of depression in a large sample of university students.[16] The findings showed that degree of alienation was a significant predictor of depression. The authors of this research report selected alienation as a provisional operationalization of modernity, making the case that alienation is the primary vehicle by which the conditions of modernity translate into depressive symptoms.

COMPETITION, DEPRESSION, AND PSYCHOLOGICAL WELL-BEING

The alienation that is so central to contemporary life is accentuated by the cultural emphasis on competition, which is a core working of mass market individualism. The imprinting of members with internalized control mechanisms, as well as an egocentric orientation toward self-interest and self-development, lends itself readily to the pitting of people against one another in a variety of competitive social contexts. This arrangement can also help to explain the current rise of depression-proneness, as well as other manifestations of the modern mental health crisis.

Competition is one of the most conspicuous qualities of life in the contemporary Western culture. It is so all-pervasive that it sometimes escapes our attention, yet competition varies greatly from one culture to another, casting doubt on any claims about its naturalness or inevitability. At one end of the continuum are cultures that are almost devoid of competition. When first discovered, many groups of Australian Aborigines were found to lack all notion of competition. Even today, elementary school teachers sometimes feel the need to build a sense of competition into young Aboriginal children in order to prepare them for the competitive academic years ahead.

Among the many other noncompetitive cultures that have appeared in the anthropological literature are the Tangu of New Guinea, who do not even have competitive games. Instead, they play a game known as *taketah*, in which two teams spin tops with the goal of reaching a draw.[17] Zuni Indian culture revolves around a nonindividualistic principle of cooperation, which discourages material possession and economic competition.[18] Sources of wealth are readily circulated among members, with little or no motivation in individuals to accumulate or horde. Traditionally, the Zuni have been avid followers of a four-mile footrace that is incorporated into religious ceremony. The way the Zuni approach the results reveals the noncooperative feature of the culture. The winner of the race receives no recognition for the victory, and repeated winners are not allowed to participate in future races. The Mixtecans of Mexico have such a taboo on competitiveness that displays of it are considered a minor crime.[19]

At the other end of the continuum we have American culture, which has adopted competition as the basis for economic and social practices. Competition has become the primary way that members define their self-worth and signify their value to the abstract social world. Winning over others has invaded almost every aspect of life. Most members are acceptant of the implicit cultural assumption that one's success is a direct extension of someone else's failure. Cooperation is largely invisible and engaged in only to the extent that it will eventually serve participating individuals.

Modernity has introduced sufficient separation between identities in order for competition to become a means by which to evaluate human behavior. In the process, cultural heroics have shifted away from traditional cooperation. From a young age, members are now conditioned to compete and to believe that competition is healthy and worthwhile. The education system socializes competition by setting children against one another, identifying winners and losers at every step of the way. The misery and dejection of losers are a cause for winners to rejoice. The typical activities taking place in American schools would be considered inhumane in many noncompetitive cultures. Yet the fact remains that the entire self-validation process has become highly reliant on the capacity of individuals to prevail over others by way of competition. Any signs of noncompetitiveness are interpreted as deficiencies of character.

A society creates certain benefits for itself, and for many individual members, in the course of maintaining a social plan revolving around hypercompetition. It amplifies the motivational levels of especially fit members who anticipate victorious outcomes. Total life-styles can unfold in relation to the ongoing process of individual competitive success. The winners sometimes enjoy a quantity and quality of privilege that would be impossible in a cultural setting that stressed cooperation and sharing. When competition is working for someone, there are new and exciting opportunities to override the barriers that influenced the lives of former collectivist peoples. At its most refined levels, competitive success nearly erases the feeling that life has any bounds.

Even when positive outcomes are not expected, members often respond to their fear of competitive failure by pushing themselves to higher levels of output. The fear that operates in the background consciousness of competitive-minded people can also prompt them to participate in fresh and potentially fruitful activities that aim to enhance security and overall adaptive potential. Out of this sometimes come remarkable individual achievements that would be far less likely under cultural conditions motivated by social harmony. Competitive environments can enhance people's creativity as they probe new means of gaining strategic advantage over other competitors. In the process, they sometimes discover aspects of themselves that would have remained undiscovered if they had not been propelled by competitive forces.

It is not difficult to run across claims that competition builds character and helps to develop the resources of the individual. That may be partially true for people who are successful in their competitive undertakings, but the bulk of evidence suggests that competition is deleterious to psychological well-being. For example, it creates the conditions whereby one constantly doubts one's self-worth. This is because positive self-esteem is not unconditional, but rather dependent upon one's current and future competitive outcomes. Competition, and the proving of one's worth, never end, and the self is always a potential victim of the next competitive encounter. Avoiding competition hurts one's self-concept since we are conditioned to equate avoidance with failure and inadequacy. A vicious circle is created in which competition erodes self-esteem, causing the person to amend this deficit by trying to bolster self-esteem through further competition. As Alfie Kohn writes in *No contest: The case against competition*, "We compete to overcome fundamental doubts about our capabilities and, finally, to compensate for low self-esteem."[20]

It could be argued that competitive activities should have a positive effect on self-esteem in cultures wherein competition is the norm, but research on the relationship between self-esteem and competitiveness suggests that the dynamics of competition outweigh any norm effects. One exhaustive review of this subject concluded that cooperation, by contrast to competition, contributed to feelings of self worth, emotional maturity, a clear sense of personal identity, healthy interpersonal relations, and trust in others.[21] Quite interesting is the paradoxical finding that cooperative orientations have the effect of engendering an internal locus of control that makes people experience greater control over their lives. Research in educational settings confirms that healthy self-esteem is enhanced by cooperative systems, whereas competition-based methods have the reverse effect.

A broad cross-cultural perspective on this issue reveals that human cooperation is one of the most essential ingredients in determining positive mental health. From time to time, the extreme cultural emphasis on competition gives rise to countertrends. In California, for example, some elementary schools have tried to push the pendulum in the opposite direction by introducing programs that minimize competition in order to maximize positive self-esteem. Other states have experimented with this system even though its critics have argued that it gives children messages that are in conflict with the broader teachings and demands of contemporary Western culture.

This particular self-esteem movement, as it is called, is coming under critical scrutiny because of research studies demonstrating that it demotivates children and causes them to recoil from new challenges. It may be that the child senses that there is nothing more to be gotten in terms of reward and that any new endeavors could not benefit him or her. Or it could be that the child learns to be a passive absorber of reinforcements that are not contingent upon equivalent reciprocations. This attitude could establish a mind-set in which people expect the world to come to them. The specific methods employed in self-esteem programs may be flawed in terms of the almost ludicrous amounts of praise that are lavished on children regardless of the nature or quality of their behavior. The radically unconditioned nature of the rewards, when delivered in a context of social unreality, can actually produce mutant forms and levels of self-esteem that deplete empathy for others. In many respects, this resembles the noxious type of pseudo self-esteem that is emerging within the indulgent but socially unreal climate of consumer society. If self-esteem programs do in fact inhibit the development of competitive traits, one is also left to wonder about the long-term effects on people once they attempt to adjust to the prevailing social structures, which demand an ability to get a competitive edge.

Hypercompetition between members introduces the inevitable experience of failure into the lives of people. Even the fittest competitors have the problem that it is impossible to win all the time and that, sooner or later, one is destined to lose. Furthermore, losing, even when encountered in the course of so-called individualistic pursuits, is symbolically representative of a cultural taboo. Losers understand that they have failed, not only in their own eyes, but in terms of the rules of heroism inscribed in our modern cultural template. Yet, given this template, they cannot avoid gravitating toward winning as their primary source of hope.

Increased depression-proneness is to be expected when traditional other-centered vehicles for hope relocate themselves in the alienating quest for victory. The problem is exacerbated when winning tends to be acted out in relation to objects of consumption. The impersonal commodity signs forthcoming from victorious consumer heroics offer little if any long-term comfort. Depression is an ever-present risk unless comfort and reassurance have a deeper social foundation.

In this regard, modern depression is fueled by the tarnishing effect that hypercompetition has on interpersonal relations. Competitors who feel the need to do whatever it takes to win sometimes find themselves willing to submerge their natural compassionate tendencies and to engage in behavior designed to weaken the opposition. As people override prosocial qualities within themselves, they are sometimes left with an uncomfortable disquiet and vague sense of guilt in the face of competitive success. On the other hand, human beings are inclined to react negatively to others who represent a threat or who have actually managed to defeat and outperform them. So it is very common to feel animosity and even hatred toward those whom we perceive as victors.

Although open hostility may be suppressed, social interactions between competitors still suffer from superficiality and residual distrust. If all relations with one's competitors are avoided, a state of social deprivation can ensue unless the person cultivates alternative relationships. Even then, however, there remains a distinct tension due to people's generalized sense that everyone is a potential competitor, and thus a possible threat. The tension-generating properties of competition are explored further in the next chapter, which deals with contemporary sources of anxiety.

CHAPTER 5

The New Anxiety

Although depression seems to have superseded anxiety as the defining emotional state of the modern age, mental health professionals are aware that we still live in a so-called Age of Anxiety. Modernity, however, has given rise to several new sources of anxiety that are less tangible and less controllable than the anxiety determinants of earlier times. Regrettably, attempts to understand anxiety in historical and cultural contexts are often overshadowed by explanations that emphasize the biological and physiological processes and the apparent universality of anxiety. But even though most human beings have the potential to experience anxiety, there exists extensive cross-cultural variation with regard to the general magnitude of anxiety, as well as the prevalence of anxiety disorders. Indeed, there have been some striking observations made on this subject in different cultures. In a study of 2,360 Yoruba Aboriginals of Australia, not a single case of overt anxiety was found.[1] No indications whatsoever were found of such specific anxiety disorders as phobia or obsessive-compulsive disorder.

Some observers have persisted in the assumption that anxiety symptoms are present in all cultures, arguing further that an absence of symptoms means only that anxiety is expressed in alternative ways. We saw this same logic with regard to cultures that appeared to have few signs of clinical depression. It has been reported that Yoruba Aboriginals experience certain fears concerning witchcraft, evil spirits, the dark, and strangers. At times, these fears express themselves in ways that resemble "overt anxiety" (e.g., sweating, agitation, shaking), but it has also been observed that these fear responses are of short duration and subside once the object of fear is no longer present. Thus they do not resemble the persistent types of anxiety disorders with which we are familiar in the West.

Yoruba culture is unusual in its apparent total absence of anxiety disorders; in most cultures one can find evidence of pathological anxiety. It is probably possible for a culture to be organized in such a way that anxiety disorders are entirely precluded. Yoruba culture may be a case in point. In the vast majority of cultures, however, it seems that some members experience anxiety symptoms. One cross-cultural study examined the prevalence of various anxiety symptoms (nervousness, heart pounding, sleep troubles, upsetting dreams, and shortness of breath) in India, Nigeria, Chile, and Israel. The researchers found some evidence of all these symptoms in each of the four locations, but the prevalence of the different symptoms varied considerably from one culture to another.[2] Nervousness, which we often equate with anxiety, was experienced by 48 percent of Indians, 36 percent of Chileans, 27 percent of Israelis, and 9 percent of Nigerians. Whereas the Nigerians had far fewer symptoms of nervousness, they reported considerably more disturbing dreams than people from the other countries in the survey.

This latter finding reflects the cultural significance attached to dreams in traditional Nigerian culture. Unwelcomed messages contained in dreams can generate stress and anxiety. In cultures that assign less authority to dreams, anxiety is not channeled in this direction to the same extent. In general, it is evident that anxiety can ground itself on a multitude of cultural structures. This is especially obvious when one considers culture-bound syndromes, such as *koro*.

The defining feature of *koro* is a high degree of anxiety associated with penis size. The sufferer is convinced that his penis is shrinking and disappearing into his abdomen. The idea involves the same sort of body image distortion that we see in anorexia nervosa, except that the *koro* victim perceives the penis as much smaller than it is in reality. The body image distortion of the anorexic causes the victim to perceive her/his body as larger than it is. *Koro* is a disorder that is found only in some south Asian countries (e.g., China, Taiwan, Malaysia) and can be traced to the cultural cognition "Be virile" that becomes a primary motivation of many men in these cultures.

It has been suggested that *koro* is the etiological counterpart of anorexia nervosa in Western culture.[3] One could debate whether these should be classified as anxiety disorders, yet no one would question that both anorexia nervosa and *koro* involve a great deal of anxiety, in terms of the feared conditions of obesity and sexual inadequacy, respectively. So once again we see that culture determines to a large extent the form of anxiety expression.

From all we know about anxiety and culture, it would be oversimplistic to claim that modernization and/or Westernization is to be blamed entirely for the rash of anxiety problems that exist today. It may be that in the Age of Anxiety the West has a higher prevalence of anxiety disorders than many traditional non-Western cultures, but the complexity of this issue makes definitive conclusions rather difficult. An interesting study looked at the relationship between blood pressure and degree of Westernization in a number of Micronesian, Polynesian, and East African settings.[4] The results showed that blood pressure is lower in non-Western tribal peoples and that it increases as contact rises with Westernized life-styles. This difference could not be explained fully by such factors as obesity, salt intake, and envious resentment. Instead, the researchers attributed the higher blood pressure in Western locations to acculturation, information overload, and competition.

Moderns have come to embrace high levels of stress as an expected and ongoing element of their inner experience. Conspicuous signs of being stressed are even worn by some as a badge of honor signifying their faithful adherence to the success dictates calling for physical and emotional overextension.

Rather than focus on anxiety disorders, it might be more revealing to think in terms of cultural factors that affect resting levels of anxiety, or what could also be termed *general anxiety*. One can then begin to think in terms of cultures that are anxiety-prone, as compared to ones that are less likely to instill anxiety in members. Some of the most thought-provoking work on this subject is that of Raoul Naroll, who analyzed all available cross-cultural anxiety research in an attempt to isolate the factors that predisposed cultures to the experience of anxiety.[5] Working from the sizable body of data contained in the Human Relations Area Files, Naroll found that a culture was more likely to produce anxious members if it was competitive; individualistic; futuristic and anticipatory, with an emphasis on planning, saving, and working toward; restrictive of emotional freedom, with reliance on artificiality for success; repressive of sexuality; and lacking in overall integration (i.e., a weak "moral net"). Some of these characteristics are especially relevant to the Age of Anxiety phenomenon and need to be considered in more detail. We might begin by looking once again at competition, this time as it contributes to the experience of anxiety.

COMPETITION, SOCIAL FRAUDULENCE, AND ANXIETY

As with depression, the history of modern anxiety parallels the shift of location of the self from the group to the individual.[6] The rise of the powerful individual provided the basis for the current cultural strategy of competitive individualism, which in turn has shaped the new forms of anxiety experienced by moderns. The exceptionally intense competitive arrangements that exist in many segments of modern society have the effect of emphasizing technique and outcome. Individual participants often experience so much competitive anxiety that they disengage their private imagination in favor of situational pragmatics. Some people with strong creative inclinations experience frustration as they compromise this aspect of themselves in order to maximize the likelihood of competitive success.[7] If the rewards are high, they are often able to persist in their compromise, but smaller payoffs frequently fail to mask their discontent.

Research on the emotional consequences of competition shows consistently that competitive arrangements are associated with greater anxiety.[8] When anxiety levels are high, there is a concomitant impairment of performance. The competition-anxiety relationship is so well established that researchers often expose their participants to competition when they want to create anxiety in the experimental situation. This is referred to as *competition-induced anxiety*.

Over long periods, this type of anxiety can create a state of *competition fatigue*, wherein the person is drained of the ability to compete with intensity and determination. In the leadup to this syndrome, the fatigued person often reports feelings of emptiness and an acute awareness that social needs are not being satisfied. Sometimes the individual remains in the competitive environment, in which he or she might need to live with the consequences of reduced performance. In other cases, afflicted individuals attempt to use the experience in order to construct for themselves an alternative life-style that revolves around cooperation and the cultivation of positive social relations. This may involve a physical retreat to a remote geographical area, which is intended to facilitate a life-style and attitude change. Those who are burned out by excesses of competition may employ isolation as a form of refuge, or they may seek out groups or communities that reflect their need for change. It is quite remarkable, for example, how many members of communes and dropout communities have former lives as aggressive competitors in a range of professional occupations. They frequently report that competition had become an intolerable substitute for true personal control in their lives.

Rather than viewing competition fatigue as a disorder, it is better to understand it as a creative diagnosis by individuals who gradually recognize that a relentlessly competitive orientation deprives them of much that is important in life. It often represents a new maturity that rests on the awareness that hypercompetition builds barricades between people, while also furthering anxiety, isolation, and alienation. But most modern-day competitors find it difficult to escape the cultural mind-set that equates survival and desirability with triumphant competition. Most will respond to the isolating and anxiety-arousing effects of competitive striving by redoubling their effort or shifting their energies toward different competitive pursuits.

The prospect of easing away from a competitive approach to life conjures up catastrophic fantasies about failure and destitution. To some extent, these worries have a basis in reality since the entire economic structure of Western life implies a certain degree of competitive willingness. In this regard, many people now find themselves in what has been termed a *competition trap* wherein they cannot find relief from the pernicious effects of highly competitive life orientations.[9]

The world of competition invites an intrapersonal fraudulence that paves the way for additional anxiety. Humanistic psychologists have long known that artificiality lies at the heart of anxiety and that a successful cure lies in the restoration of authenticity to people's lives. Yet the radical reliance on competition for purposes of self-marketing has led moderns to package themselves in such a way that any semblance of an authentic person is disguised beyond recognition. It is not uncommon to hear people referring to themselves, and their abilities and qualities, as a package that is on offer.

Although the hope is that this package will be competitive and thus able to attract a good valuation, the fraudulence (both to self and others) involved is almost certain to take a toll. Anxiety becomes more likely as we continue to sacrifice authenticity for purposes of becoming competitively fit standardized units.[10] Without the inner knowledge that we *are* someone, we are confronted by the unsettling feeling that survival, and reality itself, rest on the ever-shifting demands of surface impression. With these intrapsychic dynamics, the nervous self-as-package cannot even savor many of the fruits of victorious competition.

WORK, LEISURE, AND OVEREFFORT PATHOLOGIES

Despite enormous advantages in technology that make most types of work faster and easier, individuals are actually working more than they did prior to these advances. Research in the United States shows that, between 1970 and 1990, the number of hours worked per week increased by 3 hours.[11] Thus, even though the real need to work has decreased, people's perceived need to work is increasing. The decision to push themselves until they exceed their coping ability is often regarded by modern "working beings" as legitimate in light of the high cost of servicing a materialistic consumption-oriented life.

The force behind cultural avarice can be so powerful as to blind members entirely to the falseness of their needs. Thus we see multitudes of people who let themselves be exposed to high levels of work-related stress and to the risk of pathological manifestations of anxiety. This is compounded by sleep problems, which have reached epidemic proportions in the modern postindustrial world. Surveys show, for example, that over 40 percent of Americans suffer sleep deprivation to the extent that it interferes with performance of their daily activities. In response to this, a growing number of workplaces have created rules requiring employees to take naps.

Of course, many people derive a great deal of satisfaction from their work. It can be the central means by which social, intellectual, and creative needs are met, but in a culture that does not distinguish clearly between greed and success, work can easily take on a compulsive quality. It is estimated that 5 percent of the American population suffer from unrelenting workaholism[12]; a much higher percentage are afflicted with less extreme, and less destructive, degrees.

There are a variety of factors that contribute to the onset of workaholism. It has been said that this pattern of behavior can represent a compensation for fear of failure, a response to earlier deprivation, or an escape from intimacy. However, one factor that cannot be ignored is that our culture encourages and rewards this addiction.[13] The associations between work and the fruits of material success have become so close that work can represent an indirect form of consumption and a symbolic enactment of the American Dream. At the same time, work fever, as it is sometimes called, carries many mental health penalties. It has been related to anxiety, stress, worry, hopelessness, frustration, grief, sleeplessness, and marital breakdown.[14]

Significant changes have transpired with regard to the actual nature of work. Traditional command structures have given way to ones that emphasize individual incentive and responsibility, as well as the ability to achieve competent performance with small teams operating on a project-by-project basis.[15] The new workplace is well-suited for flexible personality types that can tolerate stress, high arousal levels, ambiguity, lack of certainty, and risk. A good match in this regard can increase the likelihood that work will prove gratifying, and act as a catalyst for personal growth. Conversely, as work continues to become an exercise in self-management, potential problems are created for the rigid personality that has strong needs for security, formality, and external structure.

Regardless of one's temperament and personality makeup, however, the modern workplace is more prone to generate anxiety than the work structures of the past. The overall level of tension is increased by the permeable nature of work boundaries, as well as the need to operate as one's own authority.[16] Well-established work parameters have given way to less defined ones that demand continual invention and revision. Pacifying historical elements are disappearing as work becomes more situational and less safeguarded by proven routine. Workers need to perform without the outside indicators that once afforded direction and rationale. Additional complexities have been introduced as work has come to entail more negotiation, personal accountability, and knowledge management.

Employment itself no longer affords convincing security since the new worker must offer ongoing proof of value and efficiency within the organization. Career advancement now depends largely on successful self-propulsion rather than reliable performance within clear organizational frameworks. The trend toward compulsive work patterns is an expected overkill response to the experience of being the primary, or sole, determinant of one's fate as a provider. It also represents a sort of antidote for the insecurity stemming from the tenuous bond between worker and workplace. Workers who punish themselves by assuming, or inventing, more work for themselves are repaid in the knowledge that they are bolstering their marketability and employability.

In a more general sense, work is becoming the social center of contemporary life. It has taken on new meanings for individuals who perceive it as their only voice for communicating their cultural fitness and for achieving social validation. Work has also become a mechanism by which to replace the cultural dramatics that have disappeared from modern life. These dramatics once overlapped with a wide range of activities and rituals that enabled members to engage in social celebrations characterized by mutuality as well as recognition of individual contributions.

Leisure has also taken on new meanings in the consumer age. Great amounts of effort, and even overeffort, are often poured into leisure pursuits. Rather than creating opportunities for rejuvenation, many leisure activities resemble strenuous forms of work that have compulsive and frantic overtones. An example might be the growing mass of people who train for and run grueling marathons for "fun." Mental health professionals are becoming concerned about the growing problem of *leisure burnout*, wherein leisure pursuits exacerbate already existing conditions of work burnout.

The increasingly theatrical nature of leisure displays has introduced a new element of danger into the lives of performers. Although often excused as thrill seeking or epinephrine (adrenaline) addiction, modern leisure fanaticism entails new sources of stress, fear, and physical demand. Helping to maintain it is a situation wherein leisure becomes a mode of consumption that, like heroic work, flags one's cultural valuation. Given the tight restrictions on people's busy schedules, brief but attention-grabbing bursts of leisure are often the only opportunities whereby to disseminate messages about their competence as working beings.

INFINITE POSSIBILITY AND CHOICE FATIGUE

The word *acculturation* refers to the process whereby members of a culture are put in the position of needing to learn the rules of another culture. Although adaptation to a new culture may have some positive outcomes, it is also a potentially stressful exercise. Various terms have been used to describe the type of stress that accompanies adaptation to new cultural settings (e.g., *culture stress, culture shock*). In recent years, the term *acculturative stress* has become popular.

The process of change tends to be stressful and anxiety-arousing, especially in dealing with changes to the cultural structures that underlie and support one's constructions of reality. Acculturative stress has been explained partially in terms of the loss of identity and the decrease in social support that accompanies cultural transition. This is in addition to whatever forms of discrimination, prejudice, and marginalization people face in their new culture.

Acculturative stress is also generated when people are deprived of the information that is needed to make meaningful self-evaluations. It has been shown that when one lacks the information to achieve certainty about one's social status and place in the community, anxiety results. This is because decision making, judgments, and appraisals are made more difficult as a consequence of diminished environmental clarity. This makes day-to-day living ambiguous and likely to promote anxiety in those who lack sufficient structure and mechanisms of control.[17]

One especially stressful element of acculturation is the reevaluation process wherein people struggle to establish a role, and a sense of belonging, in the new culture. Large numbers of migrants, refugees, and displaced people around the world are in this difficult position, but a discussion of acculturative stress could be expanded to include the masses of people today who must cope with culture change on an ongoing basis. More than anything else, modern culture is identified by its changing nature. Even if some overarching themes remain constant, there is still continual fluctuation with regard to how these themes are to be understood or approached.

It is not only new cultural arrivals who must battle to forge roles and identities. Everyone today encounters stress that is due to a lack of communal grounding and the perpetual free-floating condition that threatens constantly to fragment the self.[18] In this way, modernity involves an ongoing dissolution and reconstruction of social arrangements and their associated psychological messages, leaving us in a constant state of exploration for certainty, with a background sense of vulnerability. It is very possible that our explorations will prove rewarding, but once again the process can be stressful. The persistent need to define and redefine oneself in a constantly shifting world usually translates into a vague type of acculturative stress.

Stated otherwise, a rapid rate of change makes it unclear to what we belong. As conditions change, so too does our position in the larger scheme of things. Cultural structures that do not account for belongingness needs are not conducive to well-being. Research on the relationship between belongingness and mental health shows that belongingness is negatively correlated with measures of anxiety and neuroticism.[19] Not many of us will ever experience the premodern situation of belonging to something that has continuity and predictability, or of being able simply to imitate rather than forever innovate.

The reward for living in constant cultural flux is that members have available to them an unprecedented amount of possibility, which has the potential to enrich life experience. Consumer society operates optimally when members are made to drift about in a sea of limitless options. The body and mind have themselves become commodities that represent new sources of possibility via the commercial industries that have been built up around them. At the same time, it has been pointed out that modernity is a type of psychological whirlwind in which the person is perpetually disoriented by incommensurable themes and messages.[20] The chaos of "languages" that confronts modern people can place them in contradiction with themselves and others. With the exception of materialism and consumption, it is difficult to pinpoint many areas of consensus in modern culture. Yet even those are fluid and in a constant state of revision.

A world of unlimited possibility requires us to be highly malleable and always prepared to update our attitudes, beliefs, and values. Like perpetual change, infinite possibility has a way of dissolving the self and making it difficult to locate ourselves, or to find a frame of orientation by which to comprehend the world. Indeed, the modern world floods us with a dazzling array of possibilities, many of which are lodged in the consumer-based foundation of the culture and its economy. We are inclined to evaluate ourselves, and our success, in relation to our conquest of these endless possibilities.

Choice itself can be emotionally taxing since it requires the effort of appraisals, decisions, and actions. Since the possibilities are always changing, the task of taking advantage of infinite possibility is an ongoing one that can prove stressful, despite whatever pleasures are accumulated along the way. Additional frustration is sometimes precipitated when people recognize that choice and social variety are largely for fantasy and consumption purposes, rather than actual practice.[21] Their imaginative freedoms often do not materialize into real life-style opportunities. Logistically, the problem is that choices never remain the same long enough for supporting infrastructures to be installed around them.

The values that are shaped as we acclimatize to infinite possibility take us further away from each other and from a sense of belongingness and orientation. One reason for this is the sheer scope of possibility that confronts people, which itself takes us in myriad disparate directions that are nearly impossible to coordinate with the pursuits of others. As we turn in on our own private desires, we become servants of our own yearnings.[22] On the surface, this orientation paints a superficial impression of excitement and optimism, but, on a deeper level, a devotion to the consumption of possibility has social alienation and anxiety as its price.

The quantity of choice available to moderns is no longer rationed by the fatalistic mind-sets that were common in premodern times. Choice is also not limited by ignominy, an experience that is being eradicated for reasons of commercial expediency. The Internet, which has become a dominant player with regard to the construction of reality, is perceived by many as the central warehouse of new and eventual possibility. In general, the spread of Internet consciousness has reinforced the contemporary experience of infinite possibility. Whatever the method of exploiting infinite possibility, however, the quest often culminates in a stressful subjectivity in which promise resides in making right choices or chancing upon the right website. The self-directed journey of these new psychological nomads takes them away from their basically social nature, as well as the comfort that stems from an awareness of some limitation.

It is not easy to sustain a sense of personal control in the role of choice maker within the impersonal expanse of total possibility. Although we usually associate the act of choosing with being in control, a mass consumer society offers few opportunities for members actively to construct available options. The best that most can achieve is a passive type of control that results from a thorough and critical assessment of consumable choices. This resembles the superficial control that a shopper has while perusing a market. Yet even this false sense of control requires the canny new age shopper to digest enormous quantities of information, a process that in itself can be exhausting. Coupled with the information overload that has become a poorly tolerated cognitive companion of modern consciousness, there has been a growing trend toward coping strategies that entail radical disengagement.

The weariness of infinite possibility and information management has led many people to search out regenerative dissociation solutions. An entire consumer industry, consisting of many diverse services, has surfaced in order to meet the burgeoning dissociative needs of people. People are tuning out with numerous variations of meditation and traditional Eastern practices that produce a contentless state of mind. They are following a plethora of gurus who show them the way to a therapeutic emptiness that can eliminate their buildup of psychic static. Vacuous mental states are being aided by designer drugs, hypnogogic music, consciousness-dissolving techniques that use electronic screens as trance facilitators, compulsive exercise, trivia mesmerization, collecting fetishism, and endless other monotony devices. All of these have the effect of specializing and downsizing the mental world of people and reducing its scope of content. The same trend can be seen with regard to the madness techniques that have become popular in recent times.

TRAUMA-PRONENESS AND ALIENATED DISSOCIATION

The full range of so-called dissociative disorders has become more common as vulnerable people diagnose the need for wholesale detachment as a remedy for an extreme oversupply of cognitive and emotional inputs. These are coping specializations that engage dissociation in order to reduce the realm of possibility and the quantity of elements that beckon consideration. They often involve a focal target that becomes the sole referent for their lives, and the foundation of their adaptive self-imposed system of restriction.

As the perfect body has become the crowning symbol of consumer competence, we have seen aspects of bodily appearance become the absorption points that facilitate the dissociation process. For example, body dysmorphic disorders, which are on the rise today, enable the person to miniaturize his or her world through dissociative fixations on imagined bodily flaws. Although this and other such disorders such as anorexia nervosa are not classified officially as dissociative pathologies, they nonetheless offer dissociative relief from a threatening loss of control. Aside from the heightened risk of psychological overload and subsequent loss of control, another reason for the spate of dissociative disorders is an increased vulnerability to trauma that has arisen under conditions of modernity.

Historically, culture served as the first line of psychological defense for intrapersonal, interpersonal, and situational problems. This role is so important that some social analysts literally have equated culture with coping. Modernity has seen the arrival of an almost opposite relationship, as culture is often associated with emotional chaos, coping failure, and psychopathology. Most viable cultures have an elaborate emotional defense structure constructed of shared beliefs and rituals, as well as identifiable guidelines for attribution, rationalization, and utilization of social support resources. These are especially important during times of extreme crisis, when the individual is exposed to high levels of emotional stress and arousal that require the adaptive deployment of dissociation.

When cultures perform their usual role as the governors of the dissociation process, it is unlikely that individual members will become traumatized or need to embark on a private program of dissociative pathology. Such cultures offer normalized ritual pathways that permit transient emotional distancing via dissociation. This arrangement avoids the problems that surface when people enact dissociation in social isolation. In a broader sense, a working culture teaches members how to suffer. Cultural suffering strategies afford power and confidence, while also eliminating the need for members to drain energy on personalized coping discoveries. But far-reaching changes have transpired that affect the ability of culture to construct and preserve suffering strategies. A cross-cultural examination reveals a large degree of variation with regard to the prevalence of psychological trauma. In some non-Western settings, members have a high degree of emotional hardiness and a strong resistance to trauma. By contrast, moderns have become exceedingly delicate from the standpoint of resisting the stressors of life. Today we see an unprecedented level of trauma-proneness, as even minor conflicts cause individuals to exceed their coping limits and to lapse into a state of trauma.

Moderns who need to engage dissociation do so in an arbitrary idiosyncratic manner that often does little more than intercept the memory process in order to isolate the problem from consciousness. This does almost nothing to combat the source of the stress. In fact, crude dissociation techniques of this sort keep alive the emotional distress, and hamper final resolution, as they simply banish toxic memories from conscious awareness. Long painstaking psychotherapies are usually needed in order to permit the memories to be emotionally absolved by supported gradual exposure to conscious recognition.

The retreat into the private self has diminished the sense that suffering can be absorbed by the group. Our amplified emphasis on ourselves increases the suffering that we experience in the face of adversity. The limited amount of communal support that is attracted by modern modes of suffering is inferior in quality and does almost nothing to slow the breakdown of the person's defenses. The number of traumatized people will continue to grow as the burden of suffering, and of maintaining emotional order, transfers increasingly from the collective to the individual. More conflicts will become irreconcilable as members find themselves unable to subscribe to culture and to be rewarded with the mental health prophylactics of a social identity.

Trauma counseling will keep expanding as a profession, even though its therapeutic structure does little to address the fundamental social alienation that underlies the current outbreak of trauma-proneness. The loneliness of the modern sufferer will be characterized by a continued reliance on privatized dissociative symptoms, rather than the more efficient madness techniques that were once on offer at the cultural level. A partial solution may lie in a deeper understanding of the cultural designs that were once able to minimize the experience of chaos for members.

FUTURE-MINDEDNESS AND COLLECTIVE AGITATION

It is not difficult to understand why future-oriented cultures have members with elevated anxiety levels. Humanistic psychologists preach about the therapeutic value of immediacy and warn of the emotional risks of abandoning the moment in favor of anticipation and concern about future occurrences. The rationale for a relationship between anxiety and future-mindedness involves issues such as control, predictability, and reliability of experience.

Some thinkers have described modernity as a process that encourages a type of dandyism that causes the person to become lost in presentness.[23] This idea is based on the rationale that the modern dandy must occupy the moment as part of the ongoing process of idealized self-fashioning. It also assumes that the impossibility of maintaining a unified personality in a collapsed cultural sphere demands a transient identity that depends on moment by moment adaptations. Yet, with the cultural shaping of *Homo consumens*, the moment has progressively succumbed to the drive to be somewhere else, and to have something else. This activates a future orientation that is transported by consumer motives, in particular the compulsion to dispose of and replace. The act of replacing has been endowed with so much cultural currency that the replacers cannot accurately compare the new to the old. Their habit is maintained by a blind faith in the cultural assumption that something else is an improvement.

A general consciousness pattern has evolved in which the present is understood as a hindrance, and an impediment to absolute fulfillment. The quest to overcome the limitations of the moment engages a process of planning and anticipation designed to procure future gain. This combines with the modern appetite for *everything*, which further deports the person from the moment. As the future achieves final precedence, immediate streams of awareness conjure up disturbing feelings of discontent and guilty self-betrayal. Along these lines, the moment has become an irritant in that it provides distracting cues that threaten progress toward a worthier tomorrow.

Future consciousness has the potential to translate into anxiety because the moment is lost as a source of grounding, and also because the future is tainted with uncertainty and the risk of failure. Frequently these are not neutralized by the perception of the future as a potential deliverer of hope and betterment. Also, we can no longer trust elements of the present to survive for any length of time. Our own survival has become linked to our ability to adjust to future developments. Unlike in the past, when we operated in the realm of the known, or what we felt we knew, today our fate is tied to the unknown. We are committed to the moment only for the purpose of being able to gauge when conditions will change.

Yet the claim that modernity fosters future focus and anxiety needs to be qualified somewhat. In fact, as is the moment, the future is nearly extinct. It has become an illusory commodity that operates in conjunction with economic dynamics that utilize ephemerality to arrest the emotional world of moderns, and to maintain their continued participation as unsettled consumers who survive on brief punctuations of pseudogratification.[24] The future is now a manipulated illusion that functions as a compass for novelty, which is the lifeblood of consumption as a cultural strategy. As a commercialized fiction, the future not only makes the moment unfashionable and obsolete, but sets the self adrift in misgiving, confusion, and incomprehensible titillation devoid of culmination.

Responsibility for the future has declined as it has become increasingly unreal, and more of a disposable carrierbag for desire. Largely gone is the type of future anxiety wherein the person entertained distressing images of ecological disaster, mass extinction, nuclear holocaust, and the end of the world. There is no longer even much evidence of a background apprehension in relation to such matters. The new variation of future anxiety is fueled less by collective and global concerns, and more by a nagging existential-level fear that one will miss out on something.

A partial exception can be found in the form of young people who have not yet been inculcated by the magnitude of alienating self-interest needed to suppress social and cosmic sensitivities. Prior to the full arrival of their cultural discontent, they express considerable concern about the human and environmental catastrophes of which they are aware. But these vanish quite quickly when they begin to assemble their identities as restless consumers who flirt with retail-style futures that feature in an amorphous market existence. Upon entry into the market world, all aspects of their personalities are honed by cultural texts that actively strive to commercialize the reality of members. Not only the future but life itself become acts of consumption. Yet we are only beginning to recognize the mental health consequences of lengthy exposures to the conditioning patterns that result in the modern consumer.

CHAPTER 6

Modernity and Interpersonal Health

Modernity has introduced a radically different stage upon which our inherent sociality must be enacted. The form, content, and quality of interpersonal relationships have changed dramatically with important implications for psychological well-being. The redefining of the social world has sanctioned relational modes that are potentially abundant in freedom, creativity, and innovation. At the same time, it has never been more difficult for the social needs of people to unfold in a way that is satisfying and enriching.

The disappearance of the collective has had the effect of assigning relationships to individuals, but even this level of association is becoming thin.[1] The social landscape of modernity comprises solitary individuals who find increasing sanctuary in the object and cyber worlds. From this cellular position, they can still engage in a gregariousness that permits physical proximity to others. However, modern modes of human interaction involve very little real social exchange.

The social regression that corresponded to the evolution of *Homo consumens* caused relationships to be reinvented in the context of experimental individualism, and the ascending need for self-enhancement. The format of cognitive socialization is such that committed emotional relations are now coded as a threat to total self-fulfillment, and in particular to the successful exploitation of all available sources of opportunity. The advantages once associated with meaningful interpersonal relationships have been outweighed by the penalties they exact on the self-maximization process. What remains is an undeveloped social plexus that allows members to stay self-focused, devoted to the resolution of their discontents.

Previously, hypermaterialism and consumerism were analyzed in terms of their direct and indirect consequences for mental health. These processes are also important to an understanding of interpersonal health. The social mechanics of consumer society dictate to a considerable extent the types of relationships that develop between people, and also the way in which they conceive of, and relate to, themselves. Consumer culture promotes a type of existential displeasure wherein members are perpetually engaged in a cycle of searching but not finding.[2] As competitive self-interest infiltrates all relationships, the "other" becomes a secondary priority, and social engagement begins to be perceived as a costly enterprise that delays elusive satisfactions. Gradually, consumption becomes more alluring than other human beings.

The advertising industry has been quick to recognize, and capitalize on, the depleted state of human relations by converting consumption into a symbol of closeness. This is illustrated by a clever commercial that begins with beautiful music and images of young children playing with a wooden car. A soft loving voice sings several repetitions of the phrase "If you want to get to know someone, *really* get to know someone." Viewers feel suspense as they wonder what they must do to really know someone. Since children feature in the commercial, people wonder what must be done if they really want to know their children. The tension is resolved when the lyrics add, "Just wait till you drive it, just wait till you drive it." The "it" in this case is a big new automobile. This is a good example of the common practice of selling people more of their problem as a supposed cure.

The desolation of modern relationships has been interpreted in terms of the concept of *conformist consumption*, in which the quality of interpersonal life deteriorates as people adopt a total life-style based on consumption, and in particular on overwork that enables them to overconsume.[3] When the consumer program is fully internalized, it becomes a social vision that, with ongoing media assistance, insulates members from a conscious awareness of their loneliness. Consumption as a cultural code has become so prominent that few members find themselves capable of the healthy disobedience required to develop a personal code that makes ample room for the "other."[4] Even if this were possible, it is likely that self-motivated consumer defiance would have the reverse effect of increasing the amount of estrangement experienced as a result of this cultural disobedience.

PUBLIC ORIENTATIONS, MODERN VOYEURISM, AND SOCIAL ALLERGIES

The consumption of information has become a primary motivation that is restructuring our social lives. For example, Internet usage, which is the fastest growing mode of consumption, has major implications for the depth and quality of our interpersonal relationships. Research reveals that regular Internet consumers (i.e., more than 5 hours per week) spend significantly less time with other people and participate in significantly fewer social events than nonusers or less frequent users. One obvious explanation is the time allocation factor; as more time is devoted to the Internet, less time is available to those in one's local social environment. Another explanation concerns a shift away from the local other as a preferred social partner. Greater priority is being given to the limitless universe of social possibilities that reside in cyberspace.

Although Internet consumption can be thoroughly asocial, it is also giving birth to a new voyeuristic interpersonal style wherein participants beguile themselves with the experience of being connected to the whole world. This heralds a turn of events in which the public has become the new extended family. Moderns are now seeking to forge relationships with far-off audiences, rather than those who inhabit their immediate surroundings. In fact, localness has become a disincentive for social investment, with some people concentrated almost exclusively on their relationship to the public. Evaluations of the self are reliant on ever larger recognition groups, as local heroics is no longer able to fortify identity.

The void left by an absence of committed local relationships is filled partially by personal statements that are aimed at the generalized public. Often the body is used as a billboard for announcing personal tastes, novel values, elite identifications, unique orientations, or exceptional consumer conquests. The simple broadcasting of one's allegiance to prized brand names can serve as a primitive form of public statement. The person making a public statement is driven to stand out, but, unlike for outmoded forms of showing off, there is little prospect of a social response. Although targeted to an unlimited audience, the statement is made in psychological seclusion. The performers are even likely to feel repulsed and embarrassed by unwanted reactions from inconsequential local observers. They are private broadcasters whose signal is aimed at the outlying and unknown reaches of social space, but with no one to register their signals, moderns have in effect become their own seducers.

Statements to the public audience are by no means limited to positive depictions of the self. In fact, ugliness, outrageousness, and preposterousness are popular themes for such statements, especially for young people who are quick to realize the potency of such themes. However, as many parents fail to understand, these statements have little to do with the effects they can generate in the immediate social sphere. Certain consumer gadgets are well suited for purposes of public communication and, as do perfection and ugliness, have great appeal to the young. For example, public displays of mobile phone usage convey not only one's technological currentness, but also the impression that one is in great demand in the world at large. It does not matter that there is no singular listener, as long as the person appears to have something going with all of humanity.

The new social entrepreneur uses the public statement as a creative propaganda strategy that extracts a vague hope of eventual discovery. But this discovery almost never eventuates because people have set their sites on the whole world, and few of them have the self-promotion resources to make an impact at that media level. So their statement remains an imperceptible beacon that stays lit in case fate would somehow conspire to actuate their public discovery. Locals tend to be kept at a distance since they have a knack for tarnishing one's statement and causing one to forfeit some of the effort that has been invested in the public.

A public social orientation weds itself well to the current condition of alienation, while also giving maneuverability to the type of self-servicing that is jeopardized by emotional commitments. Relationships to the public can be maintained quite economically by a surface exhibitionism that does not tax the poorly formed empty self or diminish credibility by virtue of unauthentic encounters. Taking the place of old-fashioned sociality we have personality magnetism that is better designed for bonding to the anonymous public.[5] Also, by adding psychological distance between us and the immediate social environment, we facilitate our capitalist values and ambitions by reducing the guilt we experience through the manipulation of locals.

This shift of the heart from the private to public realm has been aided by an economic plan that has institutionalized and marketed the audience in order to nurture the illusion of communication between self and public. From this has arisen a revolutionary type of undesignated relationship that requires neutralization of honest human inputs. The modern preoccupation with fame represents a new mode of relating that does not entail any people who are actually known to one another.

It might seem that, as with other-directed moral anxiety, the demise of the local "other" would lessen the likelihood of social fear since, in theory, people are not emotionally invested in those around them. However, the past decade has witnessed a well-documented spate of social anxiety disorders, in particular social phobia. Major drug companies have responded robustly to the social phobia boom by developing new medications to treat the estimated 12 to 15 percent of the population who will become psychologically "allergic" to other people.

Whereas cynics have argued that the social phobia phenomenon is still another example of a manufactured commercial pathology aimed at stimulating medical consumption, it is probably better to fathom it as an additional consequence of the loss of the local social sphere. More specifically, it reflects a situation in which performance-driven actors are unable to evaluate themselves as a result of the absence of a local audience. Social anxiety accumulates rapidly when individual performances, directed at nonexistent figmental audiences, have no way of offering the person the type of feedback that assists in self-evaluation or future planning. With no means to pacify themselves through normal local social channels, performance anxiety escalates and becomes cued to a variety of social contexts, thus creating the psychic conditions for social phobia.

BEYOND MUTUALITY AND THE PURE RELATIONSHIP

Not long ago, social theorists were commenting that modernity lends itself to the *pure relationship*.[6] The reasoning was that modernity has disengaged social relations from nearly all external restraints and economic realities, leading to unencumbered relationships that are powered only by the emotional satisfactions that they can deliver. Marriage, like all other forms of relationships, became more "pure" as togetherness was less and less determined by financial survival and division of labor factors. Beyond that, many of the elements that held partners together in former times, which included children, have now become potential nuisances to the new types of relationships that are motivated primarily by internal reward contingencies. The advance of modernity, however, has generated additional changes that no longer allow us to speak of the pure relationship.

One of these is the draining away of commitment. Mutuality, intimacy, trust, and sacrifice are necessary in order to sustain commitment, but all of these have declined as relationships have come to revolve around self-actualization. Ever greater amounts of privatized and idiosyncratic input are funneled into decisions about who will be our partner and friend, as well as the nature and duration of those relationships. The emotionally unaccompanied approach to interpersonal relations has taken on the overriding signature of a culture that has redefined intimacy as an economic entity. Thus we see more technical types of relationships that are no longer founded on substance, character, and resignation.[7]

Whereas all cultures throughout history have put forward some sort of human ideal, the situation now is much different. In former ages, the cultural messages concerning desirable human traits had considerable stability. However, relationships today are updated continually in relation to one's marketability, and to the quickly changing ambitions of all involved. As this unfolds, intense bonding is made less likely, except in short-lived strategic bursts. Further reducing the prospect of deep local attachment is the fact that the structure of our affections is being forged by media-generated images that invite celebrity fantasies as the basis of evaluating others. As the celebrity has invaded consciousness, the job of generating appeal at the local level has become exceedingly difficult.

Modernity has seen the "other" become largely hypothetical, a development that has been magnified by the disappearance of local space and the subsequent rise of cyber caring and purely conjectural relationships. Cul-

tural greed has thinned human involvements even more and replaced uni-
fication tendencies with an accounting process that assesses the exchange
value of the relational investment. One of the most interesting social compensation strategies is *petism*, as increasing numbers of people develop
overly close relationships to pets. Petism has been described as a new culture-bound disorder that is becoming increasingly common in modern
Western culture. By contrast, it does not exist in traditional non-Western
cultures, where social relations and community ties are relatively intact.[8]
The interpersonal vacuum that fuels petism has seen a proliferation of pet
hotels, pet restaurants, and pet psychologists.

In its new role, the pet can help to fill the void left by the disappearance
of the confidant in modern life. Pet owners can communicate their
thoughts and emotions, and obtain comfort in the knowledge that they
have a listening ear. Many moderns cannot access this form of mutual receptivity via human channels. Ultimately, the hypothetical public proves
unable to meet people's relatedness needs, thereby increasing the attraction of the nonhuman world. Pets are the great unsung social heroes of the
modern age, and their psychological value as antidotes to loneliness cannot
be overestimated. Closely behind, and also very important as social surrogates, are collectibles, which are becoming the only friend of the modern
stranger. Menageries of collectibles, which are reliable and unchanging, are
the social and psychological salvation of innumerable moderns who experience a profound sense of abandonment.

SOLITARINESS AND THE INTIMACY CRISIS

As culturally constructed bundles of desire, moderns have the expectation that they will relate to their desires in a relatively private manner.[9] This
augments the sort of individualism that can interfere with interpersonal relations. One cross-cultural study of eleven cultures found that healthy and
lasting relationships between parents and children were more likely in collective than individualistic cultures.[10] Robert Putnam's influential essay
Bowling Alone: America's Declining Social Capital examines individualism
and related cultural processes that diminish *social capital*, "the features of
social organization such as networks, norms, and social trust that facilitate
coordination and cooperation for mutual benefit."[11] An understanding of
the ongoing decline in social capital can shed light on the state of our relationships to other individuals and the wider community.

Generally speaking, life is easier and more satisfying if a society or community has a rich store of social capital since it creates the foundation for social trust and generalized reciprocity. It also underlies civic engagement as
well as the motivation to participate in activities that transcend
self-interest. However, our lives today have become more self-defined and
characterized by a high degree of self-containedness. A wide range of re-

search demonstrates that, in America, there is a significant shift away from nearly all activities that contribute to social capital. The result is that we are doing more and more things alone.

For example, recent years have seen a dramatic fall in participation in local political events, public meetings, school affairs, volunteer work for civic organizations (e.g., Boy Scouts, Red Cross), fraternal organizations, women's clubs, and so forth. In less than 20 years, participation in the Parent-Teacher Association dropped from 12 million to less than 7 million. Research that considered all forms of group membership found that, from 1970 to 1995 in America, aggregate associational membership has declined by approximately 25 percent. As the number of bowlers in America increased by 10 percent from 1980 to 1993, league bowling fell by 40 percent during that period. Again, the trend is to do things alone.

Some countertrends seem to be at work. For example, recent decades have seen an increase in the membership of environmental organizations (e.g., Green Peace, Sierra Club), retired persons groups (e.g., American Association of Retired Persons), and feminist groups (e.g., National Organization of Women). In analyzing this trend toward participation in mass organizations, Putnam points out that most members have only a tertiary relationship with the group. For most, the extent of their involvement is limited to the annual writing of a check to cover dues, plus the occasional glance at a monthly newsletter. Only a small percentage of members attend meetings, and very few have contact with other group members. They usually do not even know that each other exists. So there is almost no foundation upon which social capital can be built.

Another countertrend is the ongoing rise of self-help and support groups. Although these offer some basis for the development of social capital, there is only a very weak bond between members, despite the fact that many people are drawn to these groups in an attempt to compensate for relational deficits with family, neighbors, and general community.[12] In most cases, the actual meetings are merely a forum for individuals to focus on themselves in the company of others. Ultimately, most self-help and support groups do not begin to satisfy the hunger for community that is experienced by many people today.

The disappearance of social capital points to a worrying pattern of social disengagement that has consequences in terms of social trust and "good neighborliness." In 1960, for instance, 58 percent of Americans surveyed endorsed the sentiment that "most people can be trusted." By 1993, this had fallen to only 37 percent.[13] Research from thirty-five countries shows that social trust is closely linked to degree of associational membership. Trust and engagement are two dimensions of the same fundamental factor, namely, social capital.

People today are surrounded by a growing assortment of disinterested specialists who will attend to their needs whenever services are required.[14]

But this new technique-driven social order promotes an intimacy crisis as people are required to relate to fragmented glimpses of the social "other."[15] The absence of a relationship to a complete person invites moderns to participate with the human world in a nomadic way that precludes deep relationships, while giving greater incentive to self-gratification by way of association to the material world. The crisis of intimacy and the demise of social gratification have refashioned all aspects of family life and given rise to an entirely new locus of socialization and affection.

TOWARD THE INVISIBLE PARENT

Historically, the family was the primary culture bearer in a society whose chief motivations were reproduction and conformity. With the parents at the hub, the family provided the clearest pathway to the values, principles, and assumptions of the wider culture. This is less true today as the media overshadow the family as the focal point of cultural transmission, and as the workplace becomes the new physical and psychological home for family leaders. The nuclear family has given way to a diverse multiplicity of family patterns and household arrangements.

The existing culture of consumption has altered goals and life-styles, further reducing the influence of the family as culture bearer. It is now common to find families located in "floating" communities that lack closeness, purpose, and stability. The primary motivations for such communities consist of convenience, consumption, and leisure.[16] As floating families accommodate themselves to consumer society, relationships between family members are made on the basis of economic decisions.

Modern cultural conditions have forged a wide emotional gap between parents and their offspring. Research shows that during the years 1960 to 1986 the amount of parental time available to children decreased by 10 hours per week.[17] This trend appears to be continuing as historical conceptions of family life are being dissolved by asocial motivations that surface in the context of hyperindividualistic consumer society. The cultural transition from family-mindedness to work-mindedness amplifies the effects of all other factors that are sapping strength from the family. In surveys of working couples, upward of 40 percent of respondents report that their jobs interfere with family life. Yet, except for a small countertrend in which some people are rethinking their work and family priorities, the general trend continues to be in the direction of more work and less time for the family.

A growing number of parents are simply unable to find the time for their children. Some observers have begun to speak of the emerging antichild society, which is thought to explain some of the antisocial trends among our youth. Escalating work (and leisure) zeal has, quite literally, prevented many parents from actually knowing their children. The child-as-stranger phenomenon has created a challenging situation for mental health professionals as they try to assess its impact on child development, as well as the family as a basis for social integration. The same is true of the relentless swing toward proxy-style child rearing methods.

Millions of day-cared children are being spawned by the modern precept that children need not prevent us from pursuing private ambitions. Children may be part of our package of wants, but they can no longer expect to have a *psychological parent*.[18] In order for someone to become a psychological parent, he or she must be proximally and emotionally close to the child in a relatively uninterrupted way. Research shows that even relatively brief separations can impede the development of this type of relationship and have long-term negative consequences on the child. So-called quality time does not compensate for actual quantity of time spent with one's child.

Many new age parents like to believe that day care centers are not harmful to a child's development, and furthermore that their children receive benefits through increased exposure to other nurturing adults and to other children who add to their friendship network. Parents who are concerned about the quality of day care settings are turning to new technologies that give them the impression that they are still participating in the care of their children.

This practice has taken the form of Internet websites that allow working parents to access periodic visual images of their children as they go about their activities. It takes them only a few seconds to log in to the site and locate the phantasm that corresponds to their little boy or girl. If all looks well, they can log off and resume their work without any significant loss of time or productivity. This system proves to be especially popular when the child is very young since it provides Internet parents with the illusion that they themselves are doing the supervision, thus freeing them from the instincts that would otherwise incline them to be physically present with the child. Aside from whatever comfort this gives the parents, there is a sizable body of research that demonstrates quite clearly that nonparental child care practices are detrimental to the social and emotional well-being of the child.[19]

One consistent finding is that children raised in day care are more physically aggressive and more verbally abusive to peers and adults. They also tend to display identity confusion, lower frustration tolerance, and diminished ability to persist in task fulfillment than children raised in full-time parental care. Long-term research shows that teenagers who were raised in day care settings were more nonconforming and more likely to use alcohol and drugs. They were also found to be more prone to delinquent behavior and more likely to withdraw from school than teenagers raised in full-time parent care.

Other research has shown that children who spent over 20 hours per week in day care exhibited a reluctance to make contact with their own parents. Research also shows that day care children have greater difficulty in developing a "moral center" and a conscience.[20] They are more inclined to believe that they have full and unrestricted freedom to do whatever they like, regardless of the social consequences. There is a risk that we may be producing many undersocialized children who lack basic social skills and trust.[21]

As the self becomes the consumer, the importance attached to cravings can easily overshadow family devotion and loyalties. Although child neglect can be a result of parental materialistic ambitions, there is a partially competing trend wherein parenthood is conceived as an extension of ownership prerogatives. This translates into a parental desire to maximize the potential of children, to get the utmost from them, and in general to use parenthood as a vehicle to personal fulfillment. In contradiction to the underlying situation of neglect we sometimes find a hyperscrupulous passion to overbond with children. When neglect combines with overindulgence and overbonding, the result is children who do not develop fully in terms of cooperation, sensitivity to the needs of others, and ability to work effectively in groups.[22]

Prior to 2 years of age, children show the ability to feel for, and respond sympathetically to, the suffering and misfortune of other people. But there is mounting evidence demonstrating that children are being socialized in a way that suppresses this natural response capability.[23] In one research study, both mother and child were placed in a situation wherein both were exposed to the distress of another child. Then the mother was observed for her own reaction to the distress and the extent to which she conveyed to her own child the feeling of personal responsibility for the distressed child. The following passage reflects the revealing outcome of this research:

> Far from conveying intense messages about children's responsibilities when they are bystanders to others' suffering, the mothers tend either to ignore the suffering or, more frequently, to reassure the children and tell them not to worry about it! This lack of involvement in others' pain, when their own children have not had a hand in it, is startling.[24]

The wider conclusion drawn from this and similar studies is that altruism is waning in modern society. Social instruction in basic kindness has been supplanted by teaching and modeling that engender a robust sense of entitlement. Humility and gratitude, which have also been removed from society's curriculum, no longer function to curb self-interest. Parents extinguish "good samaritan" tendencies while encouraging aggressive and competitive personality traits. This emphasis raises their children's fitness as lone individuals who must rely on themselves to cope in their unassisted worlds, but the cost of this enculturation design lies in an undercurrent of social insecurity that stems from the progressive breakdown of bonds between people. In conjunction with the general poverty of modern relationships, this insecurity disposes many people toward still greater reliance on consumption.

Children, like adults, are replacing sociality with buying and acquisition strategies aimed at forging for themselves a sense of belongingness, even though they ultimately belong more to the economy than to a cohesive network of other human beings. The child-as-customer phenomenon has been explained by the rise of the "absent other" and of distanced relations in modern society, in stark contrast to premodern social structures that were characterized by the obvious presence of others.[25]

The antiquated notion of maternal instinct is no longer taken seriously as a primary source of cultural motivation, and the same is true of instinctual drives toward parental nurturance in general. Increasingly children are becoming an extension of the impression management strategies used by alienated parents who have retreated into a romance with their own potential. If one's children can also be made to realize their potential, this is even more proof for the anonymous public that the parent is realizing his or her full potential. The child's new role as impression manager of the parent is the reason many parents today feel a compulsive urge to push their children to their limits and beyond in order to achieve conspicuous victories. The emotional costs to the children tend to be rationalized with the assumed logic that excellence and fame will open doors and give them a grounding for future happiness.

The age of unquestioning devotion to the child is gone; parents are now able to negotiate their affections with their own interests at the forefront of their mind. The presumption of compromise has given way to parent-child relationships wherein both parties receive equal consideration. Children have joined the expanding ranks of those who must be responsible for their own psychological welfare, freeing former parental captives to develop their own personality into a worthwhile commodity.

The physical deportation of one's children is being experienced as less and less sinful in light of the elevated status of personal profit, and the new understanding of self-sufficiency as the key to a thoroughly profitable life. The debut of the whimsical self-seeking parent has been made possible by the psychological compartmentalization of children, wherein cultural permission has been granted to deem children as part-time entities that have been stripped of most of their historical powers of restriction, limitation, and inhibition. The dreary, but pacifying, resignations of earlier versions of parenthood are no longer inevitable.

However, the social sanctioning of the invisible parent is not yet complete; as a result some parents are still confronted by guilt about their general absence from their children's lives. In fact, there has emerged a rather characteristic pattern that could be labeled *self-actualization guilt* in which parents use negative emotion to punish themselves for giving priority to their own program of self-fulfillment. Some parents engage in a daily routine of mourning for their children as they deposit them with their care givers; residual guilt stays with them the rest of the day. The mourning-guilt syndrome is especially prevalent in women who are choosing to work because it is more satisfying and pleasurable than being at home.

In this regard, research confirms that a growing number of mothers are outsourcing their children, not for financial reasons, but for the more stimulating types of arrangements that exist in the workplace.[26] A similar reaction has appeared in men who become married to work, and thus even less available to the family, because work offers more than home in terms of recognition and positive feedback. It has become easier for parents to justify career moves that are designed as escapes from the pandemonium and urgency of children and their needs.[27]

Yet for those whose old style of conditioning is still alive, considerable conflict can arise during moments of awareness of the emotional cost to their children. Those most affected by this conflict find themselves wavering in confusion, not able to resolve the work-family dilemma. A small percentage of conflicted parents are sacrificing their work pleasures in order to make more time for their children and family. But the broader trend is for parents to dissociate from their guilt and sadness in order to devote more of their time to the manageable and less precarious relationships in the work environment.

One overriding trend, the choice not to have children, is being reflected in rapidly declining birth rates throughout the Western world. The childless family will continue to gain in popularity as more and more people are swayed toward life-style creations founded upon maximal freedom as a vehicle for consumer heroics. This goal will also result in a continuation of the present trend away from marriage itself, which reflects the tendency of moderns to approach commitment on a purely experimental and exchangeable basis.

EXCHANGE RELATIONSHIPS, POSTMARITAL DEPRESSION, AND DIVORCE CULTURE

Marriage has become steadily more private and voluntary in nature. Decisions about marriage are being made in light of the prospects for personal fulfillment. The institution itself has been dethroned as a supraindividual entity that supersedes both the individual and the couple. In its place, we have another possible life choice that, if taken wisely, has something to offer the individuals involved. Rather than being the basis for compromise and sacrifice, it has been reshaped into a relational investment that can pay dividends in terms of *self*-satisfaction.

In this respect, recent decades have witnessed a shift from communal marriages to exchange marriages.[28] In communal relationships, people are concerned about the welfare of others at least as much as they are concerned about their individual desires. There is a mutuality about communal relationships that carries the assumption that both participants are looking out for each other. As part of this, they do not feel a strong need for automatic reciprocity. When they give to the other person, it is assumed that this is making a contribution to the overall relationship. By contrast, in exchange relationships, participants are more self-focused, and thus more likely to view the relationship as a sort of economic exchange. Many such marriages revolve around the efficient management of work schedules and finances. An expectation exists that there should be a significant return from any investment of time, energy, or money into the relationship. Although traditional arranged marriages had some of these pragmatic qualities, the exchange involved was intended primarily to benefit the long-term *union* of two people. The "other" in a modern exchange marriage is a carefully chosen, but modifiable, component of one's life portfolio.

There is a positive side to the practice of selecting a mate realistically on the basis of an exchange. For example, entering into a relationship on a cost-benefit basis increases one's chances of financial security, while conversely reducing the risk of material deprivation. Exchange relationships also enjoy a contractual structure that allows more predictability and control than less rational love-propelled relationships. Yet one must wonder about the ability of market-style marriages to provide the intangible rewards of a blinder type of love that is not ruled by self-interest and cost-benefit calculations.[29]

People are finding it difficult to make the sort of emotional commitment that is necessary in order to enter into a marriage. One reason for this trend is that many of us now feel that marriage entails giving up too much. We hold off until we are convinced that the other person is the real thing, and that the marriage will be the sure bet that we demand. Until then, the "opportunity cost" of making a marital commitment is perceived as being too high.[30]

Modern marriages are becoming more companionate in design, and less bound to mutual commitment assumptions.[31] Personal considerations have come to outweigh traditional influences and rendered obsolete the notion of lifelong devotion. Commitment has become highly tentative. Out of this development has arisen a flourishing counseling industry whose central aims are to negotiate marital relationships within the framework of the private demands of participants and to remedy the distress stemming from failed negotiation agreements. One small part of this expanding industry is the drawing up of prenuptial agreements that preserve individual interests in anticipation of marital dissolution.

The motives for divorce in companionate marriages can be quite subtle. Rather than reflecting indifference to or disregard for the partner, they seem more related to unconscious existential assessments made about one's progress with the Dream. With pragmatism no longer able to justify marital continuity, the Dream has achieved as much importance as the marital participants themselves. The modern marriage partner is expected to do his or her part in making the Dream a reality. If both have similar aspirations along these lines, some semblance of harmony will prevail, but if one partner begins to lose sight of the Dream, the other is likely to interpret this as a form of mutiny or rejection. Sometimes this is explained away with the reasoning that they have grown apart, but in reality the split has little to do with growth. With increasing frequency, marital breakdown is the result of the partners' falling out of step in their wider journeys as consumers.

The viability of marriage is always threatened by the fact that the Dream has too many variations, and too many fluctuating qualities, for it to be achieved in unison with someone else. Another problem is that a great deal of time and energy must be funneled into its quest. Among other things, it transforms the seeker into a worker who runs the continual risk of becoming invisible to the other person. The simple matter of time can account for a large number of marital collapses. Working marriages often have much more economic capital than marital capital, as a result of insufficient time to nourish a loving relationship.

Marital capital, which ultimately determines the strength of a marriage, derives from engagement in joint pursuits and activities that promote the experience of being a couple. Simultaneously, those pursuits forge a set of values and attitudes that are unique to the marriage. They give life to the relationship in which the participants are also part of a supraindividual association made up of two connected people. However, the trend is for marriages to be so individualized that they lack the necessary amounts of mutuality to generate adequate marital capital. The previously mentioned "bowling alone" phenomenon is observable in many marriages, allowing us to speak of people who have the underlying feeling that they are married alone.

The aloneness of the modern marriage experience is one reason that *postmarital depression* has become a common affliction for new Western brides and grooms. It is precipitated by some of the same social structures that predispose new Western mothers to postnatal depression. In particular, both new mothers and new marriage partners are assaulted by the postceremony reality that their new status has no recognition or support in the wider culture. In both cases, their new roles have no structures other than improvised ones that strive to assign meaning to the whole venture. Newly married people sense that new responsibilities are an aspect of their changed status, but they again struggle to identify a wider framework within which to comprehend and act upon these responsibilities. In many cases, it soon emerges that they are solely responsible for themselves.

This experience is magnified by its stark contrast to the usual pomp that precedes the occasion. The commercial hysteria that features prominently in contemporary marriages results in a demoralizing transition from consumer fantasy to relational reality. It masks only temporarily the cultural separation that young newlyweds are forced to endure in the modern age. The general isolation of modern marriage causes the couple to look toward each other for direction, guidance, and comfort. However, in most cases, the motives instilled by consumer conditioning overtake the relationship, and both soon become devoted to work and other profitable engagements. Before long, participants realize that the spouse is unable to provide emotional salvation; that recognition adds to the suspicion that marriage will be a lonely and poorly delineated experience.

Like the new Western mother who succumbs to depression as a result of perceived social abandonment, the new go-it-alone married person is predisposed in a similar way toward depressive symptoms. When this combines with the conscious awareness of disappointment and the withdrawal effects of a hypercommercialized premarital period, it is an easy step to entertain divorce as a solution to one's negative emotion.

The modern crisis of sexuality is another element that contributes to postmarital depression and the general poverty of contemporary marriage. Modernity has seen the demise of shared sexuality. The sexuality crisis that has ensued has been explained in terms of social alienation and the eclipse of intimacy.[32] Without the "other" to complete the sexual act, there is little chance for intimacy. When this happens, sex becomes just another thing to have, or another commodity to consume. Satisfying sexuality requires a deep union with the "other," but self-interested participants end up with an other-less sex that has a way of fostering confusion, doubt, and variety seeking.

Social analysts have made increasing reference to the commercialization of love and sexuality. In a noncommercial marriage, love is integrated into the relationship in such a way as to provide an antidote for individual maximization.[33] That is, a love union actually offers relief from the pursuit of immediate self-interest, and a redirection toward a subjectively higher cause in the form of the love union itself. It is even probable that the self-sacrifice entailed in this type of relationship strengthens the union and becomes a source of heightened attraction. Sexuality loses an essential component when both individuals are geared toward personal maximization. Fidelity and faithfulness are among the assumptions that have been ejected in favor of ones that relate to the new prerogative not to allow one's desires to be frustrated.

The loss of the presumption of permanence has an impact on "emotional insurance" and, in turn, the quality of sexual relations.[34] The experience of emotional insurance is unlikely when individualistic calculation is the primary motivation underlying sexual engagement. When sexuality is perceived as a consumer right, loneliness pervades the union, and the sex act itself becomes dominated by technique. Since sexual technique cannot compensate for a loss of mutuality or bridge the gulf of loneliness, sexual incompetence is never far behind. This explains the rising rate of all types of sexual dysfunction and sexual inadequacy that feature in the modern sexuality crisis.

Estimates indicate that over 30 million American men suffer from either complete or partial erectile dysfunction. One must wonder whether the human being has ever had sexual problems on this scale. Reports are appearing about the modern "Impotency Boom" and the epidemic proportions this problem has reached in the West. This phenomenon has become a financial boom for many, not unlike the gold rush of the nineteenth century. A prosperous drug and sex therapy industry has arisen to capitalize on this sexual problem.

Sexual desire disorders have also been increasing at a very rapid rate over the past two decades.[35] The most common disorder is classified as *hypoactive sexual desire disorder*, a deficiency or total absence of sexual urges, which currently affects over 20 percent of the adult population. Different causes have been suggested, such as fear of loss of control, fear of pregnancy, depression, and a history of sexual trauma. Of these factors, depression is the only one that could account for the sharp increases in sexual desire disorders, but we probably need to go beyond depression as a causal agent and to look at the shifting focus of our desires. Passion that normally would be directed to the social realm is drained off as culture imbues members with the type of desire, including sexual desire, that does not promote self-transcendence or human interest.

As the market absorbs greater amounts of our emotional attention, the "other" becomes more generalized, and the strength of emotional bonding is depleted.[36] Even our closest "loved ones" have become more generalized, and less capable of being circumscribed with lasting deep emotion. The inability to differentiate others from a diffuse market experience has resulted in a different definition of marriage. It has uncoupled itself from traditional societal goals and redefined itself as a personal gamble that could pay off in terms of self-fulfillment for both parties. The market mentality and the subsequent loss of the distinct other have also rewritten the meaning of divorce. Rather than being perceived as failed cultural heroics, or even as an arrangement that went wrong, divorce has become a wager that did not come in, a bet that did not work out. Consumer society has remolded marriage into a wearable consumer product that may or may not fit.

The option to divorce is a consumer's right if the product proves unsatisfactory, and if the contractors want to cut their losses. Unlike in former times when divorce was constrained by social morality, now the marital customer is always right. In this environment, there is no need for divorce to be accompanied by punishing social dramatics, lengthy self-flagellation, soul searching, or self-improvement. Instead it is thought that, in time, the market will swing in one's direction and make obvious another choice.

As divorce has been embraced by consumer dynamics, it has achieved a new respectability that liberates participants from restrictive social dominion. The whole process of divorce, from initial fantasy through to new partner shopping, is becoming a type of consumer distraction that somehow compensates for the barrenness of actual relationships. Despite the emptiness and social craving that intermingles with modern divorce culture, permanent marriage is largely unfathomable, and already quaintly unfashionable, to the new generation of the interpersonal consumer. Historically, children have represented a reason for disregarding or delaying the option of divorce, but the swing toward viewing children as an optional extra to marriage will make divorce an even easier course of action in the future.

We are all familiar with the statistics about the rising divorce rates. In some parts of the Western world, more than 50 percent of marriages end in divorce. In the United States, nearly 10 million children currently live in single-parent families: a sixfold increase over the past four decades. The divorce rate is rising steadily all over the Westernized world, even in countries like Israel that have a deep tradition of family unity. There are a few exceptions where the percentage of marriages ending in divorce has stabilized for the time being, but the assumption of impermanence continues to permeate the marital contract. There is an implicit background expectation that the time will come when the relationship will no longer be *worth* it to the contractual participants.

Although modernity has shortened the lifespan of marriages, some aspects of modernity appear to enhance marital satisfaction. In one study in Israel, for example, researchers assessed quality of marriage in relation to a number of modernization variables, including education, maternal employment, and equality of conjugal power.[37] These factors were found to correlate with increased marital satisfaction, despite the overriding fact that contemporary Israeli marriages are more precarious than traditional ones. This was the case for both males and females. The investigators concluded that the growing voluntariness and equality of modern marriages in Israel, which produce instability and vulnerability, have the effect of improving the quality of marital relations. Therefore, the truncated lifespan of marriages today does not automatically imply diminished marital satisfaction during the actual course of the relationship. A divorce option may be especially liberating for women who have run the historical risk of marital imprisonment, and the exploitation and oppression that this has entailed.

There is some evidence that, under certain conditions, features of modernization can lessen the likelihood of divorce. In Islamic Southeast Asia, for example, decreasing rates of divorce have been explained by social changes that allow greater freedom to make personal choices about marriage partners, as well as greater opportunities for women to receive an education and thereby postpone marriage to a later age.[38] The greatest advantage of these alterations to traditional practices is that the person can reduce the risk of an unsatisfactory marriage. In contrast, Western countries give primary emphasis to the dissolution of disappointing marriages.

Research still identifies money matters as the number one reason for marital disintegration in contemporary Western society. Concerns about money and all things material has actually become a greater determinant of marital well-being even though we live in a period of unprecedented economic prosperity. It is common even for couples basking in vast surpluses of wealth to identify money matters as the primary reason for divorce.

Other frequently cited reasons for divorce include loss of mutual respect, waning feelings of love, and conflict of various sorts in addition to those related to money, but an interesting trend that has appeared is that increasing numbers of divorces unfold without any obvious signs of conflict. Nearly one-third of divorces are now of this conflict-free variety, in which one or both partners simply experience the feeling that they would be happier elsewhere.

The upsurgence of friendly divorces is proving especially troublesome for the children who must come to terms with this type of breakup. In addition to whatever other emotional problems they face because of the divorce, they struggle with a profound puzzlement. The children cannot understand why their seemingly happily married parents would choose to divorce. In the absence of a plausible explanation, they frequently turn the blame onto themselves, despite reassurances from their parents. Not surprisingly, research shows that the postdivorce adjustment of such children is less favorable than that of children who go through parental divorces that are characterized by open conflict. In general, divorce culture has created many new mental health challenges for children today.

A large body of research has chronicled the potential ill effects of divorce on children. Some types of postdivorce custody arrangements are quite difficult for children. For example, girls in paternal custody and boys in maternal custody have been found to be especially disadvantaged in terms of deficiencies of prosocial behavior, impulse control, anger management, and self-concept.[39] The loss of wider sources of social support, as well as a deterioration of the quality of living environment, can add to the problems of children in divorce culture. These harmful effects can be assuaged partially when supportive networks and adequate physical resources can be maintained after the divorce.

Beyond the potential psychological pitfalls of divorce, marriage as an institution has lost so much social credibility that it is vanishing as a prerequisite for childbearing. Throughout the modern world, the number of children being born to single mothers and unmarried parents has nearly matched the number who find themselves outside dual-parent families as a result of divorce. In the United States, one-third of children are being born to unmarried mothers, and the same trend is occurring in other Western countries. This has many complex mental health ramifications for growing numbers of children who are being raised in alternative family environments.

Children reared in single-parent arrangements are not necessarily destined to suffer psychological ill effects, but childhood stress is more likely as a result of the multiple transitions often accompanying this situation.[40] Children who undergo numerous transitions, as well as exposure to changing care-giver patterns, have reduced educational success and a greater risk of emotional difficulties. Inconsistent and contradictory socialization practices are among the reasons cited for the deleterious impact of some styles of family organization and for the inablility of parents to meet the socioemotional needs of children. Even in traditional family designs, we find that parents are making smaller and smaller socioemotional investments in their children. This affects in a negative way the self-image, coping ability, comfort level, and overall adjustment of the children who find themselves victims of this increasingly common form of deprivation.

ANTISOCIAL, IMPULSIVE, AND BORDERLINE-NARCISSISTIC TRENDS

In looking at interpersonal health from another angle, we might consider the many statistics that suggest that contemporary Western culture has gravitated toward destruction, death, and violence. For instance, between 1950 and 1970, there was a doubling of the murder rate in the United States.[41] The murder rate among boys aged 14 and 17 doubled between 1985 and 1995.[42] Increasingly we hear of children under 10 years of age who murder other children, sometimes for a few dollars, sometimes for no apparent reason other than boredom. Over 2 million Americans are currently in jail, and many American states opt for the death penalty out of general frustration with the burgeoning problem of violent crime.

Medical practitioners in many urban hospital emergency rooms compare their work to that of doctors who mop up on the front lines of battle during war. Murder has become the single most common cause of death in some age groups. In the United States, the leading cause of death for women in the workplace is murder; for men it is the third most common cause of death. Each year in America, the number of murders is more than half of the number of American lives lost in the combined years of the Vietnam War. More than 2,000 murders are committed annually in the city of

Los Angeles. Not long ago, 34,000 wreaths were laid out near the White House, each representing a child or adolescent who had been murdered in the preceding few years. A considerable number of these deaths were the result of the increasingly popular pastime of thrill killing. When interviewed after their crimes, thrill killers speak as if they had done nothing more serious than kill a little time. In most instances, no signs of social conscience can be found.

The motivation for this phenomenon has little to do with achieving the basics of survival. The former correlations between crime and poverty, or crime and unemployment, are disappearing. Acts of brutality are being committed by people who have no excuse on the grounds of need. Rather, they reflect a desensitization to antisocial behavior that stems from a moral code that lacks a social foundation.

Alarmists have begun to speak of the suicidal and necrophilic tendencies of modern Western culture, but this stance is not warranted, for several reasons. It is true that the new cultural conditioning project has replaced public virtue and other-directed empathy with a profit mentality whose primary allegiance is to the market,[43] but the vast majority of asocial profiteers continue to operate within a set of cooperative arrangements and self-constraints that maximize their efficiency and adaptability and make for profitable business with others.[44] In this way, considerable degrees of dishonesty and deception can be acted out as part of the normal interaction between partakers. The law itself is revamping itself in order to accommodate mutual exploitation practices wherein all parties are both criminal and victim.

Psychological symptoms tended historically to mirror cultural prohibitions that were propounded by mainstream social institutions. For example, obsessive and compulsive symptoms were almost exclusively religious in nature, such as intrusive negative thoughts about God or unstoppable urges to commit some type of sin. Hypervirtuous symptoms, in which the patient symbolically enacted social contrition, were also a feature of premodern madness techniques. When religion faded as the moral purveyor, obsessive-compulsive symptoms still had a distinctly other-related aspect, as when a woman feared that she might hurt her husband or children. Although drawing on more localized themes for pathological structure, they nonetheless continued to echo the inclination of individuals to transcend themselves and to locate meaning in a larger social framework. However, these patterns of symptom formation are becoming less common as cultural wrongs become less salient, fewer in number, and more reflective of infractions against oneself. The symptom constellations that are becoming prevalent today are those that communicate pathological degrees of self-attention. Characterological and self-control symptoms are becoming highly prevalent as a consequence of the social deregulation of madness.

What were once called character disorders are now sometimes classified as personality disorders in the official psychiatric diagnosis manuals. Even so, some mental health professionals still refer to character disorders in an attempt to describe symptoms that are more than, or other than, overtly psychiatric in nature. The diagnosis of character disorder often involves a value judgment that the disturbance somehow relates to deeper flaws at the level of the self. In this regard, an assessment is made that something is wrong with the person, rather than simply with the "mind" of that person. The potential confusion that stems from the diagnosis of a character disorder relates to the possibility that the disorder might be normal (in the sense of being the norm) and also that the afflicted often do not experience suffering. The diagnosis then becomes a matter of what the diagnostician assumes to be acceptable behavior and, more generally, what constitutes human nature.

A grandiose dimension has been added to the private self that curtails social perspective and produces narcissistic individuals who become their own most compelling cause in life. It has been claimed that narcissistic personality disorder (NPD) is the defining characterological disturbance of the contemporary world, and that it is a direct by-product of modernity.[45] In support of this claim, there is ample clinical evidence that the diagnosis of pathological narcissism is being made much more frequently than in previous decades.

A similar picture has emerged in relation to borderline personality disorder (BPD), which some scholars believe is simply a more disorganized manifestation of NPD. Research indicates that BPD is far more common in modern, as compared to traditional, societies and also that it is increasing within Western cultural settings.[46] BPD is defined officially as *a pervasive pattern of instability of interpersonal relationships, self-image, and emotion* that is associated with high levels of impulsivity. It is this impulsivity that represents the core element of BPD.

Certain contemporary social structures combine to generate an impulsivity-proneness that predisposes members to personality styles that attract a borderline label. The nebulous and uninformed nature of current cultural institutions leaves members with a similarly ill-defined psychic framework that cannot support social inducements or values that adulterate self-attention. Modern culture has also gravitated toward very broad socialization patterns that emphasize individual preferences rather than the conformity-based behavior that stems from narrow socialization strategies.[47]

The narrow socialization of traditional societies is usually supported by close living and working relationships between adolescents and adults. The high degree of monitoring and mentoring that this affords inclines the adolescent to adopt the values and beliefs that have social approval, while reducing the likelihood of embarkation on a course of reckless, idiosyncratic, and whimsical action. Their close physical and mental proximity to respected sources of enculturation augments their motivation to succeed within the historical constraints and guidelines of the culture. They develop and engage impulse control in an effort to accomplish the challenge of repeating prosocial cultural formulas toward the end of locating a recognized role and paving the way for entry into the adult world. The acceptance of prohibitions and responsibilities is typically a part of this process.

Societies employing narrow socialization formats usually have institutionalized methods by which to usher adolescents into the adult world; this structure rewards prosocial conformity and connects self-concept to social harmony and the assumption of adult responsibility. Research demonstrates that cultures that offer adulthood challenges and subsequent initiations for official recognition of adult status have low rates of reckless and antisocial behavior.[48] Broad socialization patterns as they exist in the modern age leave the young person undisciplined for an indeterminate period, without any guarantee that this individual will ever achieve much self-control or mastery of primitive impulses. In fact, modernity has stretched the lifespan of adolescence to the extent that it is possible to fend off adulthood almost indefinitely.

This development has been assisted by media socialization that mesmerizes members with youthful advantage, while also inspiring them to entertain continually any private or dissociated urges that could be satisfied through creative consumption. The end product is that the perpetual adolescent of the modern era has become immune to the regulating influence of maturity, while enjoying permission to act impetuously on even the most covert motivations that might be detected. This explains in part the steady increase in the prevalence of various impulsivity disorders that have been documented in recent years. The cultural invention of the temporally arrested adolescent offers choice and fluidity and seduces a titillating exploration of one's fantasies. At the same time, it programs the perpetual adolescent with certain traits, most notably impulsivity and social unconnectedness, that increase the risk that borderline and narcissistic orientations will become dysfunctional.

The narcissism-borderline category is the most frequently diagnosed of all the personality disorders. Looking more closely at NPD, we see a disorder characterized by a preoccupation with unlimited success, a greatly exaggerated sense of self-importance, exhibitionistic appeals for attention, unresponsiveness to social criticism, disturbed interpersonal relations, and a tendency to respond with rage to disappointment or restriction. The terms *depressed narcissism* and *negative narcissism* are being used with increasing frequency to emphasize the negative emotion that stems from an oscillation between self-glorification and self-loathing. It is also sometimes referred to as *middle-class narcissism*, an attempt to identify it as a class of pathology that is not necessarily defined by abnormality in the sense of deviating from the norm.

In NPD we see a character structure that displays intense feelings of entitlement that permit the person to exploit and control others without much inhibition, anxiety, or guilt. From their highly self-centered perspective, it is difficult to experience motivations that do not relate to immediate benefits to the self, even though they can sometimes manipulate social circumstances to their gain. Their general disregard for others is often accompanied by intermittent cravings for their approval. Narcissistic disorders are associated with a proneness toward hostility, due in part to the pronounced inferiority and diminished frustration tolerance that characterize this personality style.

Modern cultural conditions provide the ideal breeding grounds for personality disorders such as NPD and BPD. Their design is such that there is no longer a place for strategic barriers to unregulated self-expression and self-gratification. Modern culture has also seen a significant depletion of easily identifiable social roles. When that depletion is combined with exceedingly fast social change, the result is an environment wherein members must forge a personal identity that is not structured through community affiliation.[49]

The full range of personality disorders may be encouraged under conditions of cultural disintegration and rapid change. One reason for this may involve the loss of family cohesiveness, and the failure of children to receive necessary amounts of nurturance and consistent emotional support. Out of this comes a family structure that is virtually opposite to the traditional "Confucian family" that stresses structure, rules, cohesion, and marital stability. Although tensions can arise in a Confucian family, its supports and networks are able to buffer most encounters with adversity. To illustrate this point, cross-cultural research related to antisocial personality disorder shows that this form of psychopathology is rare or is nonexistent in cultures that have a Confucian family structure.[50] According to some thinkers, the increasing prevalence of personality disorders and related forms of psychopathology is due to the combined effects of family and community breakdown. Temperamentally vulnerable individuals often collapse under the weight of multiple stressors related to normlessness, depletion of social roles and consensual values, and the general failure of social structures as coping devices.[51]

With specific reference to narcissistic personality features, modernity has constructed a private sphere that has fragmented away from the constraining institutions that once governed instinctual impulses and thereby discouraged purely selfish gratification.[52] This arrangement leaves little room for the installation of ideals and motivational motifs that recognize external authority beyond the bare minimum required for safe operation. As contemporary cultural ideals take people further into the materialistic

and purely informational world, there is even less impetus for them to sub-
limate self-interest. In the absence of perceived prohibitions, modern culture places very few demands on its members to communicate substance,
or to develop beyond the level of exhibitionism and the creative scratching
of one's consumer itches.

Today both narcissists and normal individuals display a deliberative
technique-driven self-structure that demotes the status of sharing relationships. Likewise, both emphasize manipulation and control in order to maximize personal outcomes, simultaneously creating a social veneer designed
to mask disinterest. In a paradoxical way, the plague of narcissistic pathology is being cured to some extent by the rapid cultural normalization of
narcissism itself. As a product of collective regression, normal narcissism
expresses itself in many ways, including enthusiasm for personal achievement, health and fitness, bodily perfection, diet, the ultimate orgasm, spiritual bestowals, and all sorts of self-improvement prescriptions. This is all
part of a cultural situation in which radical self-preoccupation is an acceptable, and even admirable, approach to life.

CHAPTER 7

Spiritual and Existential Health

A long-standing debate concerns the relation of religion to mental health. Recent years have seen the publication of several books and many research articles on this and related topics. My own book *Religion and Mental Health* was an attempt to synthesize empirical studies that could demonstrate the effects of religious belief and practice on a range of mental health variables.[1] In the introduction to that book, I spell out some of the reasons why religion is generally thought to be beneficial to psychological well-being. These include its ability to reduce anxiety by providing cognitive structures (e.g., pacifying attributions and explanations) that help to impose order on a chaotic world; offer existential grounding in the form of meaning, purpose, and hope which, in turn, generates an emotional well-being; instill followers with a reassuring fatalism that enhances coping ability; yield solutions to situational and emotional conflicts; provide a partial solution to the fact of earthly mortality; offer a feeling of control and power by way of identification with an omnipotent force; provide the basis for self-serving and other-serving moral guidelines; foster social cohesion and a sense of community; afford members a social identity, and a sense of belongingness, by uniting people around shared understandings; and establish a foundation and outlet for cathartic ritual.

No one would dispute the fact that religion can transform completely the life of an individual. Endless cases can be found of people whom religious enlightenment rescued from the brink of despair or suicide, and for whom it paved the way for new life directions. We hear of hopelessly addicted drug users for whom religion was the only pathway to a drug-free life. Aside from religion's being helpful in a healing role, it is not difficult to find ordinary people who derive a great deal of day-to-day joy and meaning through a close association with religion.

There is no doubt that religion also has the potential to go very wrong and to play a destructive role in terms of mental health. Religion is easily contaminated by individuals in authority who twist the process in order to accommodate their own perversions, control ambitions, and eccentric interpretations. Additionally, it is possible for religions to incorporate beliefs and worldviews that can prove disturbing to members, and ritual practices that are sometimes the source of emotional scarring, but the fact that all cultures throughout history have created religion speaks to some extent of religion's capacity to afford members with certain benefits. Even so, modernity has ushered in dramatic changes that have important implications for religion's ability to function as a mental health prophylactic.

SELF-ABSOLUTION AND PRIVATE RELIGION

Being alive as a human being is not easy, in part because of the difficult task of believing, which in the past was assisted greatly by the wider culture. Many of the advantages of religion mentioned here stem from its social dimension, but the modern quest for belief and spiritual transcendence has been reshaped by self-containedness. Modernity has seen an ongoing privatization of religion wherein the inner self and individual consciousness become the primary guidelines for transcendence.[2] As part of this, God has become more accessible, albeit in ways that have become detached from larger social meanings. Religious privatization has placed God in a better position to respond to our specific needs.

Unlike in premodern times, when followers were the instruments of God, they have now taken the initiative and made God into an instrument of progress and advancement.[3] Old-fashioned forms of faith have disappeared since they rely upon a constant self that is not fostered under existing cultural conditions. Additionally, they demand too much patience and equanimity, and that requirement has caused them to yield to more assertive spiritual capitalizations. The active exploitation of a demystified and more progressive God reflects the trend of moderns to assume greater responsibility for their own wants.

Religion inhabits an increasingly separate world, and religious institutions have been besieged by techniques from other segments of society. More specifically, religion is being cordoned off by new attitudes, languages, interests, and styles of institutional life that have emerged from the requirements of technology, science, secular education, and postreligious economics and politics.[4] In some locations, most notably the United States, popular culture has stepped in to absorb some of the spiritual slack created by the deinstitutionalization of religion.

The current innerness of religion can be understood as an aspect of the process of self-absolutization. Modernity has seen the human being become self-centered, prone to self-divinization, and inclined to construct reality in this-world ways. It is a development that has the effect of diminishing the transcendent elements of religion and creating a new sort of cognitive crisis. Robert Bellah writes that as religion becomes increasingly human, we run the risk of becoming psychological captives of a "literal and circumscribed reality which is precisely and classically to be trapped in hell, without transcendence, without manner, and without the devastating power of the sacred."[5]

Religious individualism makes more difficult the classic task of religion, namely, to construct a common world that infuses social life with ultimate meaning.[6] The distinctly self-centered nature of contemporary Western religion coincides with the shedding of universal organizing principles designed to support shared assumptions and an agreed-upon universe. The loss of religion's operational nucleus has also created a predisposition among members to experience a spiritual restlessness that has become a prominent feature of contemporary life.

Faithless Religion and the New Personality of God

Just as we have seen the disappearance of the deep relationship in other areas of life, so too has it vanished from religion. Our primary commitment is shifting to the economy, which increasingly is addressing our unreality needs and providing the myths that are indispensable in making sense of a senseless world.

In the main religions of the modern capitalistic world, God is becoming less paternalistic, less spiritually imperious, and less needy of our undivided attention. Rather than lording over us with rigid authoritarian commandments, God is being envisioned as a gifted broker who blesses in an unreliable way those who have faith enough in themselves to capitalize on earthly systems. When we ourselves are pleased, we know that God is also pleased. It is not necessary to make one's life into a prayer, as was done in premodern times by some of God's children. In becoming more spiritually adult, we no longer expect much loyalty or response from God; nor does God any longer ask much of us.

A faithless attitude toward God has given rise to purely ritualistic modes of prayer that are not targeted at any spiritual entity. Research has shown that the majority of today's adolescents and young adults feel that God has not lived up to their expectations as a provider, thereby justifying their growing doubts about God as a religious symbol and an explanatory force.[7]

Many no longer perceive God as having the means or power to satisfy the magnitude of desire that they experience.

Religion has entered the wider marketplace of consumable options that must compete with one another. In the same way that modernity has supplanted fate with choice, spiritual consumers now find themselves selecting among spiritualities on the basis of how good they feel, or what works for them as individuals. With the loss of moral consensus and shared religious meanings, God has become a matter of personal choice. More generally, religion has been released from the confines of the transcendent and placed in the domain of the individual. Expanding religious diversity has cast new doubts on the cosmic validity of group-sanctioned belief systems and further encouraged faith in oneself as the foundation for reality construals. In the process of all this, the status of public knowledge has been greatly diminished as the content source for spiritual transcendence.

The decline of the social transcendental has spawned a spirituality that is better suited to autonomous self-governing individuals, but the case has been made that the private pursuit of transcendence lacks some of the psychological advantages associated with collective religions.[8] Private religion is self-conscious in the sense that participants lose awareness of group endorsement. Historically, the group has served to normalize belief systems that otherwise would be deemed irrational or even pathological. Collective religion also managed to normalize ritual and thereby afford to members the many mental health benefits that group ritual has to offer.

The Crisis of Ritual

Human beings have a deep-rooted need for ritual that explains why all intact cultures throughout history possessed elaborate patterns of ritual that served individual members and the general community. These rituals offer a means for emotional catharsis in a socially sanctioned context that minimizes self-consciousness.[9] As self-consciousness is reduced within a supportive environment, the person is able to transcend the literal and commonsense perspectives of everyday life.

Religion and ritual are inseparable. Rituals represent the religious techniques that make spiritual transcendence accessible. They help to enchant the world, while also satisfying cravings for community. When a culture's dominant religion is viable, members can avail themselves of the therapeutic properties of ritual. When mainstream religion weakens dramatically, so too does the vehicle by which ritual is usually delivered to most members. In this case, the individual is faced with the task of meeting his or her ritual needs. This type of compensation is predictable, even though ritual was meant to be acted out in group contexts. However, once ritual departs from a socially sanctioned frame of reference, it soon takes on the label of psychopathology. Only the group can normalize ritual, which, by its nature, must be shared in order for it to be a moving and meaningful experience.

The modern crisis of ritual has been blamed on the continuing separation of the individual from the collective, and on the emanation of self-service as the prime method of social organization.[10] This is different from traditional individual-group patterns in that it lacks a center; it is therefore unable to support collective representations of the sacred. There remains little room for group ritualizations in a system that rests on the ambitions and wishes of autonomous individuals.

The decline of effective ritual is also related to an absence of shared mythologies, which are the historical building blocks of ritual. The sacred and the profane dissolve into one amorphous process that is almost devoid of transcendental potential. From this situation arises the current condition of anomie, of faulty individual-collective relations that unfold in an environment of excessive individuality wherein overly transparent societal arrangements prevent members from perceiving elements that transcend the field of personal experience. As their own myth makers, secularized individuals inevitably navigate toward self-interest without the pacifying superstructure that is made possible by collectively defined ritual.

THE PSYCHOLOGICAL CHALLENGE OF RELIGIOUS SURROGACY

Until recently, there was a tendency to associate modernity with secularization and to anticipate an eventual disappearance of religion. The reasoning has been that modernization interferes with the unity and solidarity of meaning systems, weakens the social underpinnings of religion, and calls into question the relevance of the sacred and its associated values. Now, however, certain developments have caused scholars to rethink secularization theory and to focus more on the ways in which modernity changes the appearance of religion, rather than extinguishes it.

One such development is the expanding body of data demonstrating that religious decline in any given society is almost always temporary and followed by various types of revitalization. Furthermore, during periods of religious decline one can observe manifestations of religious improvisations that appear to compensate for deficits in the dominant religion of the culture. Another development that casts doubt on traditional secularization and modernization theories involves the fundamentalistic transformations that may be a religious response to modernity.

Fundamentalism has been depicted as a religious voice that addresses the fears generated by modernity.[11] It is a reaction against the secularizing forces that threaten traditional religious foundations. The concept of the fundamentalistic self has been used to describe an emerging identity structure that is motivated to subdue the forces responsible for the unpredictable protean age.[12] The fundamentalistic self is drawn toward movements that can restore simple delineations between good and bad, God and devil, and so forth. These types of religious designs mitigate the modern experience of insecurity and chaos, while introducing antimodern elements that can restore common unifying principles as well as absolute morals and values.

In fundamentalism, religion responds to toxic historical forces by seeking to revitalize itself and to make possible the advantages traditionally associated with religion. Modern fundamentalistic religion represents a bold return to idolatry, as the Bible serves as the idol that must be followed blindly. It has responded to the need of many lost souls to find psychological sanctuary in an automatic, unquestioning, and unconscious spirituality.

There is mounting sentiment that religious motivation should be understood as a constant that seeks expression under all cultural conditions, but the means by which religious motivation tries to stay alive can take many different directions. The recent era of religious decline has been associated with a logarithmic rise in new religious movements that aim to reenchant the world. Research shows that the degeneration of dominant cultural religions is often followed by an increase in small-scale cults and other alternative religions. One study that calculated the number of cults per million people in nineteen different countries found that the highest rates of cult participation existed in the least religious countries.[13]

Europe, which contains some of the least religious countries in the world, has the highest rates of cult involvement. For example, Iceland has exceptionally low levels of mainstream religious belief and practice and five times the rate of cult participation of the somewhat more religious United States. The United Kingdom, which also has low levels of traditional religion, has seven times the cult participation of the United States, irreligious Sweden has four times, and Switzerland has ten times. This finding begins to sketch a picture of compensatory efforts aimed at achieving spiritual transcendence in the absence of broader cultural direction.

Declining rates of church participation should also not lead us to conclude that modernity is somehow incompatible with spirituality. For example, whereas only 2 percent of people in Iceland attend church on a regular basis, 77 percent profess a belief in God and 75 percent believe in life after death.[14] Similar patterns can be seen in other superficially irreligious societies such as Denmark, Belgium, and France.

Instead of becoming completely nonspiritual or nonreligious, people continue to be motivated spiritually even when they cannot avail themselves of a traditional dominant religion. That is, spiritual needs do not cease to exist when culture no longer becomes a competent supplier of religion. The apparent absence of religion in some societies almost always coincides with the appearance of invisible religion, or what has also been termed *civic religion*. Nationalism and patriotism can also serve as quasi religions that compensate partially for slumping mainstream religious systems. This strategy is quite evident in the United States. Psychotherapy also has some potential to function as a religious surrogate, as famous therapists are able to muster some credibility as high priests of personal growth and self-fulfillment.

In one well-known study, researchers examined patterns of religious change in two hundred societies.[15] They were especially interested in those locations where the dominant cultural religion was undergoing serious decline. The results showed that religious decline is almost always followed by a process of revitalization wherein several minority religions surface to replace the sickly dominant one. A good example of the resilience of the need for spiritual transcendence is in Russia, where religion was suppressed for several decades. During the actual suppression phase, religion went underground, replaced in part by an upsurge of interest in the occult and other paranormal quasi religions. With the recent lifting of religious bans, there has been a rush back to religion on a scale that has not been witnessed since the Middle Ages.[16]

An analysis of Japanese culture sheds further light on the indefatigable quality of religion. After World War II, Shintoism came under attack for its role in promoting the type of militarism that led Japan into war. Other religions, in particular Buddhism, were also greatly depreciated in the years following the war. To this day, Japan has one of the lowest rates of religious belief and participation in the world; upon closer inspection, however, it soon becomes clear that it has one of the highest rates of cult participation. Not long ago, Japan's extremist Aum Supreme Truth cult made the news as a result of Tokyo subway gas attacks. At the time of the attacks, that particular cult had only ten thousand followers, but the Aum Supreme Truth cult is only one of over three hundred cults in Japan, of which the largest has a membership in the millions.[17]

To reiterate, the weakness of religion today is the result of cultural disintegration rather than the loss of the need for transcendence. Instead of disappearing, spiritual energies transform themselves and reemerge in other forms. Therefore, it is illogical to speak of secularization as a process whereby religion ceases to be a factor in the lives of people. At most, it wanes temporarily only to find some other mode of expression.

Today's world is inhabited by an extraordinary number of paranormal and parapsychological beliefs and rituals. They are emerging at an extraordinarily fast rate, raising the question of their function. At this moment in the United States, UFOlogy is the religion growing most rapidly. UFO abductees have spiritually moving experiences, but there is also a great deal of variation in these experiences, and some abductees report sexual abuse at the hands of the aliens. Like all other types of new age religion, UFOlogy is uncoordinated and poorly patterned. The high degree of improvisation involved explains why no two abductees have the same experience. That is an ever-present limitation of all compensatory quasi religions.

Research at the level of the individual supports the claim that motivation toward transcendence remains relatively constant despite developments of conventional religion. One group of researchers tested the hypothesis that nonreligious paranormal beliefs and rituals (e.g., clairvoyance, witches, ghosts, ESP, astrology, UFOs) serve as functional equivalents to mainstream religion.[18] Specifically, they predicted that a greater amount of paranormal belief and ritual would be found in individuals with low levels of mainstream religion. As predicted, low-religion people had significantly greater belief in the paranormal than their high-religion counterparts. These results, which have been replicated by other researchers, substantiate that nonreligious paranormal belief is a type of invisible religion that tries to make up for an inadequate measure of traditional group religion.

Another line of research has focused on individuals who indicate "no religion" when asked to indicate their religion. It has been shown that the majority of these "religious nones," as they have been called, actually have religious belief of one sort or another. One researcher found that only 19 percent of these "nones" were without a personal God.[19] Granted, some people today seem to lack altogether a spiritual side, but everything tells us that this is more the result of an absence of outlets for the spirituality that lies within. Most people, even in the midst of cultural predispositions that are incompatible with human spirituality, find themselves searching for some way to meet their transcendence needs.

Some commentaries on cyberpunk culture have made reference to an absence, or rejection, of religion among its members. The cyberpunk movement has been described as one that has staged a rebellion against the illusory fantasies (including religion) of former generations, but some observers have described cyberpunk more accurately as a generation of existential seekers who are asking questions about the meaning of their lives.[20] They experiment with meaning systems that have close ties with Eastern religion, goddess worship, primitive ritual ceremonies, evangelism, spiritually based growth and recovery plans, and all varieties of new age religion.

Mysticism is especially well suited to the conditions of modernity since this type of religious experience tends to be internal, free-floating, subjective, and relatively tolerant of rationalism and scientism.[21] It responds well to the breakdown of traditional religious structures by releasing individuals to their inner freedoms, and to their compensatory predilection for personal experience and self-actualization. Rather than seeking to accommodate or transform the world, as members of churches and sects have tended to do, the modern mystic enjoys the option of remaining indifferent to the world while focusing on idiosyncratic experience. One possible shortcoming of mystical consciousness is that the person becomes lost in a meandering succession of spiritual probings that fail to engage meaningful sources of communally sanctioned myth and symbol. Therefore, mystics, like other spiritual specialists, find themselves partially exposed to the many insecurities and vagaries of modern life.

The media have become an important vehicle by which the world can be reenchanted and replenished with spiritual drama.[22] This goes far beyond the way in which the media and religion have forged a closer union in the cultural transmission of relatively traditional modes of spirituality. Television, for example, has become the display vehicle for the secular myths and melodramas of the contemporary age. It has the potential to infuse consciousness with a sense of magic that is amplified by visual spectacle and vicarious ritual involvement. Sporting events are among the most potent media-based sources of compensatory ritual and transcendent cognitive bias.

The divinization of entertainment and entertainers through the media may seem an unlikely means by which to redress the modern spiritual vacuum. However, this process does provide media consumers with some answers and meanings, even if there is the risk that life itself will come to be perceived as something that entertains and distracts us. By providing a stage upon which moderns resacralize the world, the media can foster emotions and attachments with a transcendental quality.

Charisma has been relocated from the religious to the secular arena. Popularized media heroes facilitate religious surrogacy by serving as focal points of worship. The most adored figures in the media sphere can even offer opportunities for primitive hysterical catharsis, especially when they perform live. Some people today construct entire life-styles around the following of worshipped entertainment idols.

The convergence of media and religion is evidenced further by the evolution of commercial advertisements that tap spiritual appetites and entice consumers with spiritually laced fantasy in order to sell products. Recent years have seen an increasing prevalence of advertisements that convey indirectly the message that the goods on offer will provide some sort of inner peace or illuminated state. Product developers have discovered the value of choosing brand names that carry associations with the religious domain and of making God into the tempter. Especially common are those that target educated and fashion-conscious doubters who have gravitated toward vogue Eastern spiritual themes, thus we are now tempted by Zen skin lotion, Buddha cologne, and Karma coffee. Of course, it is rather far-fetched to presume that these products can even begin to make good on their implicit spiritual promise. More than anything, they are effective at reinforcing awareness of the new spiritual evil, which is not to look after yourself and not to consume what you deserve.

Technology is another religious surrogate that can compete to some extent with the spiritual disenchantment of modernity. As the media chronicle the perfection of technique and celebrate breathtaking technological advances, people acquire a sense of unlimited possibility. Over time, this approximates an experience that technology can accomplish the impossible. This is not apprehended consciously as the type of impossibility we associate with religious miracles, but people's inability to imagine any limits to technology bewitches them with the awe of infinity. In a general environment that offers little ultimate hope, it is easy to allow oneself to channel one's faith needs into the omnipotence of future technology.

As the new cultural archetype of hope, technology speaks on behalf of a life mastery that can be achieved by way of absolute efficiency and the systematic banishing of the unknown. Our technological prophets allude continually to the positive transformations that can be delivered by way of technical progress. We come away with a sense that this will happen if, among other things, we can somehow be connected at all times to the information that makes this a hypothetical reality. Unfortunately, the human psyche is not an ideal landscape for the realization of the promise of technological bliss. The surface impression that technology makes life easier and more efficient obscures the paradoxical effects of technology on mental health and overall quality of life.[23]

Although technology can expedite the satisfaction of existing needs, it can also make the person aware of new needs that require attention. Consumers of technology are also faced with the dilemma of obsolescence, which is due to the short lifespan of new technologies. Thus, in addition to financing the replacement of outmoded technologies, the person must invest time and energy into learning about its operation. The freedom and independence that flow from technology consumption can easily be negated by an unhealthy dependency wherein technology proves more restricting than liberating.

It is not even guaranteed that technology will ultimately increase efficiency. With all the time and effort required to prepare and refresh oneself for its use, as well as the additional expenditure of energy and time needed to afford the products, it is quite possible for the result to be less efficiency and reduced coping ability. Rather than simplifying life, it often introduces complexities that escalate stress levels. Just as technology can bring people together, it can also contribute to alienation and interpersonal disengagement. All considered, technology has too many inherent structural problems that prevent it from filling the role of an emotionally sustaining religion. Technology, which has been defined as the knack for arranging the world in ways that disallow us from experiencing it, runs the risk of adding further to the psychic numbness that stalks the modern personality.[24]

Religious compensation is always difficult, and many people find themselves left with a residual hunger that keeps them always vigilant for new sources of spiritual fulfillment. One chronic problem with this-world religion is that it challenges the individual to transcend without much aid from the supernatural. A sense of spiritual aloneness is exacerbated by the additional challenge of having to maintain beliefs without the support of a tenable sanctioning body. Because most modern seekers can achieve only partial religious compensation, frequently they must draw on multiple spiritual sources.

It is not uncommon for the new religious eclectic to juxtapose widely divergent and even incompatible elements. In the United States, for instance, 25 percent of adolescents believe in reincarnation even though most of them would describe themselves as Christian.[25] Nearly two-thirds of American young people assert that it is worthwhile to explore religious teachings from a variety of faiths, rather than adhering dogmatically to a single faith. To complete the formidable task of religious compensation, many people also find it necessary to extract spiritual sustenance from cultural themes that have been sanctified and then imported for religious utilization. In this regard, modernity has seen a considerable overlap between religious principles and those that govern consumption.

THE SACRALIZATION AND RITUALIZATION OF CONSUMPTION

Western religion has been pervaded by consumer themes to the extent that some religious scholars now prefer to describe modern religion as a mode of consumption that has evolved to accommodate the realism of the political economy.[26] As religion has absorbed the themes of consumer culture, it has found its way into the object world and begun to deliver a universe that can be understood in terms of value and profit. Consumer religion has unfolded against the background of a spiritually famished desiring self that is readily converted (in the religious sense) to messages containing the promise of infinite value. In this respect, religious enterprises with capitalistic infrastructures do not embark on a search for unknown or hidden realities; nor do they seek to clarify imbalances of the inner self. Instead, they engender a rudimentary faith in abundance, and the value of immediate relations to the world of objects and information.[27]

The state of grace has become one in which the disciple moves up or forward. Salvation and immortality take on earthly meanings in terms of market success and visible signs of wealth. In particular, Christianity has opened itself to capitalistic frameworks that can atone for, and respond to, the rapacious dispositions of the modern consumer. Its traditional teachings have been amended in order to tolerate consumer themes, and to inject materialistic zealousness with an aura of piety.[28] Narcissistic cultural themes have clashed seriously with Christian love-of-other dictates, causing revisions wherein essentially self-interested followers can remain holy as long as they do not consciously hurt others in the course of their self-serving pursuits.

The contemporary breed of disciple comprehends that it is no longer necessary to give up the things of this world in order to reap the riches of the spiritual world. Material wealth and even blatant excess are now viewed as evidence of God's blessing, and a sign that God approves of the path of greed through life. Traditional religious teachings about self-denial and self-forgetting have been transformed into an unofficial doctrine that emphasizes self-enhancement and self-fulfillment.

Among the seven social sins mentioned by Mahatma Gandhi is "Worship Without Sacrifice," but that sin is not relevant today. In an opposite way, sacrifice has become the cardinal social sin of the modern age. Rather than sacrifice that enhances our ability to serve God, patterns of worship are now designed specifically to improve the lot of the individual. Our preferences in deities are even changing in such a way that they can make sacrifices for us. The current infatuation with angels is an example. They have become so popular because they are there to do something for us. Religious messages in general have come to overlap with those that are typically encountered in self-help groups. Again this is because we are drawn to religious modes that, rather than requiring sacrifice, will speed along our journey of getting something for ourselves from life.

An example of the way in which Christianity and big business have come together can be seen in the endless television ministries that are on offer in the United States, and increasingly in other Western countries. Many of these take in vast amounts of money each year, under the guise of needing to fund the cable television stations on which their programs are aired. In truth, they often own the stations outright and have great surpluses of funds. Proof of this is the extravagant life-style of the ministers themselves, many of whom are slick salespeople who exploit the spiritually hungry. Millions of people find themselves under the spell of these religious pretenders, whose main message is that the viewer should send money. Not only have Christianity and big business united in this new mode of spirituality, but Christianity has been made into big business, causing some people to speak of the Christianity industry.

Television religion secures some of its high appeal by making itself entertaining and selling a superficial theology that has good news for materialists. Its amicable nature has led it to delete from its content much of the bad news about humanity and existence generally, and to celebrate easily accomplished trivialities. However, a number of problems have been identified in terms of the ability of electronic religion to engender an adequate quality and quantity of transcendence.[29] For example, television has some characteristics that make genuine religious experience difficult, if not impossible. One concerns the fact that a worthwhile religious service is assisted if it takes place in a consecrated space with some degree of sacredness. Television offers very few prospects in this regard. It is also befouled by commercial profanities that militate against the sacred element of religion. Altough television may not lend itself to authentic religion, it is an ideal instrument by which to promote a marketing religion that sells itself as a product and gives people what they want.

In *The Consumer Society*, Jean Baudrillard claims that the end of transcendence is an inevitable consequence of the *commodity logic* that has circulated to all spheres of modern life, including religion.[30] His argument is that, in the age of consumption, the myth of the market generates a radical alienation that precludes real transcendence. In effect, the consumer trades transcendence for gain and thereby becomes absorbed completely into spectacular consumable signs, images, and symbols, none of which is any longer capable of confronting us with a real image of ourselves or entities beyond us.

But rather than speak in terms of the end of transcendence, it may be more fruitful to explore the ways in which our transcendence needs are beginning to express themselves in harmony with consumption. Religious modernity features a process whereby objects and services are able to acquire sacred status.[31] People can experience a low-level holiness through identification with sacred objects or through pilgrimages to commercial sites, in particular those that have something to do with venerated celebrities. The emotional experience of the sacred can also be accessed through the purchase of an object that is supremely fashionable as determined by advertising and other commercial promotion methods.

Volumes have been written about shopping malls as the sacred space of the modern age.[32] The case has been made that malls have become the ceremonial centers of secular society, able to provide some of the social benefits of traditional religion. The deliberate effort of some commercial planners to construct malls according to cathedral designs attests to the potential for the mall experience to have a spiritual semblance. Additionally, malls offer a rich storehouse of opportunities for ritual enactment in the context of consumer myths and commercial reality. However, the rate of mall construction has dropped off in recent years and will probably continue to do so with the ascendance of the desocialized and deritualized cybermall. If the future includes the demise of the shopping mall, it may be even more difficult for moderns to coordinate consumer themes to spiritual ends.

The current cultural obsession with collecting illustrates further the way in which elements of the material world can be sacralized. The grip of collecting on some people is so strong that it becomes a monoideism that comes to dominate their lives. Russell Belk and his colleagues reported on the case of a collector of Mickey Mouse items.[33] An entire room of his house was filled with the paraphernalia related to this cartoon character. So precious was this collection that it was kept under constant lock and key, a measure that had the effect of magnifying the power and significance of the collection. His 7-year-old son was so intimidated by the all-important collection that he was afraid to enter the inviolable Mickey Room. This particular collector spoke out about the overpowering hold that Mickey Mouse has on his life and how easy it is to fall prey to collection addiction. Mickey Mouse had become God, and anything to do with Mickey had become sacred.

Indeed it seems that everything, no matter how silly or trivial, is being collected. The collectors themselves have a reverence for their objects that bears a strong resemblance to the respect shown by religious people to sacred relics. Complete and flawless collections are regarded with heartfelt spiritual admiration. Groups of similarly oriented collectors form congregations that allow them to share their devotion to the sacred objects that inspire their lives. Being a collector also has a clear ritual component, as collectors spend many hours sorting, arranging, and labeling their sacred objects and readying them for display. All this is energized by the prospect of financial gain as the collection approximates perfection.

Sacred consumption exhibits the deification of the mundane that consumers use to achieve partial equilibrium amid the impulsive metamorphoses of modernity. As a myth-ritual technique, it expresses the developing solidarity between the object and spiritual worlds and represents a capitalistic consummation of the most revered aspects of the dominant culture. Since it generates some degree of transcendental meaning, it has the effect of filling some of the void left by retreating traditional religion, but, as never before, moderns are confronted by the void, which stems from the precarious existential condition that has been created by the depopulation of traditional realms of myth and ritual.

THE MODERN EXISTENTIAL CRISIS

Psychotherapists report that fewer and fewer patients are presenting clear-cut disorders, such as those listed in their official diagnostic manuals. With increasing frequency, they are faced with the task of helping people with problems that relate to life itself and to the nature of human existence. In fact, the past few decades have witnessed a scourge of existential disorders. It is not surprising that one study in the United States reported that 81 percent of university students considered themselves to be in an "existential vacuum."[34]

Young people are expressing a variety of existential concerns that relate to meaninglessness, purposelessness, hopelessness, indecision, isolation-related despair, dread of death, and general confusion. Escalating levels of antisocial behavior and atrophied emotion among youth have been interpreted in terms of their existential disequilibrium, a large part of which is due to their reliance on the media as the existential epicenter of their lives.[35] In turn, the media assist in making consumption the existential framework for the world, a psychological situation that is fraught with disappointments. Not even the thriving loneliness industry that has followed on the heels of the modern existential crisis can prevent the spread of this problem.

Many moderns experience an existential disorientation that expresses itself as an inability to arrive at a sense of direction. In this malaise, identity lacks almost any durability. People often do not know which way to go in life and have little confidence in their current goals and aspirations. Such individuals do not have a solid ontological edifice for their lives to allow them to impose sense on their daily activities and pursuits. They do not see where anything is leading and suspect that they are on the wrong track or, even worse, on no track at all. Haunting them is a nagging awareness that they have somehow missed the proverbial boat. Some end up in therapy, hoping that a paid professional can steer their lives for them. Various new age and pop therapies revolve around techniques aimed at grounding and centering patients. In essence, such therapies strive to combat the problem of existential disorientation.

Even though premodern religion contributed to the restrictions on self-exploration, it nonetheless was able to furnish a general life outline, and some experience of meaningful order. By contrast, modern cosmologies are more inclined to reject meaningful order since human beings tend to be perceived as natural objects. Information, which is the operative force of the modern age, also has the result of imploding meaning and removing it from its traditional social contexts.

The modern self is a type of collage made up of unrelated elements assembled by subjective whim. The repositioning of identity to the individual has promoted reality constructions that are constrained by self-understanding.[36] Although self-fulfillment is made more possible, the individual's general orientation rests on a very small foundation. Existential disorientation comes about as the self can no longer escape itself in the course of seeking understanding and explanation.

The problem with the myth of consumption as the basis for existential orientation is that it is unstable and fleeting. It is a project that entails a series of manufactured desires that vanish, often without much real satisfaction, as the person partakes in low-level meaningless consumption strategies. Instead of meeting the need for orientation, the consumer quickly fatigues and is left with little more than an opportunity for distraction. As a framework of orientation, consumption offers very little ontological security and minimal hope for convincing truths. Any sense of control that accompanies consumer consciousness is superficial and subject to haphazard mutations.

Alienation and Existential Isolation

For most of human history, cultures have provided a system whereby members could feel at one with the world, but mental health professionals now speak of the problem of *existential isolation* that affects many people to-day. This has been defined quite simply as "a separation between the indi-vidual and the world."[37] Deep loneliness and a vague all-pervasive misgiving are symptoms of existential isolation.

The term *defamiliarization* has been used to describe the way in which it is possible to become existentially removed from the world.[38] As the environment grows unfamiliar, the usual meanings we attach to our rules, roles, values, and ethical guidelines can be lost. Usually these elements serve to stabilize our sense of reality. When these begin to fade as a result of existential isolation, considerable anxiety may result. This is an existential type of anxiety that stems from the feeling that we are not at home in this world. The endless searching that we see today is a search for a psychologi-cal home. People try to find this home in any number of ways, but they re-main strangers to their own existence. The depletion of the social sphere makes it difficult to solve existential loneliness through interpersonal affili-ation. The distrust stemming from social alienation becomes the basis for still more loneliness.

Any comfort we feel in this world can usually be traced to our participa-tion in the shared beliefs that enable us to improve on this-world reality. Modernity's destruction of shared understandings leaves some people tor-mented by subjective feelings of aloneness. Such individuals often avoid any situations that would require them to be alone. Irvin Yalom uses some anecdotes from psychotherapy to illustrate the modern dread of alone-ness.[39] During a group therapy session, one of his patients was describing her extreme discomfort with being alone. The worst thing about being alone, she said, was the prospect that "no one in the world may be thinking about me." Her perception that no one was thinking about her was not en-tirely a distortion of reality; she was probably just sensing a partial truth about the modern world, which is that others are thinking primarily about themselves. Another patient, after breaking up with her boyfriend, made the statement "I'd rather be dead than alone." Still another patient had re-curring urges to kill herself because she felt that it was the only way to make people remember her.

Many existentially isolated people are hounded, both consciously and unconsciously, by the terrifying prospect that nobody knows or cares for them. In turn, they become obsessed with the notion of being immortalized in one way or another. The profound awareness of abandonment that has become commonplace today must be understood in the context of rising levels of alienation. This type of alienation has bred into moderns an irre-pressible exhibitionistic streak that seeks to redress the loss of genuine sociality, and to employ publicity as an anecdote for generalized insecurity. On a regular basis, we absorb suggestions that incline us to believe that the world will do anything for us as long as we have sufficient publicity. Even a highly publicized kitten, who might be trapped in a drain somewhere, can expect an entire city's rescue services to work day and night until it is saved, then to make it an international hero. But the huge scale of modern exhibitionism has translated into a shortage of cooperative voyeurs, which makes exhibitionism an ineffective scheme for achieving existential footing. Sometimes the exhibitionist manages to locate a voyeuristic audience, but the very nature of voyeurism prevents the person from interpreting this attention as a sign of genuine caring.

Even when exhibitionism offers temporary relief from existential alienation, nothing solves the overriding problem, which is that the group no longer mediates the identity formation process. Consequently, the modern identity comes to be characterized by loneliness and privacy, as people are required to find purpose in themselves.[40] Logic tells us that cultural systems emphasizing individualism should generate higher degrees of social alienation than those with a collectivist orientation. In a cross-cultural study of this topic, researchers identified a group of collectivist cultures and compared them to a group of individualist cultures with regard to alienation, anomie, and loneliness.[41] As expected, they found that individualist cultures produced in their members higher levels of alienation, anomie, and loneliness. Participants from collectivist cultures perceived more, and higher-quality, social support. This research also demonstrated that collectivist cultures place a high value on cooperation, equality, and trust. The opposite was found for individualist cultures.

The identity crisis and subsequent state of existential alienation corresponding to modernity are related to the disintegration of primary cultural institutions. As a result, a number of secondary institutions have taken a more central position as the purveyors of identity and belonging. For instance, youth gangs have been described as a direct consequence of inclement cultural conditions in which young people grow up without a wider community.[42] They are expected to find their own way through a mass market world that offers little recognition or dignity. Those most affected by the poverty of their social world can easily lose interest in life itself. I recall the recent words of a police officer who was talking about the inner world of the six hundred or so gangs that now roam the streets of Los Angeles. He made the interesting observation that gang members no longer even bother to duck when a bullet is fired at them. This description confirms the point that alienation and inner emptiness can become so complete that even the immediate prospect of death fails to activate people. But rather than being the vehicle for violence and self-destruction, many gangs should be understood as substitute social institutions.

An in-depth analysis of the rise of gangs reveals that young people are motivated to join them for a variety of reasons. These include money, fun, and personal safety. Above and beyond those motives, however, is the fact that gangs operate in several ways as substitute families.[43] They provide the social identity, and even the moral foundation, that is otherwise lacking in members' lives. In this respect, gangs often have a substantial part in the personal development of members. In former ages, the family was the primary mechanism whereby culture passed from one generation to the next, but as the family has receded in this traditional role, a significant percentage of our youth have had to seek out surrogate families. These give them not only a system of social instruction, but a source of emotional support that competes with alienation.

Heavy metal music has also become the framework for a subculture of alienation that responds to the missing community.[44] Those who find their way into heavy metal often are from families that have almost no influence on their lives. They grow up in a self-socialization environment wherein they were required to make their own decisions about morality, occupation, religion, and so forth. Although some adolescents thrive under these conditions, a considerable number are drawn toward social units that have shared alienation as their primary bond. Youth subcultures can have additional appeal as mechanisms for social protest. Along these lines, Jeffrey Arnett describes subcultures such as heavy metal as "a flamboyant rejection of what society seems to offer and an outcry over what it fails to offer, as well as an attempt at providing a substitute source of meaning.[45]

MEANING, BOREDOM, AND SELF-DISTRACTING PAIN

The quest for meaning is one of the most fundamental of all human drives. By their nature, human beings manufacture meaning in an attempt to impose order on an otherwise chaotic world. The concept of *meaning* has been defined as "having a purpose in life, having a sense of direction, a sense of order and a reason for existence, a clear sense of personal identity, and a greater social consciousness."[46] Research shows that meaning is positively related to psychological and physical well-being, as well as life satisfaction, positive self-regard, optimism, coping ability, and personal growth. It has also been shown to protect vulnerable populations (e.g., the institutionalized elderly) from depression.[47] Conversely, deficiencies of meaning can pose difficulties in all these areas.

Usually the experience of meaning is linked to religious, philosophical, or mythological belief systems that clarify our existence. These represent overarching mechanisms whereby the culturally constituted world can synchronize meaningful personal and societal action. In the absence of these, members try to attach meanings to a life that strikes them as an unorganized sequence of immediate adaptations that lack a greater rationale. They fall prey to the multitude of modern emotional ailments that can be traced to underlying meaninglessness. In general, the conditions that exist in contemporary Western culture pose a considerable challenge to the human search for meaning. They do not lend themselves to a clear picture of the nature of existence; nor do they provide obvious guidelines for purposeful living. A crisis of meaning becomes inevitable as moderns fail to extract substance from an incoherent scramble of cultural communications.

Carl Jung was one of the first psychologists to observe the rising frequency of meaninglessness. He estimated that one-third of his psychotherapy clients were not suffering from any clinically definable disorder, but rather from feelings of meaninglessness and senselessness.[48] Since then, a number of prominent therapists have reported that high percentages of their clients are best diagnosed with disorders of meaninglessness. Recent empirical studies have confirmed that meaning-related problems are common and on the increase.[49]

Meaninglessness entails a persistent inability to find truth or value in the things that one does or anticipates doing. The modern crisis of meaning can be understood in relation to a new cultural template that has removed meaning structures from their historical locations. A considerable number of traditional meaning structures have been transferred to the world of consumption, where pointless ingestion becomes the principal exposition for existence.[50] However, consumer meanings see the self floating across an existential expanse of surface images that do not lend themselves to explanation or interpretation. Moderns are left with a superficial chaos that cannot establish credible meaning.

As the cultural sphere of meaning shrinks, the stage is set for the experience of existential boredom and psychic deadness. This feeling of deadness is not experienced for what it is, but rather as an intense boredom. Sometimes existential boredom can activate individuals to seek distraction. If sufficient distraction is achieved, they can block out their boredom and offset their intrapsychic vacuity.

Advertising plays an important role in conditioning people to solve feelings of boredom and death through consumption. In this regard, I am reminded of a television advertisement that was used to sell a popular soft drink. The advertisement revolved around a few young people who were at a total loss about how to combat their boredom. They tried everything, including a series of death-defying activities, such as skateboarding off the edge of a cliff, surfboarding from an airplane without a parachute, and being shot out of a cannon. But, after all this, the teenage boys were still bored to death and in agreement that they must find a better way to deal with their boredom. At this point in the advertisement, salvation came in the form of a soft drink. Once the cans were opened and tasted, a look of aliveness and joy finally appeared on the faces of the teenage boys.

Undoubtedly, the developers of such advertisements are alert to the boredom that bedevils the modern, and they seize the opportunity to market products on the back of this cultural symptom. With many repetitions, powerful illusory associations are established between consumption and relief from boredom. As the distraction capability of one product fades quickly, new products must be introduced in order for that solution to boredom and nothingness to remain workable. Although boredom can give rise to activation for purposes of escape, it can also deactivate. Like many drugs that need ever increasing dosages in order to have the intended effect, activities with ever greater distracting power are required. People habituate to their activities and move on in search of alternative sources of distraction. The result is a deep sense of ennui wherein the person loses the ability to become excited; over time, not even the most arousing sorts of activities can take them away from themselves.

Our entertainment industry tries to keep pace with the losing battle for self-distraction, resorting to always more extreme tactics to jolt the audience out of chronic boredom; but, no matter how spectacular the activity or experience, these too will soon become ineffective, needing to be replaced by still more striking distraction methods. When there is almost no ability to be stimulated by the ordinary, there is a tendency to lapse into a hypnogogic daze characterized by emotional paralysis. Some must turn to pain in a final attempt to reawaken themselves.

Recent years have seen an escalating prevalence of blatant self-destructive and self-mutilative behavior. The clinical literature contains reports on a number of such cases that represent self-directed cruelty as a response to existential deadness. One is that of a man who threw rocks on to the roof of a garage and let the rocks roll down onto his head.[51] When questioned about this activity, he confessed that it was the only way he could feel something. This same man made several suicide attempts, with the similar explanation that the pain enabled him to have some feelings, indeed *any* feelings. The majority of "rocks on the head" cases do not even come to the attention of mental health professionals. A high percentage are undetected since they are acted out within the context of accepted thrill-seeking or risk-taking acts. In fact, many profitable businesses have been built up around people's increasing willingness to risk their lives in hopes of a single moment of aliveness. Extremes of pathological boredom can even lead some to seek relief by playing with the lives of other people. With the motto "I kill, therefore I am," there is a grim trend toward killing other human beings for no other reason than to have something to do and to steal a quick thrill that punctuates an overall feeling of deadness, insignificance, and meaninglessness. Killing in order to feel alive is one of the most tragic symptoms of absolute boredom that can accompany culture failure.

There is little doubt that boredom is a growing problem that should attract the attention of the mental health profession. It has been linked to a very wide range of problems, including substance abuse, delinquent behavior, family conflicts, dangerous risk taking, and academic difficulties. Any progress we can make in terms of addressing this widespread problem would benefit society as a whole.

ADDICTION AS A SOCIOEXISTENTIAL PROBLEM

Addiction has become a conspicuous feature of modern life. New addictions appear on a regular basis, and there are few things to which moderns have not become addicted. Some debate exists about the legitimacy of addiction claims, and some voice skepticism about addictions that involve love, sex, soap operas, and the like. We have less trouble accepting a diagnosis of addiction if it involves chemical substance or behavior patterns with a history of sinful connotations (e.g., avarice, gambling).

Addiction as we know it today has a relatively brief history. This fact has been downplayed by scholars who argue that the apparent epidemic of addiction is largely an artifact of modern diagnostic and reporting methods; although this practice may have the effect of exaggerating the tendency of moderns to fall prey to addictions of various sorts, it does not offer a full explanation. In fact, modernity has created the ideal psychological conditions for the deployment of addiction as a madness technique.

The symptom formation structure of addiction allows the modern person to be partially liberated from inordinate choice. By curtailing the burden of choice, the addicted individual also escapes personal responsibility, which is often experienced by moderns as excessive. In a related way, addiction qualifies to some extent as one of the "diseases of hope" that have been described in relation to modernity.[52] Although we usually conceive of hope as a positive emotion that invigorates and enlivens people, the modern age has saturated its inhabitants with petrifying degrees of hope that are conveyed through the experience of inexorable possibility. This has made them prone to fear and despair. Those suffering from diseases of hope are frequently attracted to symptom designs that can constrict the scope of options, even if this means a reduction in the actual quantity of hope. Addictions work quite well in this regard since they reduce the vast expanse of hope to the simple matter of repeating actions in response to a perceived demand.

This leads to another strategic advantage of an addiction, namely, its ability to respond to modernity's loss of ritualistic pathways to therapeutic dissociation. An addiction offers an obvious absorption point that invites obsessive repetitions that can foster dissociative disengagements from feelings of emptiness and boredom. This also helps to fill the existential vacuum left by the modern person's loss of the social other. In key respects, addictions can be understood as transcendence techniques that respond to chaos that is encountered at the existential level.[53] This can be illustrated by examining the modern drug addiction problem.

The Cultural Context of Drug Use

Drug abuse is so rampant that some social analysts fear it could undermine the integrity of the culture itself. This idea is based on the close connections between drug abuse and a number of social problems, including crime and violence, psychopathology, the breakdown of the family, and the sizable drain on the economy. Thousands of lives are destroyed each year by people who have fallen prey to drugs of an ever increasing variety. Some of these drugs are not thought to be addictive or excessively dangerous to the user. Others are so blatantly destructive that the person becomes a virtual slave to the drug and the degrading life-style that often characterizes its use.

Although it may be tempting to view drug-related disorders as problems that befall certain vulnerable individuals, it quickly becomes apparent that cultural factors are involved. For example, the decline of traditional religion is frequently cited as a determinant of substance abuse. Drug use can easily become a compensatory strategy to deal with deficits in the area of transcendence and ritual. Even the experience of ecstasy was once located in the realm of religion. As religion wanes, drugs can substitute as a vehicle for ecstatic experience.

We tend not to think of substance abuse as an existential disorder, but in many ways it is a result of the inability of many moderns to meet certain key existential needs. This socioexistential phenomenon is also a consequence of culture's failure to fulfill certain traditional roles. Historically, culture mediated altered states of consciousness for the benefit of the individual and society. When this role is enacted successfully, culture has the potential to structure unreality as well as reality. But it will be seen that cultural failure in this role shifts the management of unreality to the individual; it is at the level of the individual that pathological drug use can occur.

Western people have become self-righteous and moralistic with regard to drugs. There seems to be a general consensus that drugs are undesirable, and even evil; the widely held view is that consciousness altering drugs are unhealthy. On the other hand, we assume that, in order to be totally healthy, we should avoid all drugs that could distort consciousness. This general attitude causes the drug user in our culture to feel deviant and villainous. Such feelings are reinforced by laws that make many types of drug use illegal. In actuality, we have lost sight of the place of drugs in the cultural lives of human beings.

Drugs have been with us from a very early point in our history. They have the potential to be healthy when employed in a suitable cultural context, in rites of passage, initiation rites, and various religious rituals. Consciousness altering drugs have been a valuable feature of all functional cultures, but drugs play a much different role in traditional societies than in modern ones. When one thinks of drugs as they are consumed in the West, one generally gets a picture of drug abuse. Since drugs have always had a role in human behavior, it is essential to distinguish between drug use and drug abuse.

Today we have a large amount of drug abuse, which distinguishes us from premodern cultural settings. As the anthropologists Marlene Dobkin de Rios and David Smith have demonstrated, drug abuse does not exist in intact traditional non-Western societies. They describe traditional culturally regulated drug use:

> Plants are used to reaffirm a society's mapping of the supernatural, permitting individuals to partake of such beliefs, both visually and emotionally. The use of plant hallucinogens for the reduction of private anxiety, the dampening of personal problems, or as a general escape from social pressures, occurs only rarely except in the face of dire acculturative stresses. For the most part, drugs are used in a magico-religious context of ceremony, either to celebrate or contact the realm of the supernatural, heal illness, diagnose its causes and determine its prognosis, divine the future, or promote social solidarity.[54]

Dobkin de Rios and Smith emphasize the near universality of culturally controlled drug use, asserting that this pattern of usage is historically incompatible with drug abuse:

> Data on nonindustrialized societies show that drug use is a means to a socially approved end, such as contacting the supernatural, either to control its forces, or else to place oneself at the mercy of forces seen to be more powerful than man. Generally, drugs have been used to confirm the integrity, values, and goals of a culture. In most cases, drug use is controlled by ritual rather than legal means. The individuals who utilize such plants do so only after periods of careful apprenticeship or guidance, with specific expectation of visionary content. . . . Drugs are rarely taken by the lone individual for personal, introspective quests. . . . In all cases, where members of a society merely lounge around and indulge in a plant brew or snuff, we tend to find Euroamerican influences, cultural disorganization, and concomitant problems of alienation and alcoholism present.[55]

When cultures are fit and acting in the service of existential needs, they automatically encourage patterns of drug use that have the effect of reducing the risk of drug abuse. These patterns involve the majority of people, who, within clearly specified cultural guidelines, become drug users but not abusers. Upon hearing the case that Western culture is largely to thank for drug abuse, some people might point to the many non-Western cultures that have serious drug problems. For example, high rates of substance abuse can be observed in what remains of native American Indian culture, Australian Aboriginal culture, and various cultures of the Amazon region of South America, but these are examples of cultures that have been destroyed largely as a result of their contact with the West. Prior to that influ-ence, few if any of these cultures suffered significantly from drug abuse. Yet, like endless similar cultures, they had long-standing traditions of de-ploying reality-distorting drugs for prosocial purposes.

The use of psychoactive plants is nearly a cultural universal, but when this practice is ritualized collectively it is unlikely to foster abuse.[56] Intact cultures possess a knowledge of the benefits of drug-related pathways to altered consciousness, as well as a wisdom that leads them to incorporate drugs (typically of the hypnotic variety) into the techniques that construct the reality of its people. Western culture stands out as an exception to this universal cultural characteristic. However, although the anthropological findings on this subject are compelling, questions arise about our ancient need for reality altering drugs, as well as the optimal methods by which drugs are introduced into people's lives.

Drug Use, Reality, and Transcendence

Reality transformation is most effective if it is a group enterprise that produces agreed-upon beliefs. This is why we see that in all workable cul-tures consciousness altering techniques are patterned into the culture and thereby made available to all members of the group. When this occurs in a sanctioned cultural context, alternative constructions of reality are shared by members of that culture; in contrast, in contemporary Western culture drugs are used by individuals to improvise reality alternatives on a private (or small group) basis.

One of the earliest of all cultural discoveries was that of drugs as a simple and efficient method by which to foster a state of dissociation. Typically, this is combined with music of a highly hypnotic nature (e.g., drumming, gonging, chanting). In the dissociative state, the person becomes hypersuggestible and highly responsive to cultural suggestions, making it possible for reality to be reconstructed in any number of ways. In the premodern world, all this usually took place in a religious context. Some re-ligious conservatives in the West may be expected to renounce the intimate historical connections between drugs and religion, but the evidence is over-whelming in this regard. It is only our eroded religious techniques in the West that mislead us into thinking that religion can and should be a drug-free enterprise.

Ihsan Al-Issa elaborates on this fact in a discussion of the historical use of drugs by culture in promoting and directing hallucinations.[57] He shows that human beings are naturally inclined toward hallucination. This is a feature of cognition that, for thousands of years, has been exploited by cul-ture, usually in order to connect its members to the spiritual realm. Thus we must come to terms with the normality of hallucination. Even in rational Western culture, around 40 percent of the general population have had some sort of hallucinatory experience, although hallucinations are not encouraged and people are offered no socially approved techniques by which to interpret hallucinatory experiences.

Culturally constructed reality is usually designed as a strategic blend of fact and illusion. Hallucinations are structured by institutionalized practice, with the aim of elevating members above strictly this-world understandings. This mechanism has allowed people, quite literally, to "see" (i.e., hallucinate) and be part of an expanded and positively biased reality. These hallucinatory ventures are generally an extension of the religious, spiritual, or magical beliefs of the culture. Once more, the actual techniques usually entail the managed use of hallucinogenic drugs. The goal is to merge reality and illusion, and even to convince people of the reality of illusion, or the reality of the transcendent world.

As an example, Al-Issa refers to an account of culturally regulated drug use by the Cahuilla Indians of California to achieve strategic hallucination during a traditional religious initiation ceremony. The drug in this instance is datura. It is widely used in the non-Western world and renowned for its powerful hypnotic effects:

Datura enabled him to glimpse the ultimate reality of the creation stories in the Cahuilla cosmology. The supernatural beings and aspects of the other world that he had been told about since childhood were now brought before his eyes for the ultimate test—his own examination. He has seen them. They are real.[58]

The description reveals how the cultural orchestration of drug-induced hallucinatory experience has the effect of bringing alive traditional spiritual spheres and tattooing them in the minds of members. When used correctly, the chemical road to the supernatural is clearly demarcated and its travelers rarely deviate from the expected visions that are rooted in cultural suggestion. A celebration ensues when the initiate "sees," experiences, and communicates with the formerly unknown reality and achieves maturity. The experience itself is usually so powerful and socially significant that it leaves an indelible mark on the spiritual sojourner. No doubt remains about the reality of illusion, and other-world understandings take a legitimate place in consciousness. This is so much the case that even during times of extreme stress, the person rarely needs to repeat the actual drug ingestion in order to escape reality. Members are imprinted permanently with the cognitive skills that can compete effectively with reality.

It is also worth considering the historical interface of hallucination, drugs, and culture, and its important mental health implications. In cultures that facilitate hallucination (e.g., with dissociative drugs), there is a markedly lower number of "psychiatric" hallucinations. On the other hand, when a culture fails to govern hallucination, we find much higher rates of hallucination that are deemed to be abnormal. Al-Issa explains:

> Encouraging individuals to fantasize in non-Western societies does not only provide them with a comparative basis on which to make clear distinctions between reality and fantasy, but it also enables them to discriminate culturally sanctioned imagery and hallucinations from other experiences. It is possible that in these cultures the high frequency of reported hallucinations may not be because more of them occur, but because culturally sanctioned hallucinations come more often into the public domain through self-description. Indeed, positive attitudes tend to facilitate social control by reinforcing commonly shared hallucinations and extinguishing those that are individual and idiosyncratic. Thus, there is a high frequency of *only* culturally sanctioned hallucinatory experiences.[59]

Understandably, cultures that suppress the natural hallucinatory tendency have an overall lower rate of hallucinatory experience. This is because hallucinations are themselves viewed by such cultures as strange, unnatural, and a sign of mental dysfunction. The only reason that cultures such as our own regard hallucinations as weird and unwelcome is that they have been vanquished from collective experience and relegated to the domain of abnormality. Socially managed hallucinatory experience has a valuable and long-standing role in normal human development.

An absence of normalized hallucination may actually indicate culture failure. When a culture is still capable of utilizing humans' predisposition to hallucination, one witnesses only very small amounts of psychopathological hallucinations. With cultural disintegration, there is a shift from traditional socially sanctioned hallucinatory experiences to individual ones that are likely to be labeled pathological as a result of their lack of consensus.

Bantu culture in Africa serves to illustrate this shift. It was a traditional practice of Bantu culture to promote hallucinatory experiences that enabled members to "hear" and learn from the voices of departed relatives. As this cultural practice has waned as a result of exposure to Western culture, an increase has occurred in the number of hallucinations wherein the source or identity of the voice is unknown.[60] These more closely resemble what we in the West term *psychopathology* since they have become detached from cultural traditions. In such a context, individual hallucinators are not protected from the label of madness. They are blocked from access to normal hallucinations that function as avenues to worlds that elude rational processes.

Many moderns are deprived of direct contact with a cohesive culturally constructed world of fantasy, illusion, and imagination. During times of crisis, they find themselves unable to reshape reality according to enduring cultural prescription. Escapes from reality are usually without structure, as in the case of self-directed drug taking. As a culture departs from the business of shared unreality, its members experience deficiencies in coping skills and personal resources. With few exceptions, they are constantly at risk of overexposure to real-world crises. This is why, as we saw earlier, moderns are psychologically and emotionally frail. Even the slightest of life's importunities can precipitate psychological trauma. It is little wonder that drugs are so close at hand in Western culture, in which people are literally forced to write their own prescription for reality transcendence and existential equilibrium.

Cultures that mediate effectively in the generation of unreality sometimes only need to make very limited use of drugs when the procedures are carried out in a meaningful and historically grounded context. This can involve a single event wherein drugs are employed in order to let the initiate make contact with the spiritual or supernatural world. The experience is often so powerful that the person remains permanently convinced of the truth of the revelations that were accessed via the drug. In other cultures, one can see periodic recourse to drug-related rituals and ceremonies that act as booster sessions, again with the goal of reinforcing a positive bias of reality.

But all this does not mean that we should romanticize premodern cultures and direct our existential yearnings toward the past. Instead, moderns are forced to nurture themselves existentially, and to improvise with regard to transcendence and meaning. Each individual must engage inner creativity in order to live under the threat of what has been described as the *existential absurdity* of modernity.[61] There are inevitable problems with individual-based modes of reality transformation, as exemplified by modern patterns of drug abuse. But the future will continue to see wayward, and frequently self-destructive, existential solutions that must be dealt with by mental health professionals and social policymakers.

ONTOLOGICAL INSECURITY AND RAREFIED BANALITY

I once saw an interview with Sam Spiegel, the veteran movie producer. What struck me most about the various comments he made was the high degree of disdain he seemed to have for the public. At one point, he said: "I've lost the joy of making movies. The audience today is a bunch of galoots. People don't read anymore. They listen to noises. They have become impervious to nuance and beauty."[62]

In *American yearnings*, Richard Rapson recounts a personal experience involving the intellectual degeneracy of the modern world. While watching television one day, he was overcome with the sense that he had entered some sort of nightmare that was devoid of all intelligence and substance.

Rapson turned off the television, but the nightmare did not go away. Instead:

> I turned off the TV, hoping to escape yet another nightmare. But America itself seemed to have become the nightmare; a land of mass idiocy, a frivolous, trivial citizenry, a value system reducing everything, even the self, to a commodity. So many celebrities were no more than manufactured personalities, hardly different from Suds and Cuds and Bud. Capitalism, sports, entertainment, politics, advertising, patriotism, television, and the showbiz personality had become so intertwined that reality could no longer be identified. What was this phenomenon? Where had it come from? Where was it taking this society?[63]

Although social analysts have described the modern death of mind and the prevailing consensus of stupidity, we do not usually consider intellectual decline as a major contributor to our existential crisis. Yet some observers have begun to pay attention to the intellectual crisis that characterizes modernity, pointing out the psychosocial pitfalls of this form of domination.[64] Whereas banality was formerly a matter of disdain or curiosity, it has achieved a new status whereby moderns now turn to it for clues and answers about their existence. Rarefied banality is the backbone of the new social utopia that cajoles the modern person.

By design, consumer society gravitates naturally toward anti-intellectualism. It is generally successful in sanctifying banality and inducing members to gear their lives to this level of experience, but it does not prevent all its members from being confronted by their own lack of substance. A significant proportion of moderns find it a stressful battle to sustain themselves on a steady diet of exalted banality. This has given rise to a new type of existential uneasiness that can be traced to cerebral understimulation, and to alienation from an intellectual stage upon which to address the larger questions of life. Some people become sufficiently adverse to cultural banality that they embark on a continual, albeit unsystematic, psychospiritual journey that can afford them some answers.

Ontological insecurity is generated whenever the person is unable to answer the big existential questions.[65] These answers were once contained in traditional ontological frameworks that delivered reasons for being and for participating in the world. The actual size of the existential question has decreased, and the locus of the answer has been subsumed by the dynamics of consumption. In many respects, the intellect has become a commodity. There is no more commitment to the intellect, and to intellectual development, as there is toward the other consumables that litter the mental landscape of the modern consumer. Rather, we hear many references to the

modern assault on the intellect that is a feature of the *dumbing down* phenomenon of the contemporary era.[66]

There are lots of statistics to support the argument that the intellect has
declined to the extent that existential disturbances could arise. For example, survey research shows that 50 percent of American university students
spend less than 2 hours per week in the university library, and 25 percent
spend no time whatsoever in the library. Of those surveyed, 80 percent
never bought any books except those used in the classroom, and only 10
percent read more than the bare minimum for their classes. This research
also found that 40 percent of the books sold at university bookstores in
America were comic books.[67]

Surveys of the actual goals of university students reflect a shift from intellectual and personal development, and toward material prosperity. In
1970, 80 percent of students surveyed indicated as a goal "the development
of a meaningful philosophy of life." When the same survey was carried out
in 1989, that percentage had fallen to 41 percent. During this same period,
those who cited as a goal "to be very well off financially" increased from 39
percent to 75 percent. These shifting goals are mirrored by changing patterns of university study. For example, the percentage of students majoring
in business-related subjects nearly doubled from 1970 to 1989, while the
percentage majoring in the social sciences declined by nearly 50 percent.

Higher education has also suffered from a commercialization trend that
has made universities little more than supermarkets of information that
teach knowledge-by-numbers. In his book *The University in Ruins*, Bill
Reading writes that, among other things, the university is supposed to
keep alive the collective cultural conscience and the ideals contained
therein.[68] Instead it finds itself operating as a profit-oriented business and
catering increasingly to whatever forces will increase its marketability.
Rather than a scholar with adjunct motives related to personal growth, the
modern student has become a consumer of educational services. Another
of the seven social sins proclaimed by Mahatma Gandhi was "education
without character." It would appear that modern education has become
more than a little sinful in this regard.

Knowledge, truth, and meaning have established a new bond with the
tenets of consumer culture. Education has been taken over by the forces of
market discipline and has redefined itself in terms of its capacity to generate wealth.[69] It has become system-centered, rather than student-centered,
and geared toward the production of formulaic dealers and manipulators
whose primary attribute is that they are economically acceptable.[70] Moreover, many of our manipulative dealers are not even coming away with the
most basic learning skills. For instance, one 1996 national survey showed
that 60 percent of high school graduates in America read at or below the
seventh-grade (12 years old) level.[71]

The trend toward dumb education has seen a countertrend toward home education. A number of research studies have shown that home educated children are 5 to 10 years ahead of their school-trained peers. It is not surprising that one and a half million American children are being educated entirely by their parents. The home education movement has been a direct response to the educational pathologies that are of growing concern to parents.

Some of these pathologies are summarized by John Taylor Gotto, a former New York city teacher and winner of many teaching awards, who describes the growing number of children in our classrooms who are passive, dependent, and cringing in the face of new challenges. Frequently this is disguised by aggressiveness and hostility, but it cannot hide what he terms the "vacuum without fortitude" that lies inside.[72] Our children are developing an indifference to the adult world. In previous ages, the younger generation was enthusiastically occupied with a study of the adult world, but more and more young people display very little tendency to grow up, and that characteristic may explain their lack of interest in the world around them. Educational observers also mention the declining levels of inquisitiveness, and the atrophied attention spans, of modern school-aged children.

We also hear about the burgeoning numbers of schoolchildren who display cruelty to each other, have little or no compassion for misfortune, and show contempt for anyone who appears vulnerable. A high percentage of children cannot handle genuine intimacy but rather seem inclined toward an artificial secret self consisting of borrowed pieces of television behavior that enables them to keep others at a distance or to manipulate others effectively. As a consequence, it is becoming difficult for them to forge meaningful relationships as they grow older. In this regard, modern educational philosophies and practices provide fertile soil for existential loneliness and social alienation.

Our schools are also having the effect of instilling children with strong materialistic inclinations. Grades have become a type of currency that rewards students on the basis of their suitability for consumer society. Individual teachers may wish more than this for their students, but they are hampered by the larger educational context, which has devalued critical thought and the guiding ideals that are intended to convey wisdom and to promote character development.

Instead of aiming at the whole person, contemporary educational approaches have become overspecialized and unable to offer true education. According to E. F. Schumacher, a truly educated person is one who is in touch with the *center*, the existential focal point that the person employs in order to consolidate an orderly system of ideas about the self and world that, in turn, help to regulate the content and direction of one's energies.[73] When in touch with this center, people have the ability to coordinate intelligently their various urges, impulses, and aspirations. They have the basis on which to clarify and comprehend their inner convictions, but most modern education methods preclude teaching people about their central convictions. The outcome is often confusion, contradiction, and life-style orientations characterized by motivational imbalances.

Psychologists have had surprisingly little to say about possible ways to revive our current educational system. It is possible that we are ignoring the existential suffering of millions of people who have been made dumber than they want to be, or were designed to be. This is not to say that moderns have actually become one-dimensional and barren of substance. On the contrary, the cultural neglect that has led them to repress their intellectual needs is crying out for creative release. The restoration of key aspects of the intellect may be a task of future mental health workers. Otherwise, the death of the mind phenomenon may continue to exert existential stress and reveal itself in previously unknown pathologies of the intellect. It may add still further to the ontological destitution of the modernist.

CHAPTER 8

Mental Health and the Physical World

Human identity has many inputs. One of these is the physical space in which we find ourselves. We often hear, for example, how the physical landscape of a country molds some of the characteristics of its people. An environment such as outback Australia exerts certain personality and characterological influences that are different from the physical landscape of inner city Detroit. Although a host of other factors contribute to the overall identity structure of the person, physical space is a key consideration. Our sociospatial identity, as it is sometimes called, is shaped by the physical environment at the local, intermediate, and global levels. This chapter focuses on aspects of the modern physical world that have implications for mental health and general well-being. It also explores features of modern consciousness that determine the ways in which we treat and mistreat the environment. We might begin by considering the worldwide population shift toward urban living.

URBANIZATION, INDUSTRIALIZATION, AND MENTAL HEALTH

When we think of cities, our attention is often dominated by statistics related to size or population. Indeed, some of these are astonishing, especially with regard to the rapidly expanding megacities. For example, Tokyo, Bombay, Mexico City, and Shanghai each have a population approaching 30 million. Some of the most explosive growth is taking place in the developing world, where there are now almost three hundred cities with populations in excess of 1 million. At the moment, approximately 40 percent of people in the developing world live in cities. In the developed world, this percentage is 75 percent.

A city is far more than a mere quantity of people, or an assemblance of physical materials that constitute its surface appearance. It is also a complex interaction of values, routines, and interests that operate in a diverse set of contexts."[1] In acknowledging the human dimension of the city, one should also point out that city life offers certain advantages over that in other settings. Many people are attracted to urban centers for the opportunities and sources of stimulation that they provide. Some individuals could not imagine life outside the city. They speak of the commercial, cultural, intellectual, and ethical options that only exist in larger urban settings. Cities offer freedoms, excitements, and services that are difficult to find in rural, semirural, or small town locations. They enjoy improved communications that can enhance efficiency and speed decision making. Cities usually offer a greater quality of health care and a wider range of medical services.

Mental health professionals have become concerned, however, about the exceedingly rapid rate of growth of many cities (e.g., pollution, crowding, noise, anonymity, erosion of community life, public transport frustrations, infrastructure collapse) and the psychological problems that this creates for its inhabitants. They have pointed out that certain basic needs (e.g., security, relatedness) cannot always be met under such conditions. A number of critics are speaking of the impersonal, indifferent, and self-absorbed quality of our burgeoning cities.

The fact that crime is positively correlated with city size is another reason for concern. Research shows that crime rates are nearly twice as high in large cities as in nonurban areas. For major crimes this difference is even greater.[2] Studies on the relationship between aggression and urbanization demonstrate that people react more violently in urban settings, in part as a result of the individual's perceived lack of control over the situation.[3] More generally, urban life often entails a buildup of aversive conditions that turn people in on themselves and neutralize the many advantages of city living. The inward orientation of urban life helps to explain the research showing that a much lower percentage of urban residents, when compared to their nonurban counterparts, reciprocate a simple social greeting.[4] Although it may be unrealistic to make token social gestures to all of our fellow urbanities, the accumulated unconscious effects of the perceived indifference of others are fear, aloneness, and distrust.

As a social process, urbanization has introduced a number of significant changes. These include the erosion of primary group relationships, the weakening of kinship ties, and the diversification and dilution of traditional social functions.[5] Urban life-style structures are associated with longer working hours, a greater division between home and workplace, and a loss of meaning for both work and leisure. They also lend themselves to stress, burnout, and impaired mental and physical health. The urban way of life can impose so much complexity, and make so many additional demands on time and energy, that the overall quality of life for the individual and family is reduced.

Before one can ascertain the mental health consequences of urbanization, it is necessary somehow to circumscribe and define this process. Sometimes it is understood in terms of increases in the size of city populations. This often involves an analysis of population distributions, such as the ratio of rural to urban, or the percentage of the overall population living in urban settings. But there are also a range of social and economic dynamics to consider as part of the urbanization process. The following definition of *urbanization* captures the complex of factors that are involved.

> Urbanization is a dynamic process and product that emerges from the complex interaction of population (size, density, and heterogeneity), spatial-geographical (i.e., location, climate, terrain), historical, cultural, economic, and political forces for socioenvironmental formation (i.e., societal differentiation, segmentalization, marginalization, stratification, and segregation) with resulting patterns of psychosocial adjustment and adaptation.[6]

One of the simplest ways to gauge the positive or negative impact of urban living is to ask urban residents whether they enjoy living in a city. One discovers that the majority of people in large urban centers would prefer to live elsewhere. In one nationwide survey in America, for example, only 33 percent stated a preference to live in a large city.[7] Two-thirds of those surveyed indicated that they would rather live in a smaller town. These and similar findings demonstrate that, even though most people now live in cities, most of those individuals do so out of some set of compromises. Yet the discontent generated by urban life has brought about some degree of demographic reversal as some people seek a higher quality of life in rural and small town settings. In a related way, suburbanization is sometimes seen as a compromise between the practicalities of urban life and the desire for a small town location.

Often the drive to escape large urban centers has to do with an urge to reclaim a sense of community, belongingness, and shared commitment. One extensive research survey found that 50 percent of Americans were actively involved in the "search for community."[8] Among the frequently cited explanations for their quest was the need to compensate for the negative effects of urban living. The researchers concluded that urbanization (as measured by city size, density, and heterogeneity) had the effect of weakening people's overall sense of community.

The consequences of urbanization may be more apparent in certain vulnerable populations. For example, research on the mental health of children from low-income urban settings demonstrated that many cities around the world have infrastructure deficiencies that deprive children of a number of vital services and opportunities.[9] When living conditions deteriorate, stress is generated, extended families begin to disintegrate, less emphasis is given to the promotion of prosocial behavior, and more tolerance is shown toward deviant actions.

The actual statistics on child poverty in urban settings are cause for great concern. For example, the percentage of American children living in "poor neighborhoods" increased from 3 percent to 17 percent from 1970 to 1990. Child poverty rose from 18 percent to 27 percent from 1969 to 1989. Inner city children have an increased likelihood of growing up on public assistance, and a greater dropout rate.

Research reviews dealing with the mental health of children from low-income urban families reveal a worrying picture. Children from these settings have been shown to have higher rates of depression, delinquency, violence, aggression, behavior problems, maltreatment, and trauma-related disorders. Some doubt remains about the etiological connections between urbanization and mental health for children from low-income families. To some extent, the effects found may indicate the tendency for inner city locations to attract individuals with a variety of problems, including mental health ones, but this argument does not seem sufficient. It appears that there are multiple stressors inherent in low-quality city settings that translate into urban stress as well as a variety of psychological disturbance.

On the other hand, some factors and conditions are able to minimize the negative input from urbanization. A number of these are family-related, such as the robust kinship ties, strong religious and spiritual orientations, and ethnic awareness that can be found in many African American families. Other factors include an emphasis on education, the promotion of self-respect, and the availability of safe structured activities of urban children.

In an attempt to delineate the psychological impact of urbanization, psychologists have begun to study the dynamics of socially toxic neighborhoods. This has involved the identification of neighborhood structures that are especially toxic to mental health. Research in this area reveals, for example, that nearly 20 percent of children in some neighborhoods experience so much disturbance from environmental stress that they require psychotherapy.[10] When these results are compared to the findings of similar studies conducted two or three decades ago, it becomes clear that children, as well as adults, are at increased risk of environmental stress and its effects. Adding to the toxicity of many modern urban environments are the availability of guns, exposure to violence, potential lethality of childhood interactions, presence of drugs, and precarious family and marital relationships.

The effects of urbanization have been grouped into four broad categories.[11] As can be seen, each of these involves a number of factors that exert an influence on social and psychological health.

> *Environmental*: Noise, air pollution, toxins, visual pollution, sensory overload, population density and distribution, traffic congestion, urban sprawl, contagious diseases
>
> *Sociological and economic*: crime, violence, gangs, migration (rural to urban), housing, crowding, marginalization, segmentalization, poverty, unemployment, industrialization, absence of community
>
> *Psychosocial*: social structure, homelessness, life complexity, family disintegration/divorce, rapid social change, acculturation/assimilation, social drift, cultural disintegration, cultural confusion/conflict, secularization, social stress
>
> *Psychological*: quality of life, sense of coherence, powerlessness, marginality, alienation, rootedness, fear, anxiety, identity, isolation, loneliness

The sheer number of urban life variables underscores the importance of developing additional research programs in this general area. This would allow us to learn a great deal more about contemporary patterns of mental disturbance. One factor that is becoming especially problematic for millions of urban residents is pollution.

Pollution: Emotional and Cognitive Responses

When we think of urban pollution, it is usually the impact on our physical health that comes to mind first. Environmental pollutants of all sorts contribute to pulmonary, immunological, and neurobehavioral diseases. The field of environmental medicine is a rapidly growing area of practice that strives to assess, diagnose, and treat environmentally induced disorders and to seek ways to control and prevent the environmental factors that cause these disorders. The scale of the problem is immense. For example, it was recently estimated that 1.2 billion people worldwide are exposed to levels of sulfur dioxide that exceed the health guidelines of the World Health Organization. It was also estimated that 1.4 billion people daily breathe air that contains harmful levels of smoke and suspended particulate matter.[12] Vast numbers of individuals live in urban environments that force them to inhale dangerous carcinogens, including chromium, nickel, arsenic, asbestos, benzene, and radon. The effects on the physical health of the affected people are well documented, but less attention has been paid to the indirect effects of pollution on psychological well-being.

The disadvantages and suffering stemming from air pollution can be found at the behavioral, cognitive, and emotional levels. At the behavioral level, air pollution can deter people from spending time outdoors, participating in recreational activities, and enjoying the psychological benefits of physical activity. If tasks are performed in a polluted surrounding, the quality and enjoyment of the performance can be hindered. When it comes to employment, many people do not enjoy the luxury of being able to avoid pollution, even on days when the dangers are especially high. This is especially true in the developing world, where urban pollution is a fact of life. Yet many of those exposed are aware of the risks and live with the depressing knowledge that their health is deteriorating daily.

Research relating air pollution to human task performance shows that prolonged exposure to various air pollutants can decrease visual acuity, interfere with sensorimotor balance, impair time estimation, diminish attention span, disrupt memory and problem-solving ability, and reduce overall work capacity.[13] There are a number of moderating variables, such as the perception that the pollution is controllable and individual differences in adaptability and environmental stress tolerance, but the fact remains that, for far too many people, air pollutants carry a high cost in terms of psychological well-being.

A research team led by Stephen Jacobs looked specifically at the relationship between air pollution and depression.[14] They surveyed English-speaking and Spanish-speaking residents of the Los Angeles metropolitan area and obtained measures of depressive symptomatology and exposure to air pollution. The results showed that perceived air pollution was a significant predictor of depression when combined with one or more other stressful life events. This study controlled for other factors (e.g., socioeconomic status, prior psychiatric status) that could have contributed to depression scores.

A study carried out in Santiago, Chile, sought to determine whether high levels of air pollution could increase level of anxiety.[15] Air pollution, and awareness of a lack of antipollution measures, had the effect of increasing anxiety levels. This may be one of many manifestations of the rising tide of *ecological psychopathology*.[16] It also lends support to those who are calling for a psychiatry of the environment that focuses on many of the disorders that are being created by urban and industrial factors.[17]

The modern industrial age has seen greater numbers of human-made catastrophic events that expose people to enormous amounts of pollution. Sometimes this happens in industrial locations; at other times it occurs in areas previously unaffected by pollution. Whatever the case, the effects go well beyond damage to the physical environment. For example, researchers examined the psychological, cultural, and social impacts of the infamous *Exxon Valdez* oil spill that took place in Valdez, Alaska, in 1989.[18] In the course of studying thirteen Alaskan communities, they found a clear dose-response relationship on a number of social and mental health variables. As exposure to the oil and the disruptive cleanup procedures increased, there were declines in traditional social relations with family, friends, neighbors, and work mates. Problems such as drinking, substance abuse, and domestic violence became more common. After the spill, there was a greater frequency of depression, posttraumatic stress disorder, and generalized anxiety disorder. Alaskan natives and women were especially prone to psychiatric disorders in the postspill period.

The researchers concluded that pollution disasters, such as that caused by the *Exxon Valdez*, have just as much effect on the psychosocial environment as they do on the physical environment. Among other questions, future research will need to determine whether the effects of such disasters are permanent, or whether the victims somehow find ways to adjust. This and related issues will become more important as hyperindustrialization increasingly creates the conditions under which these dreadful events can occur.

Noise Pollution

According to the U.S. Census Bureau, excessive noise is the most common complaint of community residents, reflective of widespread annoyance, frustration, and resentment. It has been estimated that noise levels in our cities have increased by 30 decibels in the past 30 years. Evidence also indicates that noise levels continue to rise at a worrying rate. In Sydney, Australia, 40 percent of households encounter noise pollution. In Hong Kong, 80 percent of households are affected negatively by noise. Although noise tends to be overshadowed by other urban predicaments, it constitutes a serious problem that must be addressed. Ignorance and apathy explain some of the tolerance for auditory regression, but there is also active resistance at the institutional level since the goal of noise control may conflict with the goals of profit and growth.[19]

Victims of noise pollution tend to feel that they are helpless to deal with the problem. They often perceive the noise itself as an indication of progress. Although most inhabitants of noise-affected areas would like relief, it is common for them to see the scale of the problem as too large for remediation. For these reasons, the majority of noise sufferers do not make active efforts to alleviate the situation.

Noise, unlike sound, is a psychological concept that implies a negative response by the exposed person. Thus it is not surprising that the literature tends to indicate that excessive amounts of noise have negative psychological consequences.[20] Noise is one of the most salient features of the increasingly urban world, but only a small amount of research has focused on the direct psychosocial consequences of this element of modern living. The studies that have been done demonstrate that high levels of noise can interfere with vigilance and multisource tasks and cause a deterioration of efficiency on arithmetic, reaction time, and clerical tasks.[21] One well-known study was carried out at a New York City school that was located adjacent to noisy elevated railway tracks.[22] Researchers who compared the academic achievement of children located on the quieter side of the building to that of children in the more noise-affected side found that academic achievement was significantly worse for students in the noisy classrooms.

Some research involved the artificial introduction of noise into a classroom setting in order to assess the effects of elevated noise level on scholastic performance.[23] In one study, researchers amplified traffic noise outside a large university classroom. The effect was that students participated less and showed a diminished attention span when compared to that of a no-noise control group. A similar study increased ambient noise level in classrooms of fifth and sixth graders. The result was an impairment of visual motor skills, auditory discrimination, and visual discrimination. Academic deficits have also been reported from schools that are in the flight paths of large aircraft.[24] Improvements in academic performance resulted when noise-affected classrooms were renovated in order to reduce level of aircraft noise.

A recent study of chronic noise exposure measured psychophysiological stress indicators in children (aged 9–11) before and after the opening of a new international airport in Munich, Germany.[25] After the airport became operational, a significant increase was found in the resting blood pressure, as well as the epinephrine and norepinephrine levels, of the children. These rises were interpreted as indications of environmental stress resulting from exceedingly high levels of aircraft noise. It has been suggested that the performance impairments associated with noise in schools are the cumulative result of an interference with the teaching-learning process. Difficulties arise when students and teachers struggle to hear each other. It may also be that noise has direct negative effects on information-processing ability, in part the result of hyperarousal.

Children living in noisy apartment buildings have been shown to suffer from deficits of reading ability, puzzle-solving ability, and auditory discrimination.[26] Results showed that these deficits persisted even when the children were removed to quieter settings. Evidence exists that high noise levels in the home hamper the cognitive development of young children. An inverse relationship was found between scores on a Piagetian test and reported levels of home noise. Especially poor results were obtained from children living in homes that did not offer a means for children to be isolated from the sources of noise.[27]

Studies on the effect of noise on social behavior have found that high levels of ambient noise reduce people's sensitivity to one another.[28] They become less willing to offer assistance to those in need, to offer aid to those who have had minor accidents, or to give directions to someone who is lost. Research also found that noisy settings reduce the likelihood of casual social interaction and promote distorted and oversimplified perceptions of complex social relationships. Noise has the effect of diverting the person's attention to the most prominent situational cues, ignoring a range of more subtle cues, such as interpersonal ones. Social impairments may also relate to negative emotion generated by the noise. In a different sort of study, conducted in low-income urban areas, high levels of noise were found to be associated with increased numbers of arrests and a disinclination to look after the yards of houses.[29]

The aftereffects of noise pollution have also been shown to affect a number of human abilities.[30] Research shows that prior exposure to high levels of noise lowers frustration tolerance and impairs performance on certain tasks (e.g., proofreading). These types of studies demonstrate that the poststimulation effects of noise are comparable to those found in research employing electric shock and other unpleasant modes of stimulation.

Urban development has seen the forced relocation of considerable numbers of city residents. Some research has assessed the psychological and social costs of forced relocations that were due to new road and rail construction. The effects included depression, disrupted emotional ties with neighbors and community, and early death in the elderly.[31]

In light of the many negative effects of excessive noise on cognition, performance, and affect, one would expect to find similar results for direct measures of mental disturbance. Here again, much more research is required to give a complete picture of the mental health consequences of excessive noise, but the available studies on this topic already indicate noise as a significant contributor to a number of psychological problems. Research from industrial settings has shown that prolonged exposure to excessive noise is associated with increased anxiety and emotional stress, as well as a greater frequency of argumentativeness, emotional lability, and mood fluctuations.[32] Interpersonal conflicts were found to be more common in the noisiest parts of steel plants.

A number of studies have found higher rates of psychiatric admissions in communities that are badly affected by noise pollution.[33] This line of research has been criticized for failures to use appropriate control groups, but replication studies have also found a connection, albeit a modest one, between noise levels and rates of psychiatric admissions. Higher rates of mental hospital admissions were found in the maximum noise areas around Los Angeles International Airport. In this case, the effect was a very small one. It is undoubtedly the case that many other factors contribute to a situation wherein a person would require admission to a psychiatric institution. One could also argue that the rate of psychiatric admission is too extreme a measure to ascertain the more subtle psychological effects of noise.

Yet, despite the shortcomings of available research, there are ample signs that prolonged exposures to high levels of noise can result in negative emotional, cognitive, and social outcomes.

HOMELESSNESS: A MODERN SIN

Homeless individuals have become a prominent feature of the urban landscape. All sorts of emotions are conjured up as urban residents pass by these unfortunate people who lack the most basic of all needs, namely, shelter, but indifference has come to dominate our experience of the homeless. Our ability to adapt to this human tragedy may explain the relatively small amount of time, energy, and money that is being spent on solutions. With some exceptions, mental health professionals have paid little attention to this problem.

Even the most conservative statistics reveal homelessness as a social pathology that exists on a large scale. Although the numbers are difficult to gauge, it is estimated that there are between 600,000 and 3 million homeless people in the United States alone. For New York City, the estimates vary between 35,000 and 70,000. Los Angeles has approximately 30,000 homeless, whereas Chicago has around 25,000.[34] The number of homeless in the United Kingdom has been estimated at 121,000, up from 80,000 in 1984, but down from a peak of 140,000 in 1990. This does not take into account the large numbers of "hidden homeless."

The problem of homelessness extends far beyond the social policy changes of the mid-1960s that brought about mass deinstitutionalization of the mentally ill; even so, this development is the most widely held explanatory account of the homelessness phenomenon. Although changes to mental health policy undoubtedly contributed to the problem, other evidence tells us that this is not a sufficient explanation. For example, even though many homeless people suffer from mental disorders, research shows that the majority of homeless individuals are not mentally disturbed.[35]

The likelihood of someone's becoming homeless has increased as a result of housing market changes that have occurred in many modern cities. A process of urban revitalization has led to a shortage of low-cost housing and forced some residents to seek cheaper and more modest housing. At the bottom end of this trend, we find a group of vulnerable people who cannot afford housing of any kind. In support of this explanation, statistics from the United States show that the quantity of cheap rental units declined from 17.9 million in 1970 to 6.4 million in 1980.[36] This particular type of housing shortage poses a serious challenge for vulnerable poor people. Not all of them are able to resolve it, and some of them become homeless.

A related factor contributing to homelessness is the intensifying competition for space in the dilapidated neighborhoods that were once the habitat of skid row and homeless people. City planners often target the most decayed urban areas for beautification. These are home to considerable numbers of vulnerable low-income, mentally ill, and elderly people. Once revitalization work begins, the quantity of low-cost accommodation declines. In New York City, for example, the number of inexpensive single-room-occupancy buildings decreased by 80 percent from 1970 to 1982.[37] Whereas many displaced residents make the adjustment, once again the more vulnerable ones run the risk of becoming homeless.

Substance abuse has also been implicated in the problem of homelessness. One study found that 39 percent of young homeless people drank the equivalent of 3.5 pints of beer once or more per week, but this was no more than the figure of 40 percent for unemployed males, aged 18 to 24.[38] It was also found that 64 percent of the homeless sample had taken drugs "at some time in the past," but most were only casual users. Thus substance abuse is not a sufficient explanatory factor in youth homelessness. It must be remembered that homelessness is highly stressful and that some additional substance abuse can be expected for this reason alone. Among the young homeless, the most common pattern of substance use one finds is casual experimentation, rather than prolonged and habitual use.

Other factors have also been identified in an effort to understand the homelessness phenomenon. These include unemployment, crime, mortgage problems, sexual abuse, and family breakdown, but the most disturbing question that dominates our academic curiosity is related to our collective reluctance to put an end to homelessness. Despite the innovative efforts of some cities, the fact remains that the problem of homelessness largely has been ignored. The financial costs of a solution could be absorbed very easily by wealthy nations such as the United States. They do not have the excuse of poverty, which creates an additional obstacle in many developing countries.

In trying to comprehend our lack of collective will on this count, we need to delve into the beliefs and attitudes of modern Western culture. John McMurty lists a number of social commandments that make up the unifying belief system of contemporary global culture.[39] As the building blocks of our global market doctrine, they constitute an overall value program that orders normality, determines cultural prescriptions, and dictates social policy. Obedience to these commandments is equated with survival in the market. The specific social commandments are: human justice and liberty reside in the freedom of money exchange; the money-price system is an ideal system by which to distribute services and goods; profit-maximization is the optimal vehicle for social and personal well-being; accelerating consumer desire is good; the pursuit of maximal income and wealth is natural and good; there should be no limits to the conversion of life into salable commodities; and those who have only labor and service to sell are obliged to do so if a prosperous and free society is to be maintained.

These social commandments help to establish overriding guidelines and expectations, and to specify punishments for various types of violations. Most adherents of the new global order embrace these principles to the extent that punishments for disobedience are construed as logical and justified. It has been observed that our present capitalistic structures entail faith in the compensatory logic of the cosmos.[40] Those who invest themselves properly in the system will be compensated in a just manner. A reverse sort of logic extends from this brand of faith, namely, that those who are not compensated adequately have not made the sacrificial investments that entitle them to justice. The homeless fall into this category. They have offended the moral order of the universe, and consequently they are liable for punishment. Poverty, physical suffering, starvation, and even death are part of the social shock treatment that our marketing faith demands, and by which its disciples abide. In a sense, homelessness is deemed to be a sin of disobedience that warrants ongoing penance.

According to McMurty, the meaning of life in modern consumer culture revolves around the value inversion of increasing money demand for those making investments. It entails a social value program that establishes human worth in terms of how much money is assigned to their lives, but it also introduces a sort of cognitive slippage into our present mode of cultural consciousness:

> We have come to a point where people, societies, and the planet itself have been so subjugated to the rule of the money-sequence of value that the most life-invasive and morally grotesque consequences of its system of reasoning appear rational and impeccable to its logic. Only what fits the market's value metric is computed by it or deemed "economic." The global market sequence of choices and exclusions may be a socially instituted insanity.[41]

These social organizing principles make it easy to turn away from the plight of the homeless, especially since they are not economic. A first step toward rectifying the problem would entail cultural deprograming aimed at eradification of the implicit assumption that these people have done something wrong or that someone must be economic in order to earn dignity and respect. In addition to learning more about the specific characteristics of the homeless, mental health professionals need to concentrate on the underlying process of victimization that keeps the problem alive.

TOURISM: ENVIRONMENTAL, SOCIAL, AND PSYCHOLOGICAL CONSEQUENCES

The topic of tourism may seem out of place in a chapter devoted to mental health and the physical world, but tourism is having profound effects on the physical environment, as well as the way in which people are beginning to perceive the world. In the latter instance, one could even say that our increasingly touristy world has implications for psychological well-being. The social meanings of the dramatic upsurgence of tourism are still not fully understood. In many ways, tourism is another manifestation of the theme of consumption in modern Western culture, as tourist activities are consumed in much the same manner as other more tangible commodities.

Various attempts have been made to categorize tourist activities according to other underlying motivations. In one of these, five tourist modes were identified: *recreational*, in which the tourist is motivated by relaxation and recreation in order to restore feelings of well-being; *experiential*, wherein the tourist seeks meaning aesthetically in the lives of others; *diversionary*, in which the tourist strives to escape boredom and to cope with alienation; *existential*, which sees tourists who are "exiled" from their own homes and cultures and crave orientation by forging relations with an alternative culture; and *experimental*, in which the tourist is motivated to sample alternative life-styles in distant locations.[42]

Another typology employed the actual objectives and content of the tourist activity. In that case, tourism was classified into five categories: *ethnic*, whereby the tourist experiences exotic and indigenous cultures; *cultural*, which permits the tourist to encounter vanishing yet familiar life-style patterns; *environmental*, which puts the person into contact with novel settings and locations; *recreational*, which allows explorations in new forms of activity and morality; and *historical*, which involves a symbolic journey into the glories and adventures of former ages.[43]

The vast majority of the literature tends to extol the fruits of this industry. We hear accounts of job creation, influx of foreign exchange, increased GDP, improvements to infrastructure (e.g., roads, electricity, communications, water supply), increased public services, and new cross-cultural education contacts. Tourism is also heralded for its ability to preserve indigenous cultural traditions. There is ample truth in these claims, but there is another side to the tourism onrush that gets less attention. As tourism is growing more rapidly than any other industry worldwide, we must consider the cost of this development.

One serious cost that must be addressed is the ecological degradation brought on by megatourism ventures. Many societies lack the socioeconomic infrastructure required to deal with environmental changes brought on by the sudden encroachment of tourism. The damage caused to the host environment is often so severe that much of the aesthetic appeal of the location is destroyed. More importantly, the environment and ecosystem themselves are often damaged beyond the point of repair. What the tourist then sees is the aftermath of insensitive economic development that has done irrevocable harm to the original setting. Whether or not this reality registers with most tourists is another matter. A certain percentage of tourists remain oblivious to the environmental damage that made their tourist activities possible. Yet a growing number are becoming aware of the environmentally ruinous nature of many types of tourism. Even if they do not verbalize this observation to themselves, a faint awareness of this fact discolors their experience and inclines them toward more ecofriendly tourism consumption.

The trend toward ecotourism has allowed some regions to preserve environmental balance while still exploiting the commercial benefits of tourism. At the same time, the tourism industry is incapable of providing the degree of oversight and regulation that can safeguard the integrity of the environment.[44] Despite many innovative ecoprojects, tourism development continues to account for massive amounts of environmental damage.

The tourism experience has the potential to be depressing. The services and facilities in tourist locations cannot hide their primary motivation, which is to extract money from visitors. Tourists are also confronted by a commercialized type of hospitality that can promote annoyance and cynicism. In addition, they consume images of places and people that resemble stage sets. They are exposed to planned, contrived, artificial, overdone, and unnatural presentations that will play a role in their perceptions of the world and its inhabitants. People with only limited tolerance for artificiality and contrivance are bound to experience tension. Thirty years ago, one could travel around France, for instance, and have the distinct feeling that one was part of a real human and physical environment. In recent times, however, an annual influx of 60 million tourists has transformed the experience entirely. Today, even in the most remote regions of France, it is impossible to escape the feeling that this is a world that is all about tourism. The same situation exists in many other countries.

The depression that some people feel in the role of a tourist has much to do with a sense of loss. This loss can relate to harm that was done to the physical landscape, or it can involve cultural damage. In the past decade or so, cultural tourism has become very popular. A variety of factors may explain this. For one, some potential tourists are satiated with, and put off by, the more gaudy and crowded tourist destinations. They may want their tourist experience to be more than mere travel or leisure. Thus we see emerging a new breed of tourist who seeks cultural meaning from the tourist adventure. There has been a steady increase in tourist offerings that are designed to offer cultural adventures. Operators now sell tourist packages to exotic cultures in locations that were once beyond the reach of everyone except the most determined travelers. In the travel section of a newspaper, I recently saw an advertisement that read, "Visit the Headhunters of Borneo." No cultural group, on any continent, is currently safe from tourist operators.

It is quite revealing to examine the actual motivations of people who participate in so-called cultural tourism. One study identified the specific motivations of the large numbers of tourists who visit the hill tribes of northern Thailand.[45] When asked prior to the tour about their main reason for visiting the tribes people, only 18 percent reported that it was to visit the people themselves. Other primary motivations included scenery, escaping the city, riding an elephant, having a new experience, river rafting, a feeling of adventure, and hiking. These same individuals were surveyed after their visits, about what they found to be the most satisfying aspect of their trip. Only 14 percent said that it was their actual visit with the hill tribe people. River rafting was cited most often as the best part of the trip. Other aspects that were satisfying to tourists were hiking, the trekking group, nightlife in the village, elephant riding, scenery, and drugs.

One observer concluded that hill tribe trekking does not actually represent cultural tourism in any real way. Instead, tourists tend to move around in an environmental bubble that insulates them from meaningful cultural experience.[46] This is confirmed by the significant number of hill tribe trekkers who stated that they would not return since the trip had been too touristy, commercialized, and superficial. Some who were downright demoralized by the experience expressed negative sentiments about the attitudes and actions of the other tourists. There is an increasing prevalence of this sort of antitourist position, as the person perceives himself or herself as a moral exception to the other tourists. In such a cognitive strategy the individual enjoys the tourist experience while remaining detached from the fact that he or she is part of the insensitive group.

Those who defend the trend toward so-called cultural tourism argue that it helps the natives to maintain their identity and social cohesion in the face of accelerating global transformation. This sounds like a noble cause, but it typically relates to the tourist shows that are intended to demonstrate traditional talents, customs, and skills to the audience. In fact, these are often exercises in the calculated manufacture of the exotic.[47] Sometimes this situation can be improved, as when tourists stay with local families. Yet the authenticity of the experience is often lost as locals try to fulfill stereotypes that drew the tourists in the first place. In general, what starts out as cultural tourism can quickly degrade into a significant debaser of arts, customs, and cultural identity.[48] That too can be depressing for all involved.

Economic benefits of tourism can obscure a number of potential social problems that accompany cultural tourism. For instance, some locals are forced to leave their land in order to make way for tourist developments. This can sometimes be the result even when residents are not forcibly relocated. Local inflation in areas targeted for tourism can be so high that residents must seek out less expensive areas to live. Environmental damage stemming from tourism development can also degrade existing subsistence enterprises, with the effect of forcing people off their land.

The highly seasonal nature of tourism can disturb social harmony and alter the traditional way of life. The agricultural community can be affected quite seriously in this regard. Large-scale high-standard tourist resorts have the worst type and degree of dislocating effects, and also the ones that yield the smallest relative benefits for locals.[49] One often finds that the rapid introduction of this type of facility does not involve necessary linkages with important social and economic sectors, most notably agricultural ones. Such situations, especially when they transpire in poor and previously undeveloped areas, can lead to an unhealthy overreliance on the developers.

One group of researchers studied thirty-three components of community life as they are affected by tourism.[50] These were grouped according to several categories of community functioning: economic factors, environmental factors, medical services, citizen involvement, public services, and recreational services. The findings demonstrated that tourism had the greatest impact on environment, citizen involvement, and public services. Specifically, it was found that rises in tourism development were followed by declines in satisfaction with opportunities for citizen involvement. At the same time, residents attached less importance to citizen involvement as a consequence of tourism. Increased tourism development was also related to reported dissatisfaction with access to public services.

Hostility can be experienced by local residents when it becomes clear to them that they are missing out on the fruits of tourism. It is a myth that all local people enjoy the economic benefits of tourism. This is especially inaccurate when it comes to imported tourism operations. Statistics from small-scale societies show that 70 percent of tourism profits are returned to the countries of origin of the tourism development.[51] The powerful foreign tourism operations can actually deplete the self-sufficiency of the local economy in indigenous areas, creating heightened dependency on the outside world.

Sometimes a vast network of tourism can be tightly controlled by only a few large companies. This case has been made with regard to places such as Hawaii, where active efforts are made to confine tourist spending to outlets owned by the same company or group of companies. This sort of arrangement leaves very little financial spillage for local small-scale operators.[52] Consequently, the locals receive almost no socioeconomic advantage and inevitably have some feelings of animosity. This may explain why some studies have found Hawaii to be one of the locations that are affected by resident-visitor alienation.[53]

Other potential problems with tourism include disrupted kinship systems, inequality, crowding, increased urbanization, loss of wildlife, prostitution, and crime. Many mediating factors function to determine the valence of tourism's influence on local people. Some of these have been built into stress models that have been devised to explain the impact of tourism on individual and community health.[54] Community stress is generated when tourism reaches a point of saturation.

Tourism is often greeted with initial enthusiasm by the local residents. This is due to expectations that the new industry will deliver revenue and pleasure and that the tourists themselves will have a genuine interest in the local people, customs, and life-styles. However, this mood usually deteriorates as the volume of tourists rises and the nature of resident-visitor contact becomes more impersonal and commercialized. At this stage, the novelty begins to wear off, and residents start to become irritated by tourist demands.[55] The original enthusiasm is replaced by apathy and growing concerns about matters such as inflation, loss of tradition, congestion, and undesirable alterations to community harmony. The situation is worsened if the residents are not consulted about these problems and their possible management. As tourist development progresses even further, community stress begins to express itself in feelings that the costs of tourism have begun to exceed the benefits. Open antagonism toward the tourist industry can surface at this stage if residents come to identify tourism as the primary cause of social and economic adversity. In extreme cases, this can manifest itself in crime and attacks against tourists.

This pattern is sometimes mitigated by variables related to visitor characteristics, length of stay, nature of destination, economic structure, spatial distribution of tourism activities, local politics, and strength and integrity of local culture. Yet we must take seriously the prospect that the cost of tourism can exceed the benefit. Tourism has the potential to affect the mental well-being of those who have various types of contact with it. These are some of the factors that researchers will have to consider much further as tourism continues to expand as a feature of the modern age.

MODERNITY AND ECOLOGICAL SOCIOPATHY

It is hard to avoid the many worsening reports about atmospheric pollution, ozone depletion, global warming, out of control deforestation, climatic destabilization, loss of biological diversity, ocean degradation, and so on. Outspoken critics of existing environmental policy proclaim vehemently that we cannot continue to treat the Earth as if it were a business in a liquidation sale. Being on the verge of total environmental meltdown, we must instantly turn our full attention to the acutely pathological state of the human-nature relationship. Yet the most startling aspect of this state of affairs is that the momentum of the destructive forces shows no sign of slowing. Instead, these forces are gathering more strength despite all the informed voices warning about the disaster that looms. We are left to wonder whether the human being lacks an overarching mode of intelligence that operates to safeguard itself as a species.

It may be that the fundamental way in which moderns experience themselves and the world is creating the conditions for an environmental holocaust, and an associated indifference. Albert Schweitzer predicted that because of the incapacity of moderns to foresee and forestall, the destruction of the Earth is almost inevitable.[56] The way in which modernity has reshaped our perception of nature has also contributed to ecological ruin. Nature in the current age bears little resemblance to the relatively unmediated form that inhabited the premodern mind. The new conception of nature is a thoroughly managed one that mirrors the identity and pathologies of modern society. With the conceptual demise of primal nature, there has emerged a highly socialized version that invites aggression and a surreal indifference to environmental injury.[57] Nature, which has come to be experienced as an arm of human endeavor, and in particular technology, is no longer inscribed with trust, certainty, nurturance, or fear. Instead, it has become part of the potential payoff for the random fact of our existence.

Being poised in terms of autonomous heroics, the modern self has lost the ability to perceive its interdependence with social as well as ecological processes.[58] Consequently, many people today experience almost no motivation to attend to issues outside themselves, including those that might relate to ecological health. An empty self-contained identity structure is predisposed to focus attention inward while responding to conditioned material needs. It is reasonably well adapted to a sociopolitical context that places greater importance on economic demands than environmental survival. Likewise, it responds readily to the philosophy of personal increase that lies at the heart of the existing economic system.

The problem from an environmental standpoint is that an inner-directed materialistic orientation bears an inverse relationship to ecological awareness, thus creating an ever-worsening set of conditions for planetary health.[59] Once the self was freed from its historical connections to the natural and social world, economies could evolve into operations that were at liberty to victimize nature merely for purposes of efficiency. Individual participants in this process lack the type of ecological self required to register emotionally the adverse consequences to the natural world that result from irresponsible economic activity, thereby giving free reign to the modern ecological pathologies.[60]

Rather than regarding people as ecologically oblivious, some social theorists see moderns as capable of internalizing the dangers posed to the physical world and experiencing such ecopathologies as environmental despair, environmental guilt, and ecological grief. For example, one aspect of risk-society theory states that the new sets of environmental hazards, as well as the potentials for an ecological apocalypse, are perceived by moderns as a significant threat.[61] More specifically, the perception and/or anticipation of these hazards culminates in ecoanxiety, ecoalarmism, and a subtle state of preconscious anthropological shock. It is thought that fear becomes a permanent feature of consciousness as members internalize the end of nature and realize that they can no longer trust broader social institutions to protect them from this precarious development. The sense of being at risk is amplified by the knowledge that the high-consequence environmental risks that threaten them are not within their control.

The actual response of moderns to the experience of environmental risk has not yet been established. Some have argued that ecoanxiety and other ecological disturbances do not translate into positive motivation because the person is suffused with a powerful sense of helplessness. In this case, a negative fatalism takes over wherein the individual copes primarily by dimming the awareness of environmental risk. Others have maintained that environmental anxieties are not acted upon because the person wants to avoid the terror that would arise from a full acknowledgment of the problem. It may also be that environmental action is sometimes inhibited by a fear of appearing unpatriotic or unreligious, especially in hypercapitalistic settings where unrestrained environmental exploitation has become an economic and religious right that promises salvation by way of unceasing consumption.

A slightly more optimistic scenario is that society responds to environmental pathology through a self-critique process that has the effect of altering patterns of rationality and behavior.[62] Although this does not guarantee an improved environmental condition, nor a resolution of the personal insecurity precipitated by chronic environmental deterioration, the social impetus for change at least provides a source of hope. However, there is little indication that societal self-critique is exerting itself in any meaningful way.

Environmental Dissociation

Rather than speculate about some collective intelligence that diagnoses and reacts to environmental threat, it might be more fruitful to seek an understanding of the heavy inertia that keeps alive our environmental onslaught. Without any credible source of ecological wisdom, it is easy for the individual to slip into a defensive mode designed to contain anxiety, pessimism, and hopelessness. In addition to an identity structure that does not invite attention to external issues demanding an awareness of interconnectedness, modern consciousness has a large capacity for environmental dissociation. This enables members to perceive environmental risks but simultaneously to process that information so it stays out of working consciousness and does not activate them either cognitively or behaviorally. Society then becomes characterized by a collective dissociative amnesia that involves a complete forgetting of the human-nature relationship, and of the historical imperative to nurture this relationship in order to safeguard the continuity of human existence.

Some of the best exhibitions of environmental dissociation can be seen in the form of overconsuming celebrities who campaign and raise funds on behalf of environmental causes. Dissociation allows them somehow to reconcile their proenvironment messages with their own excesses, and in some cases with personal life-styles (including private jets) that are the full embodiment of the environmental crisis. On a lesser scale, most moderns employ a similar type of dissociative process that permits an ongoing contradiction between their surface cognitions and their manifested behavior. Self-interest overrules environmental concern in cultural formats that are barren of social security and philosophically reliant on radical manipulations of nature.

If individuals experience some degree of conscious ecoanxiety, it probably reaches them by way of a diffuse cultural foreboding that has as its source an environmentally related threat to economic viability. This threat has been described by José Prades as *contemporary sociogenic global environmental change* (CSGEC):

> a human-induced bio-geo-chemical process of planetary alteration which exerts a major pressure on our society, namely by stimulating a fundamental, increasingly powerful and generalized questioning on how can the world's socioeconomic system sustain its development without compromising irreversibly the geospheric and biospheric equilibrium necessary to the survival of the human species.[63]

CSGEC is an undesirable reality that collides with the basic tenets of capitalism, in particular the capitalistic assumption that progress will continue unabated through the unrestricted exploitation of natural and societal resources. As CSGEC becomes an inescapable consideration, economic scope and efficiency are threatened, and the impression is formed that capitalistic hope is not without bounds. Divisions within business become more likely. Anxiety and uncertainty enter into the general socioeconomic system once CSGEC becomes a source of doubt about the viability of society's philosophical underpinnings.

As Prades sees it, the only real solution to CSGEC lies in our ability to move toward a revised cultural model that is distinguished by *societal solidarity*, by which is meant a "compulsory functional interdependence which links and integrates the forces and the resources of every human society."[64] As the requisite vocation of the human being, this construction could compete with individualistic capitalism in forging new respect for ourselves as part of the larger ecosystem.

It may be that despite people's seeming inattentiveness to the environmental crisis, a preconscious awareness of environmental calamity is having a generalized effect on their outlook toward life. For instance, surveys of schoolchildren show that global ecological destruction has edged out nuclear war as the greatest perceived threat. Even if this problem does not lead to mental health problems as such, it contributes to the existential crisis affecting increasing numbers of modern people. For the first time in history, we must live with the toxic knowledge that the entirety of human existence, and all future prospects, are unsafe.

Some interesting research from Canada found that positive perceptions of the health of the environment are associated with feelings of security, optimism, and confidence.[65] On the other hand, negative perceptions are related to feelings of fear, discouragement, and frustration, but the overall findings, which were based on the responses of university students, showed that there was only a slight dissatisfaction with environmental conditions and with governmental policies toward the environment. This serves to confirm that most people do not have the magnitude of concern that would propel them to action. Any inclinations to make proenvironmental life-style changes are intercepted by intractable cultural values that are incompatible with ecological concern.[66]

John McMurty writes that the environmental crisis has been allowed to proceed unchecked because of the assumed truth and desirability of the market's regulating principles. It reaches a closed metaphysical loop that prevents reality from "kicking back" and gives people the misapprehension that any potential problems with this otherwise ideal system are external to them and not cause for deep concern.[67] Environmental irresponsibility has become socially sanctioned by economic indoctrinations that exalt the growth of consumption. The legitimacy of this form of collective irresponsibility is furthered by large corporations that deliberately ignore ecological realities for the sake of trumping up more profit.[68]

Exemplifying Environmental Sociopathy and Consumer Trance

In order to illustrate environmental sociopathy by large corporations, we could consider the current American craze regarding sport utility vehicles (SUVs). By contrast to cars, these expensive and heavy four-wheel-drive vehicles emit up to 75 percent more pollution, consume 33 percent more fuel, and require considerably more energy and natural resources for their manufacture. Over the past decade, the use of SUVs has caused Americans to waste an extra 70 billion gallons of gasoline, which translates into a vast quantity of unnecessary air pollution. The claim that this waste is unnecessary originated in various surveys that revealed that close to 90 percent of SUV drivers had never taken the vehicle off-road, presumably the whole idea of the SUV. Despite all the costs to the person and the environment, sales of SUVs have risen sharply over recent years. In 1997 alone, nearly 2 million new SUVs found their way onto American roads. The sales of these vehicles have also increased greatly in many other countries that have contracted the environmentally hostile SUV virus.

Keeping in mind that people today are exposed regularly to reports about environmental destruction and the need to reduce energy consumption, we must wonder what possesses millions to purchase SUVs. The answer takes one back to the big corporations that are more than willing to cultivate the false need for SUVs for profit purposes. In this regard, much larger profits are made on the sale of SUVs than on ordinary passenger vehicles. In the course of denying to consumers the serious environmental impact of SUVs, advertisements are designed to convey the impression that SUVs are a means by which we can reunite with nature. They hope that consumers will respond to their misleading message that SUVs can actually restore some of the lost human-nature relationship. This approach has been highly successful in masking the truth about SUVs as a destroyer of nature.

We usually think of the 1950s and 1960s as the era of the oversized inefficient automobile, and we look to the wide range of new smaller cars as evidence for improved attitudes about the automobile's effect on the environment. In actuality, however, the average fuel efficiency of all personal vehicles in the United States has been decreasing steadily since 1985. Somehow automobile manufacturers have managed to realize the "bigger and better" profit strategy, while pacifying the public with the illusion of proenvironmental trends in the car industry. This raises the question about the apparent inability of modern consumers to resist appeals for overconsumption.

Although environmental dissociation helps to explain this phenomenon, another factor is the eclipse of intellectual authority and critical culture. In most simple premodern societies, a critical culture disseminated actively its wisdom in order to assign proportion to all facets of life.[69] However, when critical culture becomes unsustainable, as it has today, individual members cannot tap sufficient cultural vision to allow them to assess themselves critically and to place their behavior in a commonsense perspective. They can readily succumb to a severe breakdown of values due to a deficiency of accumulated wisdom about the interactions of human beings with each other and the physical world.[70]

In terms of environmental issues, contemporary consumers may have contact with fragmented facts about the collapsing ecosystem, but none of this is voiced to them in an organized and convincing way that inspires positive action. Without an intellectual authority to guide them, they experience enhanced advertising suggestibility and an exaggerated tendency to employ fad as a guiding principle.

With regard to the example of SUVs, once they became part of consumer fashion, the public's motivation to possess these vehicles took on a self-sustaining life of its own, which no longer even needed a justification or rationalization. The SUV trend is unquestionably a manifestation of ecological madness, but entranced individual participants are unable to ascertain their own role in the process. Any tendencies toward self-criticism and ecoanxiety are quickly squelched by their perception that their behavior corresponds to a media norm.

Governments, like corporations, perpetuate consumer trance while blinding themselves and the electorate to the real ecological dangers. When consumption falls, borrowing is encouraged through a lowering of interest rates in order to stimulate consumption. Some token efforts, such as recycling, keep some people pacified and under the impression that things are being done to improve the environmental situation. In reality, these minisolutions are probably counterproductive, simply because they generate the false perception that enough is being done. Thus we fail to see that virtually nothing is being done, and that the scale and speed of the damage are increasing all the time. Even if people care at some level, the confidence they have in their consumer orientation makes them incapable of reading the crisis accurately or taking seriously the drastic life-style changes that would be required to improve the situation.

The spread of consumer culture to all the nations of the world is cause for additional environmental concern. Whereas growth-oriented Western economies fail to spread their wealth to people in exploited poor countries, they are adept at indoctrinating them with materialistic drives. With advances in communication, people across the globe are receiving the message that consumption and a life-style devoted to materialism are the best pathways to happiness and the good life. Of course, without the means to indulge in their new materialistic urges, they are often destined for frustration. Many can only watch as their own land and its people are depleted.

In an essay dealing with the "consumerscapes" of the less affluent world, Guliz Ger and Russell Belk describe consumerism as the main vehicle of cultural interpenetration.[71] The effect is to generate discontent and instill an insatiable desire for nonessential consumer products. They cite Romania as an example. The 1989 revolution in that country was due in large part to consumer frustration and longing. This factor was at least as important as the political tensions that are often attributed to that revolution. In the past several years, Romania has been flooded by products from other countries, which have greatly activated consumer desires. Surveys now reveal that Romanians have become preoccupied, if not obsessed, with the latest "desiderata" coming out of the West.[72] The eagerness to become acceptable consumers can be seen everywhere in Romania. It is not uncommon, for instance, for a person to smoke a pack of foreign cigarettes per day, even though those cigarettes take up an entire day of income. The status involved in consuming the right products is so great that people will sacrifice their personal and family life.

The fetish for consumer goods that we are selling to less affluent countries expresses itself in many ways. In some central African locations, one runs across individuals who are willing to spend a week's income for a *real* (i.e., imported) can of Coke. After it is drunk with great ceremony, the can is placed in a conspicuous spot so visitors can admire it and be made aware of the owner's status and affluence. To do the same with a locally produced bottle of Coke would not have the same effect. The same process that is fueling their materialism is also increasing their tolerance for destructive environmental practices that can satisfy their new desires.

Continual expansion is an imperative of the modern economic system. A type of natural selection ensures that only the fastest-growing companies survive. As they grow, more technology and natural resources are used, placing an ever increasing strain on the environment. In a short span of time, our growth principle has contributed greatly to our present ecological crisis.

TOWARD ECOLOGICAL MODERNITY

Not everyone is convinced that we still have the degree of cultural unity needed to mobilize a humanistic industrialism and a society of sane consumers. Research shows that the lifting of awareness about environmental destruction has done nothing to reverse the process. On the contrary, the environment continues to deteriorate. In one large study, twenty-one indicators of environmental quality were assessed for changes, from 1970 to 1990, in nine industrialized countries. Among the indicators were air quality, water (including groundwater) quality, acid rain, chemical pollutants, municipal and nuclear waste, size of wetlands, and land quality. The results showed that, over the span of two decades, overall environmental quality deteriorated significantly in all nine countries. The percentages of decline in the different countries were as follows.[73]

Denmark	-10.6%
Netherlands	-11.4%
Britain	-14.3%
Sweden	-15.5%
West Germany	-16.5%
Japan	-19.4%
United States	-22.1%
Canada	-38.1%
France	-41.2%

What the modern world does not have is a cultural-economic system that offers moral direction with regard to the physical world in which we live. In his later years, B. F. Skinner wrote at length about the unfolding ecological crisis, and possible ways to intervene in order to offer ourselves some hope for the future. His essay "Why We Are Not Saving The World" refs to modern people collectively as "The Uncommitted" who are doing far too little to make a difference.[74] It is not nearly enough simply to teach our children to enjoy themselves in less environmentally damaging ways. The problem is so deeply ingrained that psychologists must begin to reconstruct core features of contemporary culture. Although this sounds like a nearly impossible task, it may be our only hope. As we approach the ecological point of no return, such measures may begin to appear practical and unavoidable.

Some social psychologists have begun to identify the areas of research, evaluation, and social policy formation that could help to avert environmental disaster. Overpopulation is consistently pinpointed as a crucial factor that contributes to, and magnifies the size of, all environmental problems. In addition to addressing the overpopulation crisis, psychologists must devise ways of preventing people from receiving the types of mass media communications that shape environmentally destructive attitudes. As one of many possibilities, they could employ political and corporate persuasion techniques designed to introduce regulation requiring the broadcast media to set aside a certain amount of time for purposes of educating the public about environmental problems and their solutions.[75] The media could also be used to punish corporations that do not comply with specified codes of environmental practice.

In an effort to reshape cultural practices, it may be useful to target specific organizations that could be influential. Many sectors of the economy stand to benefit from healthier environmental practices. With small amounts of innovation, other sectors could also derive advantages from practices and products that are less harmful to the environment.[76] Through persuasion, such groups could be expected to support environmental reforms and to back such reforms in a public, high-visibility way.

It may also be possible to conceive of persuasion methods that can change certain aspects of our educational system. For example, very little attention is given to the way we train economists. If it is correct that most spheres of human behavior are influenced by economic structures, it follows logically that education of economists should be a top priority. The graduate training of economists should place more emphasis on human beings and the way they respond to certain economic conditions.[77] Likewise, future economists must be made more sensitive to the ultimate environmental cost of economic strategies and their underlying philosophies. Educators must find ways to revise the existing method for evaluating economic success, which rests primarily on profit results and the hawking of discontent. Economists should learn that economic activity must take active account of environmental realities and the rights of all life's creatures.

A group of Gestalt psychologists have sought to extend the principles of Gestalt psychology in an attempt to slow the pace of environmental destruction.[78] This approach understands positive mental health as a product of connectedness to the body and nature. Conversely, disconnection or alienation from any of these is thought to impede growth and pave the way for psychological disturbance. John Swanson describes the efforts of Gestalt psychology to make a meaningful contribution to an ecopsychology aimed at intervening in the current societal abuse of the natural environment.[79] He outlines some of the Gestalt techniques that might be able to increase Earth literacy and to reacquaint oneself with the natural world. These include exercises intended to rejuvenate dulled senses and to make the person more alert to sensations originating from the physical environment. As another strategy, the person is encouraged to develop an awareness of the ways in which hyperindividualism fosters a consciousness pattern that encourages indifference to the health and future of the external world. Individuals would even be asked to spend a certain number of hours per week communing with nature, with the rationale that this could deepen the emotional bond to nature and consequently reduce the risk of environmental abuse.

Many of the proposed Gestalt ecotherapy techniques aim ultimately to encourage the person to define himself or herself more broadly and to perceive the organismic self as inseparable from the natural world. However, as noble as their intentions might be, Gestalt ecopsychologists have yet to prescribe how their plan could be deployed in order to affect large numbers of people. Changing the attitudes and behavior of individuals on a one-to-one (or even small group) basis will not make a significant difference with regard to the environmental crisis. The success of any ecopsychological strategy must be evaluated in terms of its ability to redirect the masses.

Some thinkers maintain that the only hope of resolving the present crisis is to make the environment the basis for a spiritual reenchantment of the world.[80] This idea is based on the fact that nothing can compare to religion in moving the masses. The logic is that by resacralizing nature and the cosmos, individuals will have the basis for experiencing greater sensitivity to the environment. In turn, this could lessen their indifference to the environment and demotivate harmful expressions of their consumer desires.

Although ecological problems may eventually become the existential framework for the modern world, it may be unrealistic to expect very much from an environmental religion. It has been claimed that spiritual environmentalism would fail because it would become a religion of rejection that lacked sufficient meaning and rationale.[81] Beyond that, even though we have the social persuasion technology to move toward an environmental religion, ethical issues would be confronted all along the way. As total environmental collapse threatens to become a reality, however, there may be no other solution than to employ religious technology in order to impose an environmental conversion on consumer society.

On the subject of the relationship between religion and environmental salvation, it is interesting that a number of visionary environmentalists have referred to the *Amish answer*. As one learns about the religion of the Amish, one cannot avoid the conclusion that it lends itself to a system that, from an environmental standpoint, is far superior to that of the modern Western world.[82] In fact, no group of people is so environmentally friendly. Their per capita energy consumption is extremely low by comparison to that of modern consumers. With the exception of minor manure runoff and a small amount of diesel generator fumes, they cause very little pollution. The Amish religion and philosophy of life encourage people to reject consumerism and to turn away from unnecessary technological advances. By its design, their culture creates conservationists who value thriftiness, frugality, and moderation. To waste is a shameful activity. This is opposite to our dominant culture, which does almost nothing to discourage waste. The Amish economy thrives on conservation. Greed, avarice, and rapaciousness are considered vices, rather than virtues.

On the human front, the Amish have no poverty, no crime, and almost no violence. Their rates of mental disturbance and suicide are far lower than those found outside their culture. Some Amish youths experiment with alcohol, but alcoholism is almost nonexistent among adults. Marital conflict is quite low and marriages never end in divorce. The people themselves are never subjected to large dehumanizing institutions, such as factories, big schools, nursing homes, and mental hospitals. The family tends to be a tightly knit unit that cares for everyone, regardless of age or degree of infirmity. They do not have insurance policies since the people are each other's insurance.

The Amish have much greater immunity to depression, loneliness, alienation, meaninglessness, and ennui. They have a strong sense of belongingness, and each person is keenly aware that he or she has an important role to play. Their relatedness needs are met as people work together on most tasks, from the simple act of quilting to the complex process of barn raising. Their needs for transcendence and a sense of orientation are satisfied by their religion, which lies at the heart of their lives. Amish culture may not have the final answer to all of our economic and ecological problems, but it nonetheless has much to teach us about sane economics and sustainable environmental practices. However, moving in that direction would take us directly against the flow of current cultural conditioning. It would also mean that we forgo much of the technology, objects, services, and opportunities that are available to us.

We still do not have a full explanation for the disinclination of moderns to contemplate environmental issues and to assemble life-styles that are less damaging to the physical world. Without doubt, the collective mental health of modern people will deteriorate further as a result of a continuation of environmental dissociation and strategic cultural blindness. Social scientists are beginning to explore the potential for cultural consciousness to stage a major reversal in terms of the environment. A number of them have been developing the case that *ecological modernization* is a reflexive mechanism that has already begun to address the environmental threat. According to ecological modernization theory (EMT), which dates back to the early 1980s, economic and cultural structures have the ability to diagnose ecological threats and to initiate reconciliatory action.

Offending corporations and businesses have thrown their support behind EMT, for the obvious reason that it allows them to eschew responsibility for their destructive practices. It shifts the burden of regulation to an abstract level at which the environment is deemed to look after its own welfare because a healthy environment also means a healthy economy, and vice versa. Politicians also find themselves attracted to EMT since it gives them a credible excuse for not making hard environmental decisions that could cost votes.

At the heart of EMT is the reassuring premise that environmental problems are self-correcting by virtue of intervening sociopolitical projects. It is thought that economic institutions learn from their environmental mistakes, and that they employ this learning in order to invent more mature environmental practices and products. EMT does not assume a conflictual relationship between economic growth and environmental needs. Instead, it is a conservative procapitalistic model that portrays ecological crises as responding favorably to market forces.

The mechanisms for this process are the ecological criteria that are entered into the equations for production and consumption.[83] If EMT is correct, our current political and economic infrastructures are able to internalize these ecological criteria in order to maintain the status quo, but in a form that is supposedly sustainable from the vantage point of the environment.

The locus of the hope professed by EMT lies in the ongoing technologies that can undo partially the harmful effects of previous technologies. For example, if we return to my earlier criticisms of SUVs, an advocate of EMT would predict that, in time, the socioeconomic establishment would get the message that SUVs are polluting the environment to a dangerous degree. It would also be predicted that this diagnosis would be followed eventually by new technologies that allowed SUVs to operate more efficiently. This might even lead to the production of superlight mini-SUVs that have the same fuel efficiency as ordinary cars. The recognition of unacceptable risk may also incline political bodies to legislate against the source of the environmental toxin. Already we see indications that some American states are prepared to change legislation in order to treat SUVs as passenger cars with regard to allowable pollution levels. This would reverse the current laws, which allow them to pollute at 75 percent above the level permitted from cars.

Although EMT may be basically correct in claiming that sociopolitical responses are triggered by ecopathologies as they arise, its advocates do not comprehend fully either the source of environmental threats or the level at which change must take place. EMT is naive in assuming that economic institutions learn from their ecological blunders and that they activate the deep changes that could prevent future repeats of the problem. In reality, even if they participate in the rectification of their damaging practices, they continue to operate on the same underlying principles of indifference, profit, and growth. Regardless of the degree of ecological harm done by one project, the next project will bear the signature of the same values and capitalistic assumptions that gave birth to the previous calamity.

A true state of ecological modernity can only develop once changes have been made to the intrinsic cultural values that forgive environmental dissociation and indifference for the sake of selling something. One of the characters in Arthur Miller's *Death of a Salesman* voices what seems to be the accepted motto of the modern person: "The only thing you got in this world is what you can sell."[84] Ecopsychologists face the challenging task of disseminating, at the cultural level, a new set of values that can compete with the indifferentism and salesmanship that are represented so saliently in modern consumer society.[85]

Throughout the ages, people of many cultures have found a means to become rich in ways that did not require prodigious destruction of their physical life support systems. It may be that psychologists need to hurry along the death of the modern self-as-salesperson, while demonstrating the merits of life-giving orientations that offer more promise from the perspective of both the environment and mental health. The first step toward an ecological modernity that favors mental health may need to be one in which moderns are somehow made to feel more disturbed about the general condition of the environment. In that conscious state of ecoanxiety, there might lie the seeds for the radical changes that moderns will be required to make in the process of locating some harmony with nature.

CHAPTER 9

The New Mental Health Worker

The modern age, with all its unprecedented challenges and stresses, beckons a new breed of mental health worker who can address the types of problems that are prevalent today. This person will possess broader vision, a greater appreciation of macroscopic sociocultural determinants, and a deeper sense of social justice than those who are emerging from the current system. The new mental health worker will be more social-minded and more committed to the accomplishment of changes that will contribute to the general good of humankind, and all life on our planet.

THE NEED FOR WIDER PERSPECTIVES

It is time to move toward an eventual science of culture that would employ methods beyond the shortsighted ones currently in use. This would put us in a better position to conceive of, and implement, the culture-level changes that could benefit large numbers of people. However, present-day mental health professionals have been schooled in a system that concentrates, in a microscopic way, on factors operating at the level of the individual and in the local environment. For the most part, our energies are still being directed toward helping individuals make adjustments either within themselves or to situational difficulties that draw on personal resources.

Back in 1981, Seymour Sarason wrote an important essay about the way in which our thinking is imprisoned by individual psychology.[1] He saw its current fixation on the psychology of the individual organism as the provider of logic for the overemphasis on psychotherapy. Sarason went on to make a well-reasoned plea for clinical psychology to define itself in more far-reaching ways than as a profession that could treat individual psychopathology. He is correct in his analysis that psychology managed to get things backward as it came to see the individual as a separate entity that operated outside larger cultural contexts. We ended up with an asocial and misdirected field that was thoroughly preoccupied by the mythical disturbed individual. In the midst of this preoccupation, psychology largely forgot about the wider contexts in which these individuals operate.

TOWARD SOCIETAL THERAPY

The enormity of the modern mental health crisis throws into doubt the value of psychotherapy as the front line of intervention. Epidemiological research indicates that there is a rising pandemic of psychopathology across the globe.[2] The dimension of this problem is such that there is no possibility of individual therapists making a significant impact. It is estimated that, in the United States alone, over 50 million people suffer from a diagnosable mental/emotional disorder.[3] Despite the large psychotherapy industry in America, only a small percentage of psychologically disturbed individuals can be expected to be treated by way of psychotherapy.

There is also a tendency to exaggerate the actual number of Americans who are in therapy at any one time. The California therapy mentality receives a lot of media attention, which can give the false impression that Americans generally seek psychotherapy on a regular basis. In fact a variety of factors (e.g., financial constraints, perceived social stigma, lack of information) conspire to make individual psychotherapy an unlikely option for many Americans in need of psychological help. Even if it were possible to eliminate all barriers to psychotherapy, it has been estimated that the number of therapists would need to be increased twentyfold to meet the demand.[4]

The final proof of the futility of psychotherapy lies in the fact that it does nothing to reduce the incidence of mental disturbance in the general population. On the contrary, despite all the efforts of psychotherapists to mediate in the lives of disturbed individuals, the incidence of psychopathology continues to increase. This suggests quite clearly that the successful treatment of disturbed individuals does not have the overriding effect of slowing the development and transmission of mental disturbance. One reason for this phenomenon is related to the fundamental structures of the psychotherapy process itself, very few of which are designed to deal with social and cultural pathology.

In its present form, psychotherapy is a conservative enterprise that perpetuates the same values and aspirations that create the need for therapy. It makes little sense to foster adjustment to pathological social and economic systems. Psychotherapists today lack the wider theoretical perspectives that permit them to identify the etiological determinants that lie within the accepted assumptive worlds of their patients. The fact that most therapists share the toxic social assumptions of their patients reduces the chances that these will become part of the treatment focus.

Mainstream clinical psychology embraces a status quo that acknowledges individualism and consumption as prescriptions for positive mental health. At the very least, it does not actively challenge the psychological risks inherent in capitalistic constructions that predispose members toward alienation, loss of self, meaninglessness, and general disorientation. Rather than seeking to rekindle communitarian values and to reconnect people to social resources, psychotherapy accepts the validity of the self-serving autonomous human being who thrives on self-fulfillment, personal choice, and individual achievement. Therapy consultation rooms continue to echo with the message that we best treat ourselves by making sure that all our private needs, urges, and wishes are satisfied without compromise or sacrifice. In this way, however, it has the adverse effect of magnifying the underlying interiority that creates social and intrapsychic problems for the person. It also contaminates further the individual's values, while making it more difficult to access sources of solidarity.

Existential and Philosophical Counseling

As part of their efforts to rise above therapeutic individualism, the next generation of psychotherapists must take account of the new patterns of psychopathology that are emerging in conjunction with modernity. These patterns, which derive from cultural deficits and pathologies of various sorts, require the therapist to become skilled in the practice of *existential counseling*: therapeutic intervention that responds to modern dilemmas related to meaninglessness, alienation, emptiness, deadness, and spiritual craving.

Existential counselors would understand the emotional anarchy, and paralyzing loneliness, that prevail when cultural members cannot locate ontological structures that can frame their experience. They would recognize that the frequent inability of moderns to marshal a useful philosophy of life has serious implications for psychological well-being. Therefore, existential counseling will assist in the process of *worldview interpretation*: the search for ontological coordinates that help the person to conceptualize the self and reality.[5] It is an adjunct therapeutic system that aids in the conferring of meaning, as well as the translation of life events and experiences. Existential counselors are prepared to deal with the many metaconcerns that are ignored by most contemporary therapists. They are able to respond to the epistemological, metaphysical, and ethical issues that are components of the new philosophical maladies.

An important feature of existential counseling would be the fostering of awareness of the pathological cultural forces that contribute to existential disorientation and its related problems. For many clients, this would include an exploration of materialism as a cultural theme that has led them to define themselves primarily as atomistic consumers. They would be encouraged to construct nonmaterialistic self-definitions that promote healthier values and more meaningful interpersonal relations. At the moment, however, our therapy systems are themselves an extension of capitalistic principles and ambitions.

A CULTURALLY RELEVANT PSYCHOLOGY

Cultural psychology continues to be neglected, as is readily apparent when one examines the textbooks currently in use. A recent study analyzed the content of six introductory psychology textbooks and found that only 3 percent of the material dealt with issues related to culture, ethnicity, or race.[6] The survey found that the majority of clinical psychology textbooks made no detailed reference to culture and related issues. Some texts do not even include culture in the index, indicating that all culture-related subjects are overlooked entirely.

Clinical psychology training programs have also been criticized for failing to provide adequate education on matters related to culture. Most graduates do not grasp fully the role of culture in the etiology of psychopathology, nor its potential value in treatment. A 1994 survey of 106 accredited clinical psychology programs in the United States concluded that training is inadequate in preparing students to work eventually with diverse cultural groups.[7] Another study found that only 10 out of 115 clinical psychology programs were involved in any sort of cross-cultural research.[8] Only a slightly higher percentage of these programs had some participation in research dealing with minority mental health. A mere 5 percent of student research projects were found to include variables related to cultural issues. More than one-third of graduates openly acknowledged that their training had been deficient with regard to ethnic minority mental health, and cultural psychology more generally. Only a few rare graduates felt competent to function in a cross-cultural context.

Academic training programs must emphasize assessment and treatment modalities that consider closely each person's cultural ecology. Research must also develop a cultural language and ethos that can open up new areas of investigation, involving larger and more relevant questions than those being asked at the moment. However, it remains the case that most training programs in professional psychology have a narrow focus, as well as a decidedly white middle-class bias. In this regard, Western psychology has been described as ethnocentric in terms of its format and content.[9] This particular label seems justified for several reasons, including the employment of culture-specific concepts, the development and use of culturally inappropriate assessment devices, a research agenda limited to the needs of Western society, and treatment approaches that are mired in narrow anglophone paradigms.

In trying to create a discipline that is more informed about the cultural foundations of human behavior, Western psychology must question the validity of its current status and acknowledge that its current ethnocentric structures make it of limited utility outside its own small circle. It must teach its adherents about the limits of its applicability. This should take place in order that we can progress toward a new multicultural psychology that can meet the needs of a rapidly changing global community.[10]

One reason that culture has been neglected concerns the failure of psychology to gear its activities to the wider needs of society. In terms of clinical psychology, the structure of academia and a preoccupation with private practice have combined to cocoon psychologists from developments in the outside world. A small amount of energy has gone into cultural awareness programs that were intended to broaden the vision of clinical psychologists and to awaken them to the needs of diverse cultural groups, but this has had only limited success, in part because cultural psychologists lack a substantial power base in academic and training programs.[11]

Differing value assumptions are another cause of the inability of Western psychology to incorporate culture into its basic propositions and practices. Western psychology has assumed values related to monoculture, and its methodologies leave little room for culture as an explanatory mechanism.[12] By contrast, the thrust of cultural psychology has revolved around methods that assume cultural pluralism, as well as the need to explore the local dimension of issues and problems. The monocultural ideology that has contributed to psychology's reluctance to embrace culture stems from the wayward assumption that Anglo-Saxon culture is somehow superior to all others. Unwittingly, psychologists organize their thought and practices in a unidirectional way that corresponds to Anglo-Saxon culture, but their actual practices usually entail a separation from the whole matter of culture.

Our inattention to culture can also be explained by the assumption of psychological individualism, which translates into an emphasis on the uniqueness, autonomy, self-reliance, intrinsic worth, and freedom of the individual. It has little to say about the collectivist structures that exist in many cultures of the world. Likewise, it has almost no voice when it comes to explaining collectivist themes in Western culture that coexist with the dominant individualistic ones. In terms of clinical training, students are encouraged to employ psychotherapeutic strategies in order to foster individual self-containment and to amplify the person's sense of independence, self-determination, and self-responsibility.[13] This type of training locks the psychologist into a mind-set and mode of operation that have little room for cultural considerations.

A number of changes are necessary if our goal is a new mental health worker with sufficient vision and cultural competence to function in the global community. Training programs in psychology must make culture a central aspect of the curriculum. Rather than continuing to encourage cultural detachment, they need to introduce a number of culture-related courses. Psychology must strive toward a new relevance in the form of culturally sensitive research that asks questions about larger social problems, such as drug addiction, religious conflict, overpopulation, child abuse, alienation, undersocialization, and technology-related problems. It must embark on a course that will revise completely its ideas, policies, and institutional practices. The roles of the mental health worker that emerge from this transition will depart radically from those in place at the moment.

Larger Roles of the Mental Health Worker

The time is right for professional psychologists to reconsider their role in the provision of mental health services and to look forward to new possibilities. It has been pointed out, for example, that there is a declining role for doctoral-level clinical psychologists.[14] Traditional roles that were once the domain of clinical psychologists are now being taken over by the growing numbers of master's-level psychologists, who function in nearly all respects like their doctoral-level counterparts. Approximately six thousand master's-level psychologists are coming out of American universities every year. Additional mental health paraprofessionals from various sources are also encroaching on the former terrain of clinical psychologists. In their expanding role, social workers now perform most of the activities of clinical psychologists. Certain economic factors, such as the preference of health maintenance organizations (HMOs) for master's-level psychologists, are also contributing to the shrinking role of clinical psychologists.

The initial response to this general development was that the clinical psychology profession became defensive and clung to the status quo. This continues at the moment, but some thinkers are looking forward to a new and more productive era for clinical psychologists in which they embrace new alternatives and a revised professional identity. In fact, it may be an ideal time for doctoral-level clinical psychologists to work toward a professional maturity wherein they could become effective with global problems. In this regard, they could find ways to amplify global awareness of important matters such as environmental sustainability, world peace, and wealth distribution.

Mental health professionals could also have significantly more input on other global problems, including overpopulation, terrorism, migration, refugee populations, urban stress, overconsumption, racism, sexism, and destruction of indigenous people.[15] They could also begin to make more of a difference in the areas of health, transportation, media-based pathology, cultural disintegration, spiritual rejuvenation, and ethical advancement. All of these enable the mental health worker to rise above the constraints of individual psychology. We must develop a psychology that takes account of the wider circumstances of people's lives. The new mental health worker will seek to know the ways in which cultural forces contribute to, or interfere with, mental health and general well-being. He or she will cultivate the skills to intervene effectively, not only with individual problems, but social pathologies whose resolution can benefit the global condition of humanity.

REAWAKENING SOCIAL JUSTICE

Whereas social justice was an issue in the early days of psychology, recent years have seen the evolution of a pragmatic psychology that is not strongly motivated to promote positive social change. This orientation is another manifestation of psychology's inclination to maintain the continuity of the existing sociopolitical and economic system. This approach offers little hope that psychology will have much to say about large-scale problems of social injustice or macroscopic prescriptions for needed social restructuring. Also, since this asocial and amoral approach is not working in the West toward the cause of social justice, it is of no value to export this orientation for use in the developing world, which often finds itself in urgent need of social transformation.

It has even been argued that as stabilizers of the existing social order today's psychologists are deliberately trained not to see or consider the ideological, ethical, and moral implications of their practices. On this subject, Tod Sloan writes:

> They have little to do with social transformation in the industrialized societies, and they tend to support activities that are simply ineffective in relation to the social order or that merely grease its wheels or gloss over the emotional wounds that are systematically produced by an unjust social order.[16]

Thus, rather than making social justice a top priority, modern psychology has functioned in an opposite way to preserve injustice and inequality. This problem has been addressed at length by Isaac Prilleltensky, who explains that in the course of embracing the philosophies of individualism and self-determination, modern psychology finds itself fearful of entering into the moral space of other people.[17] Our moral inertia is so strong that the mere mention of moralistic intentions would throw into doubt one's credibility as a psychologist. To rise above this mentality, writes Prilleltensky, psychologists must be encouraged to develop a social ethics mentality that motivates them to intervene on behalf of the vulnerable and disadvantaged segments of society.

The mental health profession needs to examine its moral obligations as it searches for ways to contribute in a broader way to human welfare. Our approaches to knowledge, and our conceptions of our roles and purposes, must be refined within a meaningful moral and ethical framework. Not only must psychologists begin to articulate a moral position, they need to spell out a vision for the realization of these morals. Especially important is the cultivation of a critical attitude toward the existing social order, and the way in which newly conceived interventions can contribute to the cause of a good society.[18]

The social welfare of the population is a sorely neglected goal of contemporary psychology. In the future, this devalued system must give way to one wherein mental health workers involve themselves actively in research and practice related to such issues as power inequality, distributive justice, political values, democratic participation, organizational development, social policy, human diversity, and the dynamics of oppression.

In place of our present psychological structures, there must be an orientation that has the capacity to assess, and to influence therapeutically, the macrosystems that mediate in many types of psychosocial functioning. It would rest on the assumption that psychological problems of all sorts cannot be separated from cultural, historical, and moral contexts. In addition to being able to influence disturbed individuals, the new mental health worker will be a cultural and transcultural activist with sufficient scope of understanding to prescribe new social and political policies that stand to improve the general health of large populations. Only by refining our assumptions and practices in these ways can we hope to construct the foundation for an eventual healthy, and truly modern, society.

CONCLUDING COMMENT: CAN WE SURVIVE MODERNITY?

In the opening paragraph of this book, I mentioned Herodotus's demigod of modernity, that nagging deity who denies us rest and contentment. In closing, we might ask what the human being would actually do with a truly modern society, if indeed that would ever transpire. Would we have the collective wisdom to pause at that point, or would we want to fiddle with it? In all likelihood, what we call modernity is an ever present human trait that destines us, and possibly dooms us, to change.

When isolating any single change that has contributed to our modernization, one inevitably finds that any benefits are accompanied by costs. In the distant past, modernity revealed itself in subtle ways that did not threaten the entire species with an ultimate price. But the passage of time has seen types and degrees of change that have added to the stakes our very survival as a species.

In addition to a lethal environmental madness that we moderns have unleashed upon ourselves, we are assigning our fate to a new cultural order that may not pay much heed to our *human* nature. To survive this particular modernity, it may no longer suffice to be ourselves. If we have in fact strayed into a dangerous Age of Insanity, our salvation may require that we rise above that forever restless part of ourselves that insists on pushing forward to the end. To fend off a final modernity that sees the total undoing of us and the planet, we may need to revise completely our notions of what it means to be modern.

Notes

CHAPTER 1. INTRODUCTION: THE HUMAN CONTEXT OF MODERNITY

1. Featherstone, M. (1995). *Undoing culture: Globalization, postmodernism, and identity*. London: Sage, p. 145.

2. Mestrovic, S. G. (1997). *Postemotional society*. London: Sage.

3. Marsella, A. J., & Choi, S. C. (1993). Psychosocial aspects of modernization and economic development in East Asian nations. *Psychologia, 36*, 201–213, pp. 207–210.

4. Inkeles, A. (1966). The modernization of man. In M. Weiner (Ed.), *Modernization: The dynamics of growth*. New York: Basic Books.

5. Marsella & Choi. Psychosocial aspects of modernization.

6. Mouzelis, N. (1999). Modernity: A non-European conceptualization. *British Journal of Sociology, 50*, 141–159.

7. Thurman, R. (1998). *Inner revolution: Life, liberty and the pursuit of real happiness*. New York: Riverhead Books.

8. Hall, E. T. (1976). *Beyond culture*. Garden City, NJ: Anchor/Doubleday.

9. Lumsden, C., & Wilson, E. O. (1981). *Genes, mind, and culture*. Cambridge, MA: Harvard University Press.

10. Spiro, M. E. (1984). Reflections on cultural determinism and relativism. In R. A. Shweder & R. A. LeVine (Eds.), *Culture theory: Essays on mind, self and emotion*. Cambridge: Cambridge University Press, p. 323.

11. Serpell, R., & Boykin, A. W. (1994). Cultural dimensions of cognition: A multiplex dynamic system of constraints and possibilities. In R. J. Sternberg (Ed.), *Thinking and problem solving*. San Diego, CA: Academic Press, p. 371.

12. Shore, B. (1991). Twice-born, once conceived: Meaning construction and cultural cognition. *American Anthropologist, 93*, 9–27, p. 10.

13. Marsella, A. J. (1998). Toward a global community psychology: Meeting the needs of a changing world. *American Psychologist, 53*, 1282–1291.

14. Spiro, M. E. (1994). *Culture and human nature.* New Brunswick, NJ: Transaction Publishers, p. xxi.

15. Leighton, A. (1959). *My name is legion.* New York: Basic Books.

16. Fromm, E. (1976). *To have or to be.* New York: Harper & Row, pp. 5–6.

17. Naroll, R. (1983). *The moral order: An introduction to the human situation.* London: Sage.

18. Marsella, A. J. (1979). The modernization of traditional cultures: Consequences for the individual. In D. Hoopes, P. Pedersen & G. Renwick (Eds.), *Intercultural education, training, and research.* Washington, DC: Sietar, p. 130.

19. Berry, W. (1977). *The unsettling of America.* San Francisco: Sierra Club Books, p. 11.

20. Cited in, Marsella, A. J. (1993). Sociocultural foundations of psychopathology. *Transcultural Psychiatric Research Review, 30*, 97–142, p. 106.

CHAPTER 2. MEGATRENDS IN IDENTITY, CONSCIOUSNESS, AND PSYCHOLOGICAL DEFENSE

1. Marsella, A. J. (1985). Culture, self, and mental disorder. In A. J. Marsella, G. De Vos, & F. L. K. Hsu (Eds.), *Culture and self.* London: Tavistock, p. 286.

2. Hsu, F. L. K. (1985). The self in cross-cultural perspective. In A. J. Marsella, G. De Vos, & F. L. K. Hsu (Eds.), *Culture and self.* London: Tavistock, p. 39.

3. Marsella. Culture, self, and mental disorder, p. 290.

4. Stone, B. L. (1989). Modernity and the narcissistic self: Taking "character" disorders seriously. *Studies in Symbolic Interaction, 10*, 89–107, p. 95.

5. Barth, F. (1997). How is the self conceptualized? Variations among cultures. In U. Neisser & D. A. Jopling (Eds.), *The conceptual self in context* (pp. 75–91). Cambridge: Cambridge University Press.

6. Stone. Modernity and the narcissistic self.

7. Seligman, M. E. P. (1990). Why is there so much depression today? In R. E. Ingram (Ed.), *Contemporary approaches to depression.* New York: Plenum Press.

8. Altroochi, J., & Altroochi, L. (1995). Polyfaceted psychological acculturation in Cook Islands. *Journal of Cross-Cultural Psychology, 26*, 426–440.

9. Rotenberg, M. (1977). Alienating individualism and reciprocal individualism: A cross-cultural conceptualization. *Journal of Humanistic Psychology, 17*, 3–17.

10. Bellah, R. N., Madsen, W., Sullivan, A., Swidler, A., & Tipton, S. (1985). *Habits of the heart.* Berkeley; University of California Press, p. 111.

11. Gergen, K. J. (1991). *The saturated self.* New York: Basic Books.

12. Lifton, R. J. (1993). *The protean self.* New York: Basic Books.

13. Papastergiadis, N. (1993). *Modernity as exile.* New York: St. Martins Press.

14. Garrison, A. (1995). Psychotherapy and the modern ego. *Humanistic Psychologist, 23*, 227–238.

15. Strinati, D. (1995). *An introduction to theories of popular culture.* London: Routledge, p. 9.

16. Bellah et al., *Habits of the heart,* p. 60.

17. Aquilino, W. S. (1996). The life course of children born to unmarried mothers. *Journal of Marriage and The Family, 58,* 293–310, p. 7.

18. Poole, R. (1991). *Morality and modernity.* London: Routledge, pp. 38–40.

19. Sznaider, N. (1998). The sociology of compassion. *Cultural Values, 1,* 117–139.

20. Fromm, E. (1962). *Beyond the chains of illusion.* New York: Simon & Schuster.

21. Thompson, W. I. (1991). *The American replacement of nature.* New York: Doubleday, p. 46.

22. Berking, H. (1996). Solidarity individualism. In S. Lash, B. Szerszynski, & B. Wynne (Eds.), *Risk, environment, and modernity* (pp. 189–202). London: Sage.

23. Gerhards, J. (1989) The changing culture of emotions in modern society. *Social Science Information, 28,* 737–754.

24. Mestrovi, S. G. (1997). *Postemotional society.* London: Sage.

25. Williams, S. J. (1998). Modernity and the emotions. *Sociology, 32,* 747–769.

26. This quote is from the "Excerpts from the Diary of a Borderline" section of the BPD website: www.golden.net/~soul/borderpd.html

27. DeBerry, S. (1991). *The externalization of consciousness and the psychopathology of everyday life.* New York: Greenwood Press, p. 103.

28. Ibid., p. 104.

CHAPTER 3. MATERIALISM, CONSUMPTION, AND MENTAL HEALTH

1. Lunt, P. K., & Livingstone, S. M. (1992). *Mass consumption and personal identity.* Buckingham, England: Open University Press, p. 24.

2. Baudrillard, J. (1998). *The consumer society: Myths and structures.* London: Sage.

3. Holt, D. (1997). Poststructuralist lifestyle analysis: Conceptualizing the social patterning of consumption in postmodernity. *Journal of Consumer Research, 23,* 326–350.

4. Singer, J. (1997). *Message in a bottle.* New York: The Free Press, p. 132.

5. Bouchet, D. (1994). Rails without ties: Can postmodern consumption replace modern questioning. *International Journal of Research in Marketing, 11,* 405–422.

6. Mellor, P. A., & Shilling, C. (1997). *Reforming the body: Community and modernity.* London: Sage, p. 171.

7. Ferguson, H. (1992). *Religious transformation in Western society: The end of happiness.* London: Routledge, p. 173.

8. Becker, E. (1975). *Escape from evil.* New York: The Free Press, p. 164.

9. Braun, J. (1995). *Social pathology in comparative perspective.* Westport, CT: Praeger, pp. 92–96.

10. Baudrillard. *The consumer society,* p. 25.

11. Lunt & Livingstone. *Mass consumption and personal identity,* p. 19.

12. Mellor & Shilling. *Reforming the body,* p. 171.

13. Miller, D. (1987). *Material culture and mass consumption.* Oxford, England: Basil Blackwell, pp. 184–185.

14. Baudrillard. *The consumer society,* pp. 44–45.

15. Fromm, E. (1994). *On being human* (R. Funk, Ed.). New York: Continuum, p. 37.

16. Schor, J. B. (1998). *The overspent American.* New York: Basic Books.

17. Ibid., p. 13.

18. Wilder, T. (1947). *The bridge of San Luis Rey.* London: Longmans, Green, p. 21.

19. Cushman, P. (1990). Why the self is empty: Toward a historically situated psychology. *American Psychologist, 45,* 599–611.

20. Thurman, R. (1998). *Inner revolution: Life, liberty and the pursuit of real happiness.* New York: Doubleday.

21. Ibid., pp. 7–8.

22. Mukerji, C. (1983). *From graven images: Patterns of modern materialism.* New York: Columbia University Press, p. 8.

23. Scitovsky, T. (1976). *The joyless economy.* Oxford, England: Oxford University Press.

24. Richins, M. L. (1996). Materialism, desire, and discontent. In R. P. Hill (Ed.), *Marketing and consumer research in the public interest* (pp. 111, 125–126). London: Sage.

25. Richins, M. L., & Dawson, S. (1992). A consumer values orientation for materialism and its measurement: Scale development and validation. *Journal of Consumer Research, 19,* 303–316, p. 312.

26. Cushman. Why the self is empty.

27. Thurman. *Inner revolution,* p. 257.

28. Schumacher, E. F. (1974). *Small is beautiful: A study of economics as if people mattered.* London: Abacus.

29. Csikszentmihalyi, M., & Rochberg-Halton, E. (1978). Reflections on materialism. *University of Chicago Magazine, 70,* 6–15.

30. Easterlin, R. A., & Crimmins, E. M. (1988). Recent social trends: Changes in personal aspirations of American youth. *Sociology and Social Research, 72,* 217–223.

31. Belk, R. W. (1985). Materialism: Trait aspects of living in the material world. *Journal of Consumer Research, 12,* 265–280, p. 275.

32. Richins & Dawson. A consumer values orientation.

33. O'Guinn, T. C., & Faber, R. J. (1989). Compulsive buying: A phenomenological exploration. *Journal of Consumer Research, 16,* 147–157.

34. Schor, J. B. (1991). *The overworked American. New York: Basic Books,* p. 159.

35. Hirschman, E. C. (1992). The consciousness of addiction: Toward a general theory of compulsive consumption. *Journal of Consumer Research, 19,* 155–179.

36. O'Guinn & Faber. Compulsive buying, p. 153.

37. Rindfleisch, A., Burroughs, J., & Denton, F. (1997). Family structure, materialism, and compulsive consumption. *Journal of Consumer Research, 23,* 312–325.

38. Faber, R. J., Christenson, G. A., de Zwaan, M., & Mitchell, J. (1995). Two forms of compulsive consumption: Comorbidity of compulsive buying and binge eating. *Journal of Consumer Research, 22,* 296–304.

39. Douglas, M. (1970). *Natural symbols.* London: Cresset Press.

40. Mellor & Shilling. *Reforming the body,* p. 193.

41. Cox, E. (1995). *A truly civil society.* Sydney: ABC Books, p. 71.

42. Berry, W. (1977). *The unsettling of America.* San Francisco, Sierra Club Books, p. 137.

43. Kirkpatrick, J. (1986). A philosophic defense of advertising. *Journal of Advertising, 15,* 42–48, p. 42.

44. Calfee, J. E., & Ringold, D. J. (1994). The seventy percent majority: Enduring consumer beliefs about advertising. *Journal of Public Policy and Marketing, 13,* 228–238.

45. Robertson, T. S., & Rossiter, J. R. (1974). Children and commercial persuasion: An attribution theory analysis. *Journal of Consumer Research, 1,* 13–20.

46. Linn, M. C., de Benedictus, T., & Delucchi, K. (1982). Adolescent reasoning about advertisements. *Child Development, 53,* 1599–1613.

47. Fisher, D. A., & Magnus, P. (1981). Out of the mouths of babes: The opinions of 10 and 11 year old children regarding the advertising of cigarettes. *Community Health Studies, 5,* 22–26.

48. Ringold, D. J. (1996). Social criticisms of target marketing. In R. P. Hill (Ed.), *Marketing and consumer research in the public interest* (pp. 98–99). London: Sage, p. 99.

49. Bouchet. Rails without ties, p. 416.

50. Firat, A. F., & Venkatesh, A. (1993). Postmodernity: The age of marketing. *International Journal of Research in Marketing, 10,* 227–249, pp. 236–237.

51. Ibid., p. 237.

52. Kilpatrick, W. K. (1983). *Psychological seduction.* Nashville, TN: Thomas Nelson, p. 133.

53. Brandt, D. (1997). Along came the transnationals. *Nexus, 4,* 13–17, p. 16.

54. Waters, M. (1995). *Globalization.* London: Routledge, p. 3.

55. Marsella, A. J. (1998). *The psychosocial consequences of globalization.* Seminar presented at the University of Hawaii, Honolulu, Hawaii, Dec. 4, 1998, pp. 11–14.

56. Ibid., pp. 22–23.

57. Berger, P., Berger, B., & Kellner, H. (1973). *The homeless mind: Modernization and consciousness.* New York: Random House, p. 182.

58. Ibid., p. 183.

59. Giddens, A. (1991). *Modernity and self-identity.* Cambridge, England: Polity Press, pp. 35–40.

60. Teeple, G. (1995). *Globalization and the decline of social reform.* Toronto: Garamond Press, p. 131.

61. Chomsky, N. (1999). *Profit over people: Neoliberalism and global order.* New York: Seven Stories Press.

62. Gilligan, J. (1996). *Violence: Reflections on a national epidemic.* New York: Vintage, p. 192.

CHAPTER 4. THE CULTURAL DYNAMICS OF WESTERN DEPRESSION

1. Seligman, M. E. P. (1990). Why is there so much depression today? In R. E. Ingram (Ed.), *Contemporary approaches to depression.* New York: Plenum Press. p. 1.

2. Hagnell, O., Lanke, J., Rorsman, B., & Ojesjo, L. (1982). Are we entering an age of melancholy? Depressive illness in a prospective epidemiological study over 25 years. *Psychological Medicine, 12,* 279–289, p. 279.

3. McGuffin, P., Katz, R., Watkins, S., & Rutherford, J. (1996). A hospital-based twin registry study of heritability of DSM-IV unipolar depression. *Archives of General Psychiatry, 53,* 129–136.

4. Seligman, M. E. P. (1974). Depression and learned helplessness. In R. J. Friedman & M. M. Katz (Eds.), *The psychology of depression.* Washington, DC: Winston-Wiley.

5. Abramson, L. Y., Metalsky, G. I., & Vedak, C. (1989). Hopelessness depression. *Psychological Review, 96, 358–372.*

6. Schieffelin, E. L. (1985). The cultural analysis of depression affect: An example from New Guinea. In A. Kleinman & B. Good (Eds.), *Culture and depression.* Berkeley: University of California Press.

7. Stern, G., & Kruckman, L. (1983). Multi-disciplinary perspectives in post-partum depression: An anthropological critique. *Social Sciences and Medicine, 17,* 1027–1041.

8. Harkness, S. (1987). The cultural mediation of postpartum depression. *Medical Anthropology Quarterly, 1,* 194–209, p. 207.

9. Gaylin, W. (1984). *The rage within: Anger in modern life.* New York: Penguin.

10. Frosh, S. (1991). *Identity crises: Modernity, psychoanalysis, and the self.* London: Macmillan.

11. Hollan, D. (1988). Staying "cool" in Toraja: Informal strategies for the management of anger and hostility. *Ethos, 16,* 52–72.

12. Cornelius, A. (1989). Depression as cultural illness: A social epidemiology model of catastrophic learning. In G. J. Dacenoort (Ed.), *The paradigm of self-organization* (pp. 210–227). London: Gordon & Breach.

13. Sheppard, M. (1994). Postnatal depression, child care and social support: A review of findings and the implications for practice. *Social Work and Social Science Reveiw, 5,* 24–46.

14. Lu, L. (1995). Life events, social support, and depression among Taiwanese female homemakers. *Journal of Social Psychology, 135,* 185–190.

15. Vilhjalmsson, R. (1993). Life stress, social support and clinical depression. *Social Science and Medicine, 37,* 331–342.

16. Oliver, J. M., & Novak, B. B. (1993). Depression, Seligman's hypothesis, and birth cohort effects in university students. *Journal of Social Behavior and Personality, 8,* 99–110.

17. Leonard, G. B. (1973). Winning isn't everything: It's nothing. *Intellectual Digest, October,* 45–47.

18. Goldman, I. (1961). The Zuni Indians of New Mexico. In M. Mead (Ed.), *Cooperation and competition among primitive peoples.* Boston: Beacon.

19. Romney, K., & Romney, K. (1966). *The Mixtecans of Juxtalhuaca, Mexico.* New York: Wiley.

20. Kohn, A. (1994). *No contest: The case against competition.* New York: Random House.

21. Ibid., pp. 107–108.

CHAPTER 5. THE NEW ANXIETY

1. Jones, I. H., & Horne, D. J. (1973). Psychiatric disorders among the Aborigines of the Australian Western Desert. *Social Sciences and Medicine, 7,* 219–228.

2. Inkeles, A. (1983). *Exploring individual modernity.* New York: Columbia University Press, p. 306.

3. Schumaker, J. F. (1995). *The corruption of reality.* Amherst, NY: Prometheus.

4. Murphy, H. B. (1982). Blood pressure and culture. *Psychotherapy and Psychosomatics, 38,* 244–255.

5. Naroll, R. (1983). *The moral order: An introduction to the human situation.* London: Sage.

6. Mount, E. (1983). Individualism and our fears of death. *Death Education, 7,* 25–31.

7. Kohn, A. (1994). *No contest.* New York: Random House, p. 108.

8. Wilder, D., & Shapiro, P. N. (1989). The role of competition-induced anxiety. *Journal of Personality and Social Psychology, 56,* 60–69, p. 62.

9. Kohn. *No contest,* p. 124.

10. Leonard, G. B. (1973). Winning isn't everything: It's nothing. *Intellectual Digest, October,* 45–47, p. 46.

11. Schor, J. B. (1991). *The overworked American.* New York: Basic Books; also see, Schor, J. B. (1991). Americans work too hard. *New York Times,* July 25, 1991, p. 31.

12. Seybold, K. C., & Salomone, P. R. (1994). Understanding workaholism. *Journal of Counseling and Development, 73,* 4–9.

13. Spruell, G. (1987). Work fever. *Training and Development Journal, 4,* 41–45, p. 44.

14. Minirth, F. (1981). *The workaholic and his family.* Grand Rapids, MI: Baker Books.

15. Axelrod, S. D. (1999). *Work and the evolving self.* Hillsdale, NJ: The Analytic Press, pp. 9–10.

16. Ibid., pp. 18–19.

17. Smart, J. F., & Smart, D. W. (1995). Acculturative stress of Hispanics: Loss and challenge. *Journal of Counseling and Development, 73,* 390–396, p. 391.

18. Lifton, R. J. (1993), *The protean self.* New York: Basic Books, p. 101.

19. Anant, S. S. (1971). Belongingness and mental health. *Manas, 18,* 11–23.

20. Berman, M. (1982). *All that is solid melts into air: The experience of modernity.* London: Verso, p. 17.

21. Braun, J. (1993). *Psychological aspects of modernity.* Westport, CT: Praeger, p. 230.

22. Rapson, R. L. (1988). *American yearnings: Love, money, and endless possibility.* New York: University Press of America, p. 82.

23. Featherstone, M. (1995), *Undoing culture: Globalization, postmodernism, and identity.* London: Sage, p. 46.

24. Appadurai, A. (1996). *Modernity at large.* Minneapolis: University of Minnesota Press, pp. 81–84.

CHAPTER 6. MODERNITY AND INTERPERSONAL HEALTH

1. Tseng, M. D., & McDermott, J. F. (1981). *Culture, mind, and therapy: An introduction to cultural psychiatry.* New York: Brunner/Mazel, p. 103.

2. Bauman, Z. (1997). *Globalization: The human consequences.* New York: Columbia University Press, pp. 81–82.

3. Ozanne, J. L., & Murray, J. B. (1996). Uniting critical theory and public policy to create the reflexively defiant consumer. In R. P. Hill (Ed.), *Marketing and consumer research in the public interest* (pp. 3–15). London: Sage.

4. Ibid., p. 11.

5. Cushman, P. (1995). *Constructing the self, constructing America.* Reading, MA: Addison-Wesley.

6. Giddens, A. (1991). *Modernity and self-identity.* Cambridge, England: Polity Press, pp. 89–90.

7. Gergen, K. J. (1991). *The saturated self.* New York: Basic Books, p. 169.

8. Simon, R. C. (1985). Sorting the culture-bound syndromes. In R. C. Simons & C. C. Hughes (Eds.), *The culture-bound syndromes.* Dordrecht: Reidel Publishing.

9. Deleuze, G., & Guttari, F. (1972). *Anti-Oedipus: Capitalism and schizophrenia.* New York: Viking.

10. Hui, C. H., & Triandis, H. C. (1986). Individualism—collectivism: A study of cross-cultural researchers. *Journal of Cross-Cultural Psychology, 17*, 225–248.

11. Putnam, R. (1995). Bowling alone: America's declining social capital. *Journal of Democracy, 6*, 65–78, p. 67.

12. Wuthnow, R. (1994). *Sharing the journey.* New York: The Free Press, p. 45.

13. Putnam. Bowling alone.

14. Moghaddam, F. M. (1997). *The specialized society.* Westport, CT: Praeger, pp. 114–115.

15. Gergen. *The saturated self*, p. 127.

16. Schwartz, B. (1994). *The costs of living: How market freedom erodes the best things in life.* New York: W. W. Norton, p. 223.

17. Schor, J. (1992). *The overworked American.* New York: Basic Books.

18. Robertson, J., & Robertson, J. (1989). *Separation and the very young.* London: Free Association Books.

19. Zey, M. (1994). *Seizing the future.* New York: Simon & Schuster, pp. 202–206.

20. Ibid.

21. Cox, E. (1995). *A truly civil society.* Sydney: ABC Books, p. 33.

22. Ibid.

23. Wachtel, P. (1983). *The poverty of affluence.* New York: The Free Press, pp. 76–77.

24. Ibid., pp. 77–78.

25. Giddens, A. (1990). *The consequences of modernity.* Cambridge, England: Polity Press.

26. Hochschild, J. (1997). *The time bind.* New York: Metropolitan Books.

27. Axelrod, S. D. (1999). *Work and the evolving self.* Hillsdale, NJ: Analytic Press, p. 131.

28. Clark, M. S., & Mills, J. (1979). Interpersonal attraction in exchange and communal relationships. *Journal of Personality and Social Psychology, 37*, 12–24.

29. Schwartz. *The costs of living*, p. 196.

30. Ibid., p. 208.

31. McCarthy, P. (1997). Mediating modern marriage. *Sexual and Marital Therapy, 12*, 275–287.

32. Averill, L. J. (1974). *The problem of being human.* Valley Forge, PA: Judson Press, pp. 161–166.

33. Hirsch, F. (1976). *Social limits of growth*. Cambridge, MA: Harvard University Press, pp. 99–101.

34. Ibid., p. 100.

35. Spector, I. P., & Carey, M. P. (1990). Incidence and prevalence of sexual dysfunction: A critical review of the empirical literature. *Archives of Sexual Behavior, 19*, 389–408.

36. Valadez, J., & Clignet, R. (1987). On the ambiguities of a sociological analysis of the culture of narcissism. *The Sociological Quarterly, 28*, 455–472.

37. Katz, R., & Briger, R. (1988). Modernity and the quality of marriage in Israel. *Journal of Comparative Family Studies, 19*, 371–380.

38. Jones, G. W. (1997). Modernization and divorce. *Population and Development Review, 23*, 95–114.

39. Frydenberg, E. (1999). *Learning to cope: Developing as a person in complex societies*. Oxford: Oxford University Press.

40. Aquilino, W. S. (1996). The life course of children born to unmarried mothers. *Journal of Marriage and the Family, 58*, 293–310.

41. Schwab, J. J., & Schwab, M. E. (1978). *Sociological roots of mental illness*. New York: Plenum Press, p. 60.

42. Blumstein, A. (1995). Blumstein's research was presented at the 1995 meeting of the American association for the advancement of science. A report appeared in the *Sydney Morning Herald* newspaper, February 20, 1995.

43. Schwartz. *The costs of living*, p. 177.

44. Ibid.

45. Stone, B. L. (1989). Modernity and the narcissistic self: Taking "character" disorders seriously. *Studies in Symbolic Interaction, 10*, 89–107.

46. Paris, J. (2000). Cultural risk factors in personality disorders. In J. F. Schumaker & T. Ward (Eds.), *Cultural cognition and psychopathology* (pp. 145–156). Westport, CT: Praeger.

47. Arnett, J. J., & Taber, S. (1994). Adolescence terminable and interminable. *Journal of Youth and Adolescence, 23*, 517–537.

48. Arnett, J. J. (1992). Reckless behavior in adolescence. *Development Review, 12*, 339–373.

49. Paris. Cultural risk factors in personality disorders.

50. Ibid.

51. Lasch, C. (1979). *The culture of narcissism*. New York: W. W. Norton.

52. Valadez & Clignet. On the ambiguities of sociological analysis of the culture of narcissism.

CHAPTER 7. SPIRITUAL AND EXISTENTIAL HEALTH

1. Schumaker, J. F. (1992). *Religion and Mental Health*. New York: Oxford University Press.

2. Hsu, F. L. K. (1985). The self in cross-cultural perspective. In A. J. Marsella, G. De Vos, & F. L. K. Hsu (Eds.), *Culture and self*. London: Tavistock, p. 38.

3. Braun, J. (1995). *Psychological aspects of modernity*. Westport, CT: Praeger, p. 126.

4. Nicholls, W. (1988). Immanent transcendence. In W. Nicholls (Ed.), *Modernity and religion* (pp. 167–187). Waterloo, Canada: Wilfred Laurier University Press.

5. Bellah, R. (1971). Toward a definition of unbelief. In R. Caporale & A. Grumelli (Eds.), *The culture of unbelief.* Berkeley, CA: The University of California Press, p. 155.

6. Berger, P. (1969). *The social reality of religion.* London: Faber & Faber, pp. 132–133.

7. Nipkow, K. E., & Schweitzer, F. (1991). Adolescents' justification for faith or doubt. *New Directions for Child Development, 52,* 91–100.

8. Loy, D. (1996). *Lack and transcendence.* Atlantic Heights, NJ: Humanities Press, pp. 170–171.

9. Scheff, T. J. (1979). *Catharsis in healing, ritual, and drama.* Berkeley, CA: University of California Press.

10. Bar-Haim, G. (1997). The dispersed sacred: Anomie and the crisis of ritual. In S. M. Hoover & K. Lundby (Eds.), *Rethinking media, religion, and culture* (pp. 133–145). London: Sage, p. 135.

11. Bourguignon, E. (1992). Religion as a mediating factor in culture change. In J. F. Schumaker (Ed.), *Religion and mental health* (pp. 259–269). New York: Oxford University Press, p. 267.

12. Lifton, R. J. (1993). *The protean self.* New York: Basic Books, p. 168.

13. Stark, R. (1993). Europe's receptivity to new religious movements: Round two. *Journal for the Scientific Study of Religion, 32,* 389–397.

14. Campbell, R. A., & Curtis, J. E. (1994). Religious involvement across societies. *Journal for the Scientific Study of Religion, 33,* 215–229.

15. Duke, J. T., & Johnson, B. L. (1989). The stages of religious transformation: A study of 200 nations. *Review of Religious Research, 22,* 209–224.

16. Greeley, A. (1994). A religious revival in Russia. *Journal for the Scientific Study of religion, 33,* 253–272.

17. Garran, R. (April 27–28, 1996). *The Weekend Australian,* p. 15.

18. Emmons, C., & Sobal, J. (1981). Paranormal beliefs: Functional alternatives to mainstream religion. *Review of Religious Research, 22,* 301–312.

19. Vernon, G. M. (1968). The religious nones: A neglected category. *Journal for the Scientific Study of Religion, 2,* 219–229.

20. Roof, W. (1993). *A generation of seekers.* San Francisco: Harper & Row, pp. 4–5.

21. Roof, W. (1998). Modernity, the religious, and the spiritual. *Annals of the American Academy of Political and Social Science, 558,* 211–224, p. 213.

22. Martin-Barbero, J. (1997). Mass media as a site of resacralization of contemporary cultures. In S. M. Hoover & K. Lundby (Eds.), *Rethinking media, religion, and culture* (pp. 102–116). London: Sage.

23. Mick, D. G., & Fournier, S. (1998). Paradoxes of technology: Consumer cognizance, emotions, and coping strategies. *Journal of Consumer Research, 25,* 123–143.

24. May, R. (1991). *The cry for myth.* London: Souvenir Press, p. 57.

25. Ibid., p. 218.

26. Ferguson, H. (1992). *Religious transformation in Western society: The end of happiness.* London: Routledge, pp. 202–203.

27. Ibid., p. 203.

28. Wachtel, P. (1983). *The poverty of affluence*. New York: The Free Press, p. 171.

29. Postman, N. (1985). *Amusing ourselves to death*. London: Methuen, p. 123.

30. Baudrillard, J. (1998). *The consumer society: Myths and structures*. London: Sage, p. 191.

31. Belk, Wallendorf, & Sherry (1989). The sacred and the profane in consumer behavior. p. 22.

32. Zepp, I. G. (1997). *The new religious image of urban America*. Niwot: University of Colorado Press.

33. Belk, R. W., Wallendorf, M., & Sherry, J. F. (1989). The sacred and the profane in consumer behavior: Theodicy on the odyssey. *Journal of Consumer Research, 16*, 1–38, p. 22.

34. Frankl, V. (1969). *The will to meaning*. New York: World, p. 84.

35. Best, S., & Kellner, D. (1998). Beavis and Butt-Head: No future for post modern youth. In J. S. Epstein (Ed.), *Youth culture: Identity in a postmodern world* (pp. 74–99). Oxford, England: Blackwell.

36. Taylor, C. (1985). *Philosophy and the human sciences*, Vol. 2. Cambridge: Cambridge University Press, pp. 256–257.

37. Yalom, I. D. (1980). *Existential psychotherapy*. New York: Basic Books, p. 355.

38. Ibid., p. 360.

39. Ibid., p. 374.

40. Taylor. *Philosophy and the human sciences*, p. 232.

41. Hui, C. H., & Triandis, H. C. (1986). Individualism—collectivism: A study of cross-cultural researchers. *Journal of Cross-Cultural Psychology, 17*, 225–248.

42. Goodman, P. (1956). *Growing up absurd*. New York: Bantam Books, p. 227.

43. Spergel, I. (1995). *The youth gang problem*. New York: Oxford University Press.

44. Arnett, J. (1991). Adolescents and heavy metal music. *Youth and Society, 23*, 76–98.

45. Arnett, J. (1993). Three profiles of heavy metal fans: A taste for sensation and a subculture of alienation. *Qualitative Sociology, 16*, 423–443, p. 442.

46. Reker, G. T. (1997). Personal meaning, optimism, and choice. *The Gerontologist, 37*, 709–716, p. 710.

47. Ibid.

48. Jung, C. (1966). *Collected works: The practices of psychotherapy*. New York: Pantheon, p. 83.

49. Debats, D., Drost, J., & Hansen, P. (1995). Experiences of meaning in life. *British Journal of Psychology, 86*, 359–375.

50. McCracken, G. (1990). *Culture and consumption*. Bloomington: University of Indiana Press, p. 115.

51. Fromm, E. (1973). *The anatomy of human destructiveness*. New York: Holt, Rinehart & Winston, p. 248.

52. Omer, H., & Rosenbaum, R. (1997). Diseases of hope and the work of despair. *Psychotherapy, 34*, 225–232.

53. Dubrow-Eichel, S. K. (1993). Outpatient treatment of sex and love addictions. In E. Griffin-Shelly (Ed.), *The cultural context of sex and love addiction recovery* (pp. 113–135). Westport, CT: Praeger.

54. Dobkin de Rios, M., & Smith, D. E. (1984). Drug use and abuse in cross-cultural perspective. In J. E. Mezzich & C. Berganza (Eds.), *Culture and psychopathology*. New York: Guilford Press, pp. 390–391.

55. Ibid., pp. 395–396.

56. Ibid., pp. 390–391.

57. Al-Issa, I. (1995). The illusion of reality or the reality of illusion? Hallucinations and culture. *British Journal of Psychiatry, 166* , 368–373.

58. Bean, L. J., & Saubel, K. S. (1972). *Temalpakh: Cahuilla Indian knowledge and usage of plants*. Banning, CA: Malki Museum Press, pp. 62–63.

59. Al-Issa. The illusion of reality or the reality of illusion?

60. Ibid.

61. Nicholls. Immanent transcendence, p. 180.

62. In this interview, Sam Spiegel was discussing his movie "Betrayal."

63. Rapson, R. L. (1988). *American yearnings: Love, money, and endless possibility*. New York: University Press of America, p. 181.

64. Allen, J. S. (1979). Modernity and the evil of banality. *Centennial Review, 23*, 20–39.

65. Giddens. *Modernity and self-identity*, pp. 47–49.

66. Best & Kellner. Beavis and Butt-Head, p. 81.

67. Holtz, G. T. (1995). *Welcome to the jungle*. New York: St. Martins Griffin.

68. Reading, B. (1996). *The university in ruins*. Cambridge, MA: Harvard University Press.

69. McMurty, J. (1996). *Unequal freedoms: The global market as an ethical system*. Toronto, Canada: Garamond.

70. Goldhammer, J. (1996). *Under the influence*. Amherst, NY: Prometheus Books, p. 137.

71. Ibid., p. 137.

72. Gotto, J. T. (1997). Why schools don't educate. *Nexus June-July, 81*, 13–16, p. 15.

73. Schumacher, E. F. (1974). *Small is beautiful*: A study in economics as if people mattered. London: Abacus, p. 78.

CHAPTER 8. MENTAL HEALTH AND THE PHYSICAL WORLD

1. Ley, D. (1983). *The social geography of the city*. New York: Harper & Row, p. 369.

2. Smith, C. J. (1988). *Public problems: The management of urban distress*. New York: Guilford Press, pp. 26–27.

3. Moser, G. (1994). Environmental stress and urban behavior. *European Journal of Applied Psychology, 44*, 149–154.

4. Ibid., p. 150.

5. Fuchs, R. J., Brennan, E., Chamie, J., Lo, F., & Uitto, J. I. (1994). *Mega-city growth and the future*. New York: United Nations University Press, p. 196.

6. Marsella, A. J. (1998). Urbanization, mental health, and social deviancy. *American Psychologist, 53*, 624–634, p. 625.

7. Maizie, S. M., & Rawlings, S. (1973). Public attitudes toward population issues. In S. M. Maizei (Ed.), *Population distribution and policy* (pp. 599–630). Washington, DC: U.S. Government Printing Office.

8. Wilson, G., & Baldassare, M. (1996). Overall sense of community in a suburban region: The effects of localism, privacy, and urbanization. *Environment and Behavior, 28,* 27–43.

9. Black, M. M., & Krishnakumar, A. (1998). Children in low-income, urban settings: Interventions to promote mental health and well-being. *American Psychologist, 53,* 635–646.

10. Wandersman, A., & Nation, M. (1998). Urban neighborhoods and mental health: Psychological contributions to understanding toxicity, resilience, and interventions. *American Psychologist, 53,* 647–656.

11. Marsella. Urbanization, mental health, and social deviancy, p. 632.

12. Sokal, J., Zejda, J., Pastuszka, J., Dobowski, M., & Jarosinska, D. (1996). Environmental pollution and urban health. In *Urbanization: A Global Health Challenge.* World Health Organization.

13. Evans, G. W., & Jacobs, S. V. (1982). Air pollution and human behavior. In G. W. Evans (Ed.), *Environmental stress* (pp. 104–132). Cambridge: Cambridge University Press.

14. Jacobs, S. V., Evans, G. W., Catalano, R., & Dooley, D. (1984). Air pollution and depressive symptomatology: Exploratory analyses of intervening psychosocial factors. *Population and Environment: Behavioral and Social Issues, 7,* 260–272.

15. Navarro, P., Larrain, S., Housley, P., & de Man, A. (1987). Anxiety, locus of control and appraisal of air pollution. *Perceptual and Motor Skills, 64,* 811–814.

16. Randolf, T. G. (1970). Domiciliary chemical air pollution in the etiology of ecologic mental illness. *International Journal of Social Psychiatry, 16,* 243–265.

17. Freeman, H. L. (1988). Psychiatric aspects of environmental stress. *International Journal of Mental Health, 17,* 13–23.

18. Palinkas, L. A., Downs, M. A., Peterson, J. S., & Russell, J. (1993). Social, cultural, and psychological impacts of the Exxon Valdez oil spill. *Human Organization, 52,* 1–13.

19. Bragdon, C. R. (1970). *Noise pollution: The unquiet crisis.* Philadelphia: University of Pennsylvania Press, p. 1.

20. Cohen, S., & Weinstein, N. (1982). Nonauditory effects of noise on behavior and health. In G. W. Evans (Ed.), *Environmental stress* (pp. 45–74). Cambridge: Cambridge University Press.

21. Moser. Environmental stress and urban behavior, p. 151.

22. Bronzaft, A. L., & McCarthy, D. P. (1975). The effects of elevated train noise on reading ability. *Environment and Behavior, 7,* 517–527.

23. Cohen & Weinstein. Nonauditory effects of noise on behavior and health, pp. 52–53.

24. Ibid., p. 52.

25. Evans, G. W., Bullinger, M., & Hygge, S. (1998). Chronic noise exposure and physiological response: A prospective study of children living under environmental stress. *Psychological Science, 9,* 75–77.

26. Heft, H. (1979). Background and focal environmental conditions of the home and attention in young children. *Journal of Applied Social Psychology, 9,* 47–69.

27. Wachs, T. D., Uzgiris, I. C., & Hunt, J. (1971). Cognitive development in infants of different age levels and from different environmental backgrounds. *Merrill-Palmer Quarterly of Behavior and Development, 17,* 288–317.

28. Cohen & Weinstein. Nonauditory effects of noise on behavior and health, pp. 54–56.

29. Damon, A. (1977). The residential environment, health, and behavior. In L. E. Hinkle, Jr. & W. C. Loring (Eds.), *The effects of the man-made environment in health and behavior* (pp. 241–262). Atlanta, GA: U.S. Public Health Service, Centers for Disease Control.

30. Cohen & Weinstein. Nonauditory effects of noise on behavior and health, pp. 50–51.

31. Llewellyn, L. G. (1981). The social cost of urban transportation. *Human Behavior and Development, 5,* 169–202.

32. Miller, J. (1974). Effects of noise on people. *Journal of the Acoustical Society of America, 56,* 729–764.

33. McLean, E. K., & Tarnopolsky, A. (1977). Noise, discomfort, and mental health. *Psychological Medicine, 7,* 19–62.

34. Smith. *Public problems*, p. 226.

35. Morrissey, J. P., & Gounis, K. (1987). Homelessness and mental illness in America: Emerging issues in the construction of a social problem. In C. J. Smith & J. A. Giggs (Eds.), *Location and stigma.* London: Allen & Unwin.

36. Smith. *Public problems*, p. 238.

37. Ibid., p. 228.

38. Hutson, S., & Liddiard, M. (1994). *Youth homelessness: The construction of a social issue.* Houndsmill, England: Macmillan, p. 66.

39. McMurty, J. (1996). *Unequal freedoms: The global market as an ethical system.* Toronto: Garamond, pp. 60–61.

40. Gilder, G. (1981). *Wealth and poverty.* New York: Basic Books, p. 27.

41. McMurty. *Unequal freedoms*, p. 324.

42. Cohen, E. (1979). A phenomenology of tourism experiences. *Sociology, 13,* 179–201.

43. Smith, V. L. (1978). *Hosts and guests: The anthropology of tourism.* Oxford: Blackwell.

44. Honey, M. (1999). *Eco-tourism and sustainable development.* Washington, DC: Island Press.

45. Dearden, P., & Harron, S. (1992). Tourism and the hill tribes of Thailand. In B. Weiler & C. Hall (Eds.), *Special interest tourism.* London: Belhaven Press.

46. Cohen, E. (1989). Primitive and remote hill tribe trekking in Thailand. *Annals of Tourism Research, 16,* 30–61.

47. Rossel, P. (1988). *Tourism: Manufacturing the exotic.* Copenhagen: IWGIA

48. Cohen, E. (1984). The sociology of tourism: Approaches, issues, and findings. *Annual Review of Sociology, 10,* 373–392, p. 388.

49. Ibid., p. 384.

50. Allen, L. R., Long, P. T., Perdue, R. R., & Kieselbach, S. (1988). The impact of tourism development on residents' perceptions of community life. *Journal of Travel Research, 27,* 16–21.

51. Mansperger, M. (1995). Tourism and cultural change in small-scale societies. *Human Organization, 54,* 87–94 p. 92.

52. Kent, N. (1977). A new kind of sugar. In R. R. Finney & K. A. Watson (Eds.), *A new kind of sugar.* Santa Cruz, CA: Center for South Pacific Studies.

53. Ross, G. F. (1994). *The psychology of tourism*. Melbourne: Hospitality Press, p. 123.

54. Ibid., pp. 125–127.

55. Ibid., p. 126.

56. cited in, Smith, J. W., & Sauer-Thompson, G. (1998). Civilization's wake: Ecology, economics and the roots of environmental destruction and neglect. *Population and Environment, 19*, 541–575.

57. Maguire, J. (1996). The tears inside the stone: Reflections on the ecology of fear. In S. Lash, B. Szerszynski, & B. Wynne, (Eds.), *Risk, environment, and modernity*. London: Sage, p. 185.

58. Sewall, L., & Swift, J. (1999). The embedded self. *Psychohistory Review, 27*, 71–84.

59. Richins, M. L. & Dawson, S. (1992). A consumer values orientation for materialism and its measurement: Scale development and validation. *Journal of Consumer Research, 19*, 303–316, pp. 312–313.

60. Cock, P. (1996). Toward an ecopsychology for sustainable development. In S. C. Carr & J. F. Schumaker (Eds.), *Psychology and the developing world* (pp. 191–198). Westport, CT: Praeger, p. 195.

61. Mol, A. P., & Spaargaren, G. (1993). Environment, modernity and the risk-society: The apocalyptic horizon of environmental reform. *International Sociology, 8*, 431–459.

62. Beck, U. (1992). *Risk society: Towards a new modernity*. London: Sage.

63. Prades, J. A. (1999). Global environmental change and contemporary society. *International Sociology, 14*, 7–31.

64. Ibid., p. 17.

65. Pelletier, L. G., Legault, L. R., & Tuson, K. M. (1996). The environmental satisfaction scale. *Environment and Behavior, 29*, 5–26.

66. Minic, V., & Zivkovic, J. (1996). Ecological problems as the exstential framework of the modern world. *Facta Universitatis, 1*, 301–311, p. 301.

67. McMurty. *Unequal freedoms*, p. 77.

68. Biglan, A. (1995). *Changing cultural practices*. Reno, NV: Contex Press, p. 375.

69. Berman, M. (1999). *Adventures in Marxism*. London: Verso.

70. Funkhouser, G. R. (1989). Values changes necessary for a sustainable society. *Bulletin of the Science and Technology Society, 9*, 19–32, p. 27.

71. Ger, G., & Belk, R. W. (1996). I'd like to buy the world a coke: Consumerscapes of the less affluent world. *Journal of Consumer Policy, 19*, 271–304.

72. Belk, R. W., & Ger, G. (1994). Problems of marketing in Romania and Turkey. In C. J. Schultz (Ed.), *Consumption in marketizing economies* (pp. 123–156). Greenwich, CT: JAI Press.

73. Alparovitz, G. (1995). *Index of environmental trends*. Washington, DC: National Center for Economic and Security Alternatives.

74. Skinner, B. F. (1991). Why we are not saving the world. In W. Ishaq (Ed.), *Human behavior in today's world* (pp. 19–29). Westport, CT: Praeger, p. 27.

75. Biglan. *Changing cultural practices*, pp. 379–400.

76. Ibid., p. 380.

77. Krueger, A. O. (1993). The training of economists. In S. King & P. Lloyd (Eds.), *Economic rationalism* (pp. 49–56). Sydney: Allen & Unwin.

78. Swanson, J. L. (1995). The call for Gestalt's contribution to ecopsychology. *Gestalt Journal, 8*, 47–85.

79. Ibid.

80. Gibson, J. W. (1997). Can the cultural re-enchantment of nature help stop environmental destruction. *Negations, 2*, 17–30.

81. Appleyard, B. (1993). *Understanding the present.* London: Picador/Pan Books.

82. Kraybill, D. (1989). *The riddle of Amish culture.* Baltimore: John Hopkins University Press.

83. Blowers, A. (1997). Environmental policy: Ecological modernization or the risk society? *Urban Studies, 34*, 845–871.

84. Miller, A. (1977). *Death of a salesman.* New York: Viking (originally published in 1949).

85. Ibañez-Noé, J. A. (1994). Synopsis of a theory of modernity. *Man and World, 27*, 361–381.

CHAPTER 9. THE NEW MENTAL HEALTH WORKER

1. Sarason, S. B. (1981). An asocial psychology and a misdirected clinical psychology. *American Psychologist, 36*, 827–836.

2. Albee, G. W. (1990). The futility of psychotherapy. *Journal of Mind and Behavior, 11*, 369–384.

3. Ibid., p. 370.

4. Ibid., p. 373.

5. Lahav, R. (1995). A conceptual framework for philosophical counseling: Worldview interpretation. In R. Lahav & M. da Venza Tillmanns (Eds.), *Essays on philosophical counseling* (pp. 3–23). New York: University Press of America, p. 7.

6. Jones, J. M. (1990). Who is training our ethnic minority psychologists, and are they doing it right? In G. Stricker (Ed.), *Toward ethnic diversification in psychology education and training* (pp. 17–34). Washington, DC: American Psychological Association.

7. Bernal, M. E., & Castro, F. G. (1994). Are clinical psychologists prepared for service and research with ethnic minorities? *American Psychologist, 49*, 797–805.

8. Sayette, M. A., & Mayne, T. J. (1990). Survey of current clinical and research trends in clinical psychology. *American Psychologist, 45*, 1263–1266.

9. Berry, J. W., Poortinga, Y. H., Segall, M. H., & Dasen, P. R. (1992). *Cross-cultural psychology: Research and applications.* Cambridge, England: Cambridge University Press.

10. Marsella, A. J. (1998). Toward a global community psychology: Meeting the needs of a changing world. *American Psychologist, 53*, 1282–1291.

11. Kazarian, S., & Evans, D. (1998). Introduction to cultural clinical psychology. In S. Kazarian & D. Evans (Eds.), *Cultural clinical psychology: Theory, research, and practice* (pp. 3–38). New York: Oxford University Press.

12. Ibid., pp. 17–18.

13. Ibid., p. 18

14. Humphreys, K. (1996). Clinical psychologists as psychotherapists: History, future, and alternatives. *American Psychologist, 51*, 190–197.

15. Marsella. Toward a global community psychology, p. 14.

16. Sloan, T. (1996). Psychological research methods in developing countries. In S. Carr & J. F. Schumaker (Eds.), *Psychology and the developing world* (pp. 38–45). New York: Praeger, p. 40.

17. Prilleltensky, I. (1997). Values, assumptions, and practices: Assessing the moral implications of psychological discourse and action. *American Psychologist, 52*, 517–535.

18. Prilleltensky, I., & Walsh-Brown, R. (1993). Psychology and the moral imperative. *Theoretical and Philosophical Psychology, 13*, 90–102.

Bibliography

Abramson, L. Y., Metalsky, G. I., & Vedak, C. (1989). Hopelessness depression. *Psychological Review, 96,* 358–372.

Albee, G. W. (1990). The futility of psychotherapy. *Journal of Mind and Behavior, 11,* 369–384.

Al-Issa, I. (1995). The illusion of reality or the reality of illusion?: Hallucinations and culture. *British Journal of Psychiatry, 166,* 368–373.

Allen, J. S. (1979). Modernity and the evil of banality. *Centennial Review, 23,* 20–39.

Allen, L. R., Long, P. T., Perdue, R. R., & Kieselbach, S. (1988). The impact of tourism development on residents' perceptions of community life. *Journal of Travel Research, 27,* 16–21.

Alparovitz, G. (1995). *Index of environmental trends.* Washington, DC: National Center for Economic and Security Alternatives.

Altroochi, J., & Altroochi, L. (1995). Polyfaceted psychological acculturation in Cook Islands. *Journal of Cross-Cultural Psychology, 26,* 426–440.

Anant, S. S. (1971). Belongingness and mental health. *Manas, 18,* 11–23.

Andrews, C. (1997). *The circle of simplicity.* New York: HarperCollins.

Appadurai, A. (1996). *Modernity at large.* Minneapolis: University of Minnesota Press.

Appleyard, B. (1993). *Understanding the present.* London: Picador/Pan Books.

Aquilino, W. S. (1996). The life course of children born to unmarried mothers. *Journal of Marriage and the Family, 58,* 293–310.

Arnett, J. J. (1991). Adolescents and heavy metal music. *Youth and Society, 23,* 76–98.

Arnett, J. J. (1992). Reckless behavior in adolescence. *Development Review, 12,* 339–373.

Arnett, J. J. (1993). Three profiles of heavy metal fans: A taste for sensation and a subculture of alienation. *Qualitative Sociology, 16*, 423–443.

Arnett, J. J., & Taber, S. (1994). Adolescence terminable and interminable. *Journal of Youth and Adolescence, 23*, 517–537.

Averill, L. J. (1974). *The problem of being human*. Valley Forge, PA: Judson Press.

Axelrod, S. D. (1999). *Work and the evolving self*. Hillsdale, NJ: The Analytic Press.

Bainbridge, W. S. & Stark, R. (1981). The consciousness reformation reconsidered. *Journal for the Scientific Study of Religion, 20*, 1–16.

Bar-Haim, G. (1997). The dispersed sacred: Anomie and the crisis of ritual. In S. M. Hoover & K. Lundby (Eds.), *Rethinking media, religion, and culture* (pp. 133–145). London: Sage.

Barth, F. (1997). How is the self conceptualized? Variations among cultures. In U. Neisser & D. A. Jopling (Eds.), *The conceptual self in context*. Cambridge: Cambridge University Press.

Baudrillard, J. (1988). *Selected writings*. Stanford, CA: Stanford University Press.

Baudrillard, J. (1998). *The consumer society: Myths and structures*. London: Sage.

Bauman, Z. (1997). *Globalization: The human consequences*. New York: Columbia University Press.

Bean, L. J., & Saubel, K. S. (1972). *Temalpakh: Cahuilla Indian knowledge and usage of plants*. Banning, CA: Malki Museum Press.

Beck, U. (1992). *Risk society: Towards a new modernity*. London: Sage.

Becker, E. (1973). *The denial of death*. New York: The Free Press.

Becker, E. (1975). *Escape from evil*. New York: The Free Press.

Belk, R. W. (1984). Three scales to measure constructs related to materialism: Reliability, validity, and relationships to measures of happiness. In T. Kinnear (Ed.), *Advances in consumer research*. Provo, UT: Association for Consumer Research.

Belk, R. W. (1985). Materialism: Trait aspects of living in the material world. *Journal of Consumer Research, 12*, 265–279.

Belk, R. W., & Ger, G. (1994). Problems of marketing in Romania and Turkey. In C. J. Schultz (Ed.), *Consumption in marketizing economies*. Greenwich, CT: JAI Press.

Belk, R. W., Wallendorf, M., & Sherry, J. F. (1989). The sacred and the profane in consumer behavior: Theodicy on the odyssey. *Journal of Consumer Research, 16*, 1–38.

Bellah, R. (1971). Toward a definition of unbelief. In R. Caporale & A. Grumelli (Eds.), *The culture of unbelief*. Berkeley, CA: The University of California Press.

Bellah, R. N., Madsen, W., Sullivan, A., Swidler, A., & Tipton, S. (1985). *Habits of the heart*. Berkeley, CA: University of California Press.

Bennis, W. (1989). *Why leaders can't lead*. San Francisco: Jossey-Bass.

Berger, P. (1969). *The social reality of religion*. London: Faber & Faber.

Berger, P., Berger, B., & Kellner, H. (1973). *The homeless mind: Modernization and consciousness*. New York: Random House.

Berking, H. (1996). Solidarity individualism. In S. Lash, B. Szerszynski, & B. Wynne (Eds.), *Risk, environment, and modernity* (pp. 189–202). London: Sage.

Berman, M. (1982). *All that is solid melts into air: The experience of modernity*. London: Verso.

Berman, M. (1999). *Adventures in Marxism*. London: Verso.

Bernal, M. E., & Castro, F. G. (1994). Are clinical psychologists prepared for service and research with ethnic minorities. *American Psychologist, 49*, 797–805.

Berry, J. W., Poortinga, Y. H., Segall, M. H., & Dasen, P. R. (1992). Cross-cultural psychology: Research and applications. Cambridge, England: Cambridge University Press.

Berry, W. (1977). *The unsettling of America*. San Francisco: Sierra Club Books.

Best, S., & Kellner, D. (1998). Beavis and Butt-Head: No future for post modern youth. In J. S. Epstein (Ed.), *Youth culture: Identity in a postmodern world*. Oxford, England: Blackwell.

Biglan, A. (1995). *Changing cultural practices*. Reno, NV: Contex Press.

Black, M. M., & Krishnakumar, A. (1998). Children in low-income, urban settings: Interventions to promote mental health and well-being. *American Psychologist, 53*, 635–646.

Blowers, A. (1997). Environmental policy: Ecological modernization or the risk society? *Urban Studies, 34*, 845–871.

Blumberg, L. (1995). Money and fetishism. *Free Associations, 5*, 492–517.

Bouchet, D. (1994). Rails without ties: Can postmodern consumption replace modern questioning. *International Journal of Research in Marketing, 11*, 405–422.

Bourguignon, E. (1992). Religion as a mediating factor in culture change. In J. F. Schumaker (Ed.), *Religion and mental health*. New York: Oxford University Press.

Bragdon, C. R. (1970). *Noise pollution: The unquiet crisis*. Philadelphia: University of Pennsylvania Press.

Brandt, D. (1997). Along came the transnationals. *Nexus, 4*, 13–17.

Braun, J. (1993). *Psychological aspects of modernity*. Westport, CT: Praeger.

Braun, J. (1995). *Social pathology in comparative perspective*. Westport, CT: Praeger.

Bronzaft, A. L., & McCarthy, D. P. (1975). The effects of elevated train noise on reading ability. *Environment and Behavior, 7*, 517–527.

Buck-Morss, S. (1987). Semiotic boundaries and the politics of meaning: Modernity on tour—a village in transition. In M. G. Raskin & H. J. Bernstein (Eds.), *New ways of knowing: The sciences, society, and reconstitutive knowledge*. Totowa, NJ: Rowman & Littlefield.

Burrows, R., Nicholas, P., & Quilgars, D. (1997). *Homelessness and social policy*. London: Routledge.

Burston, D. (1991). *The legacy of Erich Fromm*. Cambridge, MA: Harvard University Press.

Cahoone, L. E. (1988). *The dilemma of modernity: Philosophy, culture, and anti-culture*. Albany, NY: State University of New York Press.

Calfee, J. E., & Ringold, D. J. (1994). The seventy percent majority: Enduring consumer beliefs about advertising. *Journal of Public Policy and Marketing, 13*, 228–238.

Campbell, J. (1973). *Myths to live by*. London: Souvenir Press.

Campbell, R. A., & Curtis, J. E. (1994). Religious involvement across societies. *Journal for the Scientific Study of Religion, 33*, 215–229.

Cantril, H. (1957). The nature of faith. *Journal of Individual Psychology, 13*, 24–37.

Capps, D. (1985). Religion and psychological well-being. In P. E. Hammond (Ed.), *The sacred in a secular age*. Berkeley: University of California Press.

Carr, S. &, Schumaker, J. F. (1996). *Psychology and the developing world*. Westport, CT: Praeger.

Chandler, T. A., & Wolf, F. (1983). Gender differences in achievement and affiliation attributions. *Journal of Cross-Cultural Psychology, 14*, 241–256.

Chomsky, N. (1999). *Profit over people: Neoliberalism and global order*. New York: Seven Stories Press.

Clark, M. S. & Mills, J. (1979). Interpersonal attraction in exchange and communal relationships. *Journal of Personality and Social Psychology, 37*, 12–24.

Cock, P. (1996). Toward an ecopsychology for sustainable development. In S. C. Carr & J. F. Schumaker (Eds.), *Psychology and the developing world* (pp. 191–198). Westport, CT: Praeger.

Cohen, E. (1979). A phenomenology of tourism experiences. *Sociology, 13*, 179–201.

Cohen, E. (1984). The sociology of tourism: Approaches issues, and findings. *Annual Review of Sociology, 10*, 373–392.

Cohen, E. (1989). Primitive and remote hill tribe trekking in Thailand. *Annals of Tourism Research, 16*, 30–61.

Cohen, E. (1998). Risk society and ecological modernization. *Futures, 29*, 105–119.

Cohen, S., & Weinstein, N. (1982). Nonauditory effects of noise on behavior and health. In G. W. Evans (Ed.), *Environmental stress*. Cambridge: Cambridge University Press.

Corman, C. (1970). *Livingdying: Poems of Cid Corman*. New York: Directions Publishers.

Cornelius, A. (1989). Depression as cultural illness: A social epistemiology model of catastrophic learning. In G. J. Dacenoort (Ed.), *The paradigm of self-organization*. London: Gordon & Breach.

Cox, E. (1995). *A truly civil society*. Sydney: ABC Books.

Cross, S. E. (1995). Self-construals, coping, and stress in cross-cultural adaptation. *Journal of Cross-Cultural Psychology, 26*, 673–697.

Csikszentmihalyi, M., & Rochberg-Halton, E. (1978). Reflections on materialism. *University of Chicago Magazine, 70*, 6–15.

Cushman, P. (1990). Why the self is empty: Toward a historically situated psychology. *American Psychologist, 45*, 599–611.

Cushman, P. (1995). *Constructing the self, constructing America*. Reading, MA: Addison-Wesley.

Damon, A. (1977). The residential environment, health, and behavior. In L. E. Hinkle, Jr. & W. C. Loring (Eds.), *The effects of the man-made environment in health and behavior*. Atlanta: U.S. Public Health Service, Centers for Disease Control.

D'Andrade, R. (1984). Cultural meaning systems. In R. A. Shweder & R. A. LeVine (Eds.), *Culture theory: Essays on mind, self, and emotion*. Cambridge: Cambridge University Press.

Dearden, P., & Harron, S. (1992). Tourism and the hill tribes of Thailand. In B. Weiler & C. Hall (Eds.), *Special interest tourism*. London: Belhaven Press.

Debats, D., Drost, J., & Hansen, P. (1995). Experiences of meaning in life. *British Journal of Psychology, 86,* 359–375.

DeBerry, S. (1991). *The externalization of consciousness and the psychopathology of everyday life.* New York: Greenwood Press.

Deleuze, G., & Guttari, F. (1972). *Anti-Oedipus: Capitalism and schizophrenia.* New York: Viking.

Desmond, W. (1962). *Magic, myth, and money: The origin of money in religious ritual.* Glencoe, IL: Free Press of Glencoe.

Dobkin de Rios, M., & Smith, D. E. (1984). Drug use and abuse in cross-cultural perspective. In J. E. Mezzich & C. Berganza (Eds.), *Culture and psychopathology.* New York: Guilford Press.

Dogan, H. Z. (1989). Forms of adjustment: Sociocultural impacts of tourism. *Annals of Tourism Research, 16,* 216–236.

Douglas, M. (1970). *Natural symbols.* London: Cresset Press.

Douthwaite, R. (1992). *The growth illusion.* Tulsa, OK: Council Oak Books.

Dubrow-Eichel, S. K. (1993). Outpatient treatment of sex and love addictions. In E. Griffin-Shelly (Ed.), *The cultural context of sex and love addiction recovery* (pp. 113–135). Westport, CT: Praeger.

Duke, J. T., & Johnson, B. L. (1989). The stages of religious transformation: A study of 200 nations. *Review of Religious Research, 22,* 209–224.

Durkheim, E. (1951). *Suicide.* New York: The Free Press (originally published 1897).

Durning, A. T. (1992). *How much is enough? The consumer society and the future of the earth.* New York: W. W. Norton.

Easterlin, R. A., & Crimmins, E. M. (1988). Recent social trends: Changes in personal aspirations of American youth. *Sociology and Social Research, 72,* 217–223.

Edoho, F. M. (1997). *Globalization and the new world order.* Westport, CT: Praeger.

Emmons, C., & Sobal, J. (1981). Paranormal beliefs: Functional alternatives to mainstream religion. *Review of Religious Research, 22,* 301–312.

Evans, G. W., Bullinger, M., & Hygge, S. (1998). Chronic noise exposure and physiological response: A prospective study of children living under environmental stress. *Psychological Science, 9,* 75–77.

Evans, G. W., & Jacobs, S. V. (1982). Air pollution and human behavior. In G. W. Evans (Ed.), *Environmental stress.* Cambridge: Cambridge University Press.

Eysenck, M. W. (1992). *Anxiety: The cognitive perspective.* Hove, England: Lawrence Erlbaum.

Faber, R. J., Christenson, G. A., de Zwaan, M. & Mitchell, J. (1995). Two forms of compulsive consumption: Comorbidity of compulsive buying and binge eating. *Journal of Consumer Research, 22,* 296–304.

Featherstone, M. (1995). *Undoing culture: Globalization, postmodernism, and identity.* London: Sage.

Ferguson, H. (1992). *Religious transformation in Western society: The end of happiness.* London: Routledge.

Firat, A. F., & Venkatesh, A. (1993). Postmodernity: The age of marketing. *International Journal of Research in Marketing, 10,* 227–249.

Fisher, D. A. & Magnus, P. (1981). Out of the mouths of babes: The opinions of 10 and 11 year old children regarding the advertising of cigarettes. *Community Health Studies, 5,* 22–26.

Frank, L. (1940). The cost of competition. *Plan Age, 6,* 314–324.

Frankl, V. (1959). *From death camp to existentialism.* Boston: Beacon.

Frankl, V. (1969). *The will to meaning.* New York: World.

Freeman, H. J. (1988). Psychiatric aspects of environmental stress. *International Journal of Mental Health, 17,* 13–23.

Freire, P. (1975). Cultural action for freedom. *Harvard Educational Review, 1,* 1–55.

Freud, S. (1927/1964). *The future of an illusion.* New York: Anchor Books.

Friedman, M. (1996). Grassroots groups confront the corporation: Contemporary strategies in historical perspective. *Journal of Social Issues, 52,* 153–167.

Fromm, E. (1955). *The dogma of Christ.* New York: Holt, Rinehart & Winston.

Fromm, E. (1955). *The sane society.* New York: Rinehart.

Fromm, E. (1956). *The art of loving.* New York: Harper & Row.

Fromm, E. (1973). *The anatomy of human destructiveness.* New York: Holt, Rinehart & Winston.

Fromm, E. (1976). *To have or to be.* New York: Harper & Row.

Fromm, E. (1981). *On disobedience and other essays.* New York: Seabury Press.

Fromm, E. (1994). *On being human.* New York: Continuum.

Fromm, E., & Xirau, R. (Eds). (1968). *The nature of man.* New York: Macmillan.

Frosh, S. (1991). *The identity crises: Modernity, psychoanalysis, and the self.* London: Macmillan.

Frydenberg, E. (1999). *Learning to cope: Developing as a person in complex societies.* Oxford: Oxford University Press.

Fuchs, R. J., Brennan, E., Chamie, J., Lo, F., & Uitto, J. I. (1994). *Mega-city growth and the future.* New York: United Nations University Press.

Fuller, R. (1986). *Americans and the unconscious.* New York: Oxford University Press.

Funkhouser, G. R. (1989). Values changes necessary for a sustainable society. *Bulletin of The Science and Technology Society, 9,* 19–32.

Garrison, A. (1995). Psychotherapy and the modern ego. *Humanistic Psychologist, 23,* 227–238.

Gaylin, W. (1984). *The rage within: Anger in modern life.* New York: Penguin.

Geertz, C. (1973). Person, time and conduct in Bali. In C. Geertz (Ed.), *The interpretation of culture.* New York: Basic Books.

Ger, G. & Belk, R. W. (1996). Cross-cultural differences in materialism. *Journal of Economic Psychology, 17,* 55–77.

Ger, G. & Belk, R. W. (1996). I'd like to buy the world a coke: Consumerscapes of the less affluent world. *Journal of Consumer Policy, 19,* 271–304.

Gergen, K. J. (1991). *The saturated self.* New York: Basic Books.

Gergen, K. J. (1994). *Realities and relationships: Soundings in social construction.* Cambridge, MA: Harvard University Press.

Gergen, K. J., Gulerce, A., Lock, A., & Misra, G. (1996). Psychological science in cultural context. *American Psychologist, 51,* 496–503.

Gerhards, J. (1989). The changing culture of emotions in modern society. *Social Science Information, 28,* 737–754.

Gibson, J. W. (1997). Can the cultural re-enchantment of nature help stop environmental destruction. *Negations, 2,* 17–30.

Giddens, A. (1990). *The consequences of modernity.* Cambridge, England: Polity Press.

Giddens, A. (1991). *Modernity and self-identity.* Cambridge, England: Polity Press.

Gilder, G. (1981). *Wealth and poverty.* New York: Basic Books.

Gilligan, J. (1996). *Violence: Reflections on a national epidemic.* New York: Vintage.

Goldhammer, J. (1996). *Under the influence.* Amherst, NY: Prometheus Books.

Goldman, I. (1961). The Zuni Indians of New Mexico. In M. Mead (Ed.), *Cooperation and competition among primitive peoples.* Boston: Beacon.

Goldman, I. (1991). Narcissism, social character, and communication. *The Psychological Record, 41,* 343–360.

Good, B. J., & Kleinman, A. M. (1985). Culture and anxiety. In A. H. Tuma & J. Maser (Ed.), *Anxiety and the anxiety disorders.* Hillsdale, NJ: Lawrence Erlbaum.

Goodman, P. (1956). *Growing up absurd.* New York: Random House.

Gordon, S. (1976). *The loneliness market.* New York: Simon & Schuster.

Gottlieb, B. H. (1983). Social support as a focus for integrative research in psychology. *American Psychologist, 38,* 278–287.

Gotto, J. T. (1997). Why schools don't educate. *Nexus, June-July,* 13–16.

Greeley, A. (1994). A religious revival in Russia? *Journal for the Scientific Study of Religion, 33,* 253–272.

Hacker, D. J. (1994). An existential view of adolescence. *Journal of Early Adolescence, 14,* 300–327.

Hagnell, O., Lanke, J., Rorsman, B. & Ojesjo, L. (1982). Are we entering an age of melancholy: Depressive illness in a prospective epidemiological study over 25 years. *Psychological Medicine, 12,* 279–289.

Hall, E. T. (1971). The paradox of culture. In B. Landis & E. S. Tauber (Eds.), *In the name of life: Essays in honor of Erich Fromm.* New York: Holt, Rinehart & Winston.

Hall, E. T. (1976). *Beyond culture.* Garden City, NJ: Anchor/Doubleday.

Hall, S., Held, D., Hubert, D., & Thompson, K. (1996). *Modernity: An introduction to modern societies.* Oxford, England: Blackwell.

Hall, S., Held, D., & McGrew, T. (1992). *Modernity and its futures.* Cambridge, England: Polity Press.

Handwerker, W. P. (1991). Origins and evolution of culture. *American Anthropologist, 91,* 313–326.

Hanley, A. & Wilhelm, M. S. (1992). Compulsive buying: An exploration into self-esteem and money attitudes. *Journal of Economic Psychology, 13,* 5–18.

Harkness, S. (1987). The cultural mediation of postpartum depression. *Medical Anthropology Quarterly, 1,* 194–209.

Healy, S. D. (1984). *Boredom, self, and culture.* London: Associated University Press.

Heft, H. (1979). Background and focal environmental conditions of the home and attention in young children. *Journal of Applied Social Psychology, 9,* 47–69.

Heller, A. (1990). *Can modernity survive?* Berkeley: University of California Press.

Henry, J. (1965). *Culture against man.* New York: Vintage Books.

Hickey, N. (1998). Money lust: How pressure for profit is perverting journalism. *Columbia Journalism Review, July/August.*

Hillman, J. (1989). *A blue fire*. New York: Harper Collins.

Hills, H. L., & Strozier, A. L. (1992). Multicultural training in APA-approved counseling psychology programs. *Professional Psychology: Research and Practice, 23*, 43–51.

Hirsch, F. (1976). *Social limits of growth*. Cambridge, MA: Harvard University Press.

Hirschman, E. C. (1992). The consciousness of addiction: Toward a general theory of compulsive consumption. *Journal of Consumer Research, 19*, 155–179.

Hobbs, N. (1962). Sources of gain in psychotherapy. *American Psychologist, 17*, 742–748.

Hochschild, J. (1997). *The time bind*. New York: Metropolitan Books.

Hollan, D. (1988). Staying "cool" in Toraja: Informal strategies for the management of anger and hostility. *Ethos, 16*, 52–72.

Holt, D. (1997). Poststructuralist lifestyle analysis: Conceptualizing the social patterning of consumption in postmodernity. *Journal of Consumer Research, 23*, 326–350.

Holtz, G. T. (1995). *Welcome to the jungle*. New York: St. Martins Griffin.

Honey, M. (1999). *Eco-tourism and sustainable development*. Washington, DC: Island Press.

Hopkins, J., Marcus, M., & Campbell, S. B. (1984). Postpartum depression: A critical review. *Psychological Bulletin, 95*, 498–515.

Hoskin, J. O., Friedman, M. I. & Cawte, J. E. (1969). A high incidence of suicide in a preliterate and primitive society. *Psychiatary, 32*, 199–210.

Hsu, F. L. K. (1985). The self in cross-cultural perspective. In A. J. Marsella, G. De Vos, & F. L. K. Hsu (Eds.), *Culture and self*. London: Tavistock.

Huffman, J. R. (1982). A psychological critique of American culture. *The American Journal of Psychoanalysis, 42 *, 27–36.

Hui, C. H., & Triandis, H. C. (1986). Individualism—collectivism: A study of cross-cultural researchers. *Journal of Cross-Cultural Psychology, 17*, 225–248.

Humphreys, K. (1996). Clinical psychologists as psychotherapists: History, future, and alternatives. *American Psychologist, 51*, 190–197.

Hutson, S., & Liddiard, M. (1994). *Youth homelessness: The construction of a social issue*. Houndsmill, England: Macmillan.

Ibañez-Noé, J. A. (1994). Synopsis of a theory of modernity. *Man and World, 27*, 361–381.

Ingleby, D. (1990). Problems in the study of the interplay between science and culture. In V. J. Vande & G. Hutschemaekers (Eds.), *The investigation of culture*. Tilburg, The Netherlands: Tilburg University Press.

Inkeles, A. (1966). The modernization of man. In M. Weiner (Ed.), *Modernization: The dynamics of growth*. New York: Basic Books.

Inkeles, A. (1983). *Exploring individual modernity*. New York: Columbia University Press.

Inkeles, A., & Smith, D. (1970). The fate of personal adjustment in the process of modernization. *International Journal of Comparative Sociology, 11*, 81–114.

Jacobs, S. V., Evans, G. W., Catalano, R., & Dooley, D. (1984). Air pollution and depressive symptomatology: Exploratory analyses of intervening psychosocial factors. *Population and Environment: Behavioral and Social Issues, 7*, 260–272.

Johnson, D. W., Johnson, R. T., & Scott, L. (1978). The effects of cooperative and individualized instruction on student attitudes and achievement. *Journal of Social Psychology, 104*, 207–216.

Jones, G. W. (1997). Modernization and divorce. *Population and Development Review, 23*, 95–114.

Jones, I. H., & Horne, D. J. (1973). Psychiatric disorders among the Aborigines of the Australian Western Desert. *Social Science and Medicine, 7*, 219–228.

Jones, J. M. (1990). Who is training our ethnic minority psychologists, and are they doing it right? In G. Stricker (Ed.), *Toward ethnic diversification in psychology education and training* (pp. 17–34). Washington, DC: American Psychological Association.

Jung, C. (1966). *Collected works: The practice of psychotherapy*. New York: Pantheon.

Katz, J., & Briger, R. (1988). Modernity and the quality of marriage in Israel. *Journal of Comparative Family Studies, 19*, 371–380.

Kazarian, S. S., & Evans, D. R. (Eds.) (1998). *Cultural clinical psychology*. New York: Oxford University Press.

Kent, N. (1977). A new kind of sugar. In R. R. Finney & K. A. Watson (Eds.), *A new kind of sugar*. Santa Cruz, CA: Center for South Pacific Studies.

Kilpatrick, W. K. (1983). *Psychological seduction*. Nashville, TN: Thomas Nelson.

Kimbrough, R., Molock, S. D., & Walton, K. (1996). Perception of social support, acculturation, depression, and suicidal ideation among African American college students. *Journal of Negro Education, 65*, 295–307.

Kirkpatrick, J. (1986). A philosophic defense of advertising. *Journal of Advertising, 15*, 42–48.

Klerman, G. (1979). The age of melancholy. *Psychology Today, 10*, 37–88.

Kohn, A. (1994). *No contest*. New York: Random House.

Kopytoff, I. (1986). The cultural biography of things: Commoditization as process. In A. Appadurai (Ed.), *The social life of things*. Cambridge: Cambridge University Press.

Kraybill, D. (1989). *The riddle of Amish culture*. Baltimore: Johns Hopkins University Press.

Krueger, A. O. (1993). The training of economists. In S. King & P. Lloyd (Eds.), *Economic rationalism*. Sydney: Allen & Unwin.

Lahav, R. (1995). A conceptual framework for philosophical counseling: Worldview interpretation. In R. Lahav & M. da Venza Tillmanns (Eds.), *Essays on philosophical counseling* (pp. 3–23). New York: University Press of America.

Lasch, C. (1979). *The culture of narcissism*. New York: W. W. Norton.

Leach, W. (1993). *Land of desire: Merchants, power, and the rise of a new American culture*. New York: Pantheon Books.

Leary, M. R. (1982). Social anxiety. In L. Wheeler (Ed.), *Review of personality and social psychology*. Beverly Hills, CA: Sage.

Lechner, F. (1992). Against modernity: Antimodernism in global perspective. In P. Colomy (Ed.), *The dynamics of social systems*. London: Sage.

Leighton, A. (1959). *My name is legion*. New York: Basic Books.

Leiss, W. (1976). *The limits to satisfaction*. Toronto: University of Toronto Press.

Leonard, G. B. (1973). Winning isn't everything: It's nothing. *Intellectual Digest,* *October,* 45–47.

Leonard-Barton, D. (1981). Voluntary simplicity lifestyles and energy conservation. *Journal of Consumer Research, 8,* 243–252.

Le Roux, J., & Smith, M. E. (1992). The anti-child culture of modern society. *Education and Society, 10,* 65–71.

Levinson, D., & Malone, M. J. (1980). *Toward explaining human culture.* New York: HRAF Press.

Ley, D. (1983). *The social geography of the city.* New York: Harper & Row.

Lifton, R. J. (1993). *The protean self.* New York: Basic Books.

Linn, M. C., de Benedictus, T. & Delucchi, K. (1982). Adolescent reasoning about advertisments. *Child Development, 53,* 1599–1613.

Llewellyn, L. G. (1981). The social cost of urban transportation. *Human Behavior and Development, 5,* 169–202.

Loy, D. (1996). *Lack and transcendence.* Atlantic Heights, NJ: Humanities Press.

Lu, L. (1995). Life events, social support, and depression among Taiwanese female homemakers. *Journal of Social Psychology, 135,* 185–190.

Lumsden, C., & Wilson, E. O. (1981). *Genes, mind, and culture.* Cambridge, MA: Cambridge University Press.

Lunt, I., & Poortinga, Y. H. (1996). Internationalizing psychology. *American Psychologist, 51,* 504–508.

Lunt, P. K., & Livingstone, S. M. (1992). *Mass consumption and personal identity* . Buckingham, England: Open University Press.

Lyons, D. (1994). *Postmodernity.* Minneapolis: University of Minnesota Press.

Maccoby, M. (1983). Social character versus the productive ideal. *Praxis International, 1,* 70–83.

Maddi, S. (1967). The existential neurosis. *Journal of Abnormal Psychology, 72,* 311–325.

Maguire, J. (1996). The tears inside the stone: Reflections on the ecology of fear. In S. Lash, B. Szerszynski, & B. Wynne (Eds.), *Risk, environment, and modernity.* London: Sage.

Maizie, S. M., & Rawlings, S. (1973). Public attitudes toward population issues. In S. M. Maizei (Ed.), *Population distribution and policy.* Washington, DC: U.S. Government Printing Office.

Mansperger, M. (1995). Tourism and cultural change in small-scale societies. *Human Organization, 54,* 87–94.

Marsella, A. J. (1979). The modernization of traditional cultures: Consequences for the individual. In D. Hoopes, P. Pedersen, & G. Renwick (Eds.), *Intercultural education, training, and research.* Washington, DC: Sietar.

Marsella, A. J. (1985). Culture, self and mental disorder. In A. J. Marsella, G. De Vos, & F. L. K. Hsu (Eds.), *Culture and self.* London: Tavistock.

Marsella, A. J. (1993). Sociocultural foundations of psychopathology. *Transcultural Psychiatric Research Review, 30,* 97–142.

Marsella, A. J. (1998). Culture and psychopathology. In A. Kazdin (Ed.), *The encyclopedia of psychology.* Washington, DC: American Psychological Association.

Marsella, A. J. (1998). *The psychosocial consequences of globalization.* Seminar presented at the University of Hawaii, Honolulu, Hawaii, Dec. 4, 1998.

Marsella, A. J. (1998). Toward a global community psychology: Meeting the needs of a changing world. *American Psychologist, 53,* 1282–1291.

Marsella, A. J. (1998). Urbanization, mental health, and social deviancy. *American Psychologist, 53,* 624–634.

Marsella, A. J., & Choi, S. C. (1993). Psychosocial aspects of modernization and economic development in East Asian nations. *Psychologia, 36,* 201–213.

Martin-Barbero, J. (1997). Mass media as a site of resacralization of contemporary cultures. In S. M. Hoover & K. Lundby (Eds.), *Rethinking media, religion, and culture* (pp. 102–116). London: Sage.

Maslow, A. H. (1968). *Toward a psychology of being.* New York: Van Nostrand.

May, R. (1950). *The meaning of anxiety.* New York: Ronald Press.

May, R. (1991). *The cry for myth.* London: Souvenir Press.

McCarthy, P. (1997). Mediating modern marriage. *Sexual and Marital Therapy, 12,* 275–287.

McConnell, J. V. (1986). *Understanding human behavior.* New York: Holt, Rinehart & Winston.

McCracken, G. (1990). *Culture and consumption.* Bloomington, IN: University of Indiana Press.

McGuffin, P., Katz, R., Watkins, S., & Rutherford, J. (1996). A hospital-based twin registry study of heritability of DSM-IV unipolar depression. *Archives of General Psychiatry, 53,* 129–136.

McKendrick, N., Brewer, J., & Plumb, J. H. (1982). *The birth of consumer society.* Bloomington, IN: Indiana University Press.

McLean, E. K., & Tarnopolsky, A. (1977). Noise, discomfort, and mental health. *Psychological Medicine, 7,* 19–62.

McMillan, D., & Chavis, D. (1986). Sense of community: A definition and theory. *Journal of Community Psychology, 14,* 6–23.

McMurty, J. (1996). *Unequal freedoms: The global market as an ethical system.* Toronto: Garamond.

Mellor, P. A., & Shilling, C. (1997). *Reforming the body: Community and modernity.* London: Sage.

Meserve, H. (1986). In search of values. *Journal of Religion and Health, 25,* 91–95.

Mestrovi, S. G. (1997). *Postemotional society.* London: Sage.

Mick, D. G., & Fournier, S. (1998). Paradoxes of technology: Consumer cognizance, emotions, and coping strategies. *Journal of Consumer Research, 25,* 123–143.

Miller, D. (1987). *Material culture and mass consumption.* Oxford, England: Basil Blackwell.

Miller, J. (1974). Effects of noise on people. *Journal of the Acoustical Society of America, 56,* 729–764.

Minic, V., & Zivkovic, J. (1996). Ecological problems as the existential framework of the modern world. *Facta Universitatis, 1,* 301–311.

Minirth, F. (1981). *The workaholic and his family.* Grand Rapids, MI: Baker Books.

Moghaddam, F. M. (1990). Modulative and generative orientations in psychology: Implications for psychology in the Three Worlds. *Journal of Social Issues, 46,* 21–41.

Moghaddam, F. M. (1997). *The specialized society.* Westport, CT: Praeger.

Mol, A. P., & Spaargaren, G. (1993). Environment, modernity and the risk-society: The apocalyptic horizon of environmental reform. *International Sociology, 8*, 431–459.

Molnar, T. (1980). *Theists and atheists*. The Hague, The Netherlands: Mouton.

Morrissey, J. P., & Gounis, K. (1987). Homelessness and mental illness in America: Emerging issues in the construction of a social problem. In C. J. Smith & J. A. Giggs (Eds.), *Location and stigma*. London: Allen & Unwin.

Moser, G. (1994). Environmental stress and urban behavior. *European Journal of Applied Psychology, 44*, 149–154.

Mount, E. (1983). Individualism and our fears of death. *Death Education, 7*, 25–31.

Mouzelis, N. (1999). Modernity: A non-European conceptualization. *British Journal of Sociology, 50*, 141-159.

Mukerji, C. (1983). *From graven images: Patterns of modern materialism*. New York: Columbia University Press.

Munro, D., Schumaker, J. F., & Carr, S. (1997). *Motivation and culture*. New York: Routledge.

Murdock, G. P., & Provost, C. (1973). Measurement of cultural complexity. *Ethnology, 12*, 379–392.

Murphy, H. (1961). Social change and mental health. In H. Murphy (Ed.), *Cases of mental disorders*. New York: Milbank Memorial Fund.

Murphy, H. B. (1982). Blood pressure and culture. *Psychotherapy and Psychosomatics, 38*, 244–255.

Naroll, R. (1969). Cultural determinants of the concept of the sick society. In S. C. Plog & R. B. Edgerton (Eds.), *Changing perspectives in mental illness*. New York: Holt, Rinehart & Winston.

Naroll, R. (1983). *The moral order: An introduction to the human situation*. London: Sage.

Nataraajan, R. & Goff, B. G. (1992). Manifestations of compulsiveness in the consumer-marketplace domain. *Psychology and Marketing, 9*, 31–44.

Navarro, P., Larrain, S., Housley, P., & de Man, A. (1987). Anxiety, locus of control and appraisal of air pollution. *Perceptual and Motor Skills, 64*, 811–814.

Neusch, M. (1982). *The sources of modern atheism*. New York: Paulist Press.

Nevin, J. A. (1991). Behavior analysis and global survival. In W. Ishaq (Ed.), *Human behavior in today's world*. Westport, CT: Praeger.

Nicholls, W. (1988). Immanent transcendence. In W. Nicholls (Ed.), *Modernity and religion*. Waterloo, Canada: Wilfred Laurier University Press.

Nikelly, A. (1992). The pleonexic personality: A new provisional personality disorder. *Individual Psychology, 48* , 253–260.

Oakley, A. (1992). *Social support and motherhood*. Oxford: Blackwell.

Ogilvy, D. (1980). *Confessions of an advertising man*. New York: Atheneum.

O'Guinn, T. C., & Faber, R. J. (1989). Compulsive buying: A phenomenological exploration. *Journal of Consumer Research, 16*, 147–157.

Oliver, J. M., & Novak, B. B. (1993). Depression, Seligman's hypothesis, and birth cohort effects in university students. *Journal of Social Behavior and Personality, 8*, 99–110.

Omer, H., & Rosenbaum, R. (1997). Diseases of hope and the work of despair. *Psychotherapy, 34*, 225–232.

Orlick, T. (1978). *Winning through cooperation*. Washington, DC: Acropolis Books.

Oskamp, S. (1995). Applying social psychology to avoid ecological disaster. *Journal of Social Issues, 51*, 217–239.

Ozanne, J. L. & Murray, J. B. (1996). Uniting critical theory and public policy to create the reflexively defiant consumer. In R. P. Hill (Ed.), *Marketing and consumer research in the public interest*. London: Sage.

Palinkas, L. A., Downs, M. A., Peterson, J. S., & Russell, J. (1993). Social, cultural, and psychological impacts of the Exxon Valdez oil spill. *Human Organization, 52*, 1–13.

Papastergiadis, N. (1993). *Modernity as exile*. New York: St. Martins Press.

Paris, J. (1996). *Social factors in borderline personality disorder*. New York: Cambridge University Press.

Paris, J. (2000). Cultural risk factors in personality disorders. In J. F. Schumaker & T. Ward (Eds.), *Cultural cognition and psychopathology*. Westport, CT: Praeger.

Pawlik, K., & d'Ydewalle, G. (1996). Psychology and the global commons: Perspectives of international psychology. *American Psychologist, 51*, 488–495.

Pelletier, L. G., Legault, L. R., & Tuson, K. M. (1996). The environmental satisfaction scale. *Environment and Behavior, 29*, 5–26.

Pennebaker, J. W. (1995). *Emotional disclosure and health*. Washington, DC: American Psychological Association.

Poole, R. (1991). *Morality and modernity*. London: Routledge.

Postman, N. (1985). *Amusing ourselves to death*. London: Methuen.

Prades, J. A. (1999). Global environmental change and contemporary society. *International Sociology, 14*, 7–31.

Pratkanis, A. R., & Turner, M. E. (1996). Persuasion and democracy: Strategies for increasing deliberative participation and enacting social change. *Journal of Social Issues, 52*, 187–205.

Price, J. (1994). The social competition hypothesis of depression. *British Journal of Psychiatry, 164*, 309–315.

Prilleltensky, I. (1994). Empowerment in mainstream psychology: Legitimacy, obstacles, and possibilities. *Canadian Psychologist, 35*, 358–375.

Prilleltensky, I. (1997). Community psychology: Reclaiming social justice. In D. Fox & I. Prilleltensky (Eds.), *Critical psychology*. London: Sage.

Prilleltensky, I. (1997). Values, assumptions, and practices: Assessing the moral implications of psychological discourse and action. *American Psychologist, 52*, 517–535.

Prilleltensky, I., & Walsh-Brown, R. (1993). Psychology and the moral imperative. *Theoretical and Philosophical Psychology, 13*, 90–102.

Proshansky, H. (1987). The field of environmental psychology: Securing its future. In D. Stokols & J. Altman (Eds.), *Handbook of environmental psychology*. New York: Wiley.

Pusey, M. (1993). Reclaiming the middle ground: From new right economic rationalism. In S. King & P. Lloyd (Eds.), *Economic rationalism*. Sydney: Allen & Unwin.

Putnam, R. (1995). Bowling alone: America's declining social capital. *Journal of Democracy, 6*, 65–78.

Quinney, R. (1995). Socialist humanism and the problem of crime. *Social Change, 23*, 147–156.

Randolf, T. G. (1970). Domiciliary chemical air pollution in the etiology of ecologic mental illness. *International Journal of Social Psychiatry, 16*, 243–265.

Rapson, R. L. (1988). *American yearnings: Love, money, and endless possibility*. New York: University Press of America.

Reading, B. (1996). *The university in ruins*. Cambridge, MA: Harvard University Press.

Reker, G. T. (1997). Personal meaning, optimism, and choice. *The Gerontologist, 37*, 709–716.

Richardson, F. C., & Manaster, G. J. (1992). Greed, psychopathology, and social interest. *Individual Psychology, 48*, 260–276.

Richins, M. L. (1996). Materialism, desire, and discontent. In R. P. Hill (Ed.), *Marketing and consumer research in the public interest*. London: Sage.

Richins, M. L. & Dawson, S. (1992). A consumer values orientation for materialism and its measurement: Scale development and validation. *Journal of Consumer Research, 19*, 303–316.

Rindfleisch, A., Burroughs, J., & Denton, F. (1997). Family structure, materialism, and compulsive consumption. *Journal of Consumer Research, 23*, 312–325.

Ringold, D. J. (1996). Social criticisms of target marketing. In R. P. Hill (Ed.), *Marketing and consumer research in the public interest*. London: Sage.

Ritzer, G. (1996). McUniversity in the postmodern consumer society. *Quality Higher Education, 2*, 185–199.

Robertson, J. & Robertson, J. (1989). *Separation and the very young*. London: Free Association Books.

Robertson, T. S. & Rossiter, J. R. (1974). Children and commercial persuasion: An attribution theory analysis. *Journal of Consumer Research, 1*, 13–20.

Rohner, R. P. (1984). Toward a conception of culture for cross-cultural psychology. *Journal for Cross-Cultural Psychology, 15*, 111–138.

Romney, K., & Romney, K. (1966). *The Mixtecans of Juxtalhuaca, Mexico*. New York: John Wiley & Sons.

Roof, W. (1993). *A generation of seekers*. San Francisco: Harper & Row.

Roof, W. (1998). Modernity, the religious, and the spiritual. *Annals of the American Academy of Political and Social Science, 558*, 211–224.

Rosenberg, M. (1965). *Society and the adolescent self-image*. Princeton, NJ: Princeton University Press.

Ross, G. F. (1994). *The psychology of tourism*. Melbourne: Hospitality Press.

Rossel, P. (1988). *Tourism: Manufacturing the exotic*. Copenhagen: IWGIA

Roszak, T., Gomes, M. E., & Kanner, A. D. (1995). *Ecopsychology: Restoring the earth, healing the mind*. San Francisco: Sierra Club Books.

Rotenberg, M. (1977). Alienating individualism and reciprocal individualism: A cross-cultural conceptualization. *Journal of Humanistic Psychology, 17*, 3–17.

Sagasti, F. (1992). International scientific and technical cooperation in a fractured world order. In U. Kirdar (Ed.), *Change: Threat or opportunity for human progress*. New York: United Nations.

Sandel, M. (1996). *Democracy's discontent*. Cambridge, MA: Harvard University Press.

Sarason, S. B. (1981). An asocial psychology and a misdirected clinical psychology. *American Psychologist, 36*, 827–836.

Sayette, M. A., & Mayne, T. J. (1990). Survey of current clinical and research trends in clinical psychology. *American Psychologist, 45,* 1263–1266.

Scheff, T. J. (1979). *Catharsis in healing, ritual, and drama.* Berkeley, CA: University of California Press.

Schieffelin, E. L. (1985). The cultural analysis of depressive affect: An example from New Guinea. In A. Kleinman & B. Good (Eds.), *Culture and depression.* Berkeley: University of California Press.

Schneider, D. (1976). Notes toward a theory of culture. In K. Basso & H. Selby (Eds.), *Meaning in anthropology.* Albuquerque, NM: University of New Mexico Press.

Schor, J. B. (1991). *The overworked American.* New York: Basic Books.

Schor, J. B. (1998). *The overspent American.* New York: Basic Books.

Schultz, D. (1969). *A history of modern psychology.* New York: Academic Press.

Schumacher, E. F. (1974). *Small is beautiful: A study of economics as if people mattered.* London: Abacus.

Schumaker, J. F. (1990). *Wings of illusion: The origin, nature, and future of paranormal belief.* Amherst, NY: Prometheus.

Schumaker, J. F. (1991). *Human suggestibility: Advances in theory, research, and application.* New York: Routledge.

Schumaker, J. F. (1992). *Religion and Mental Health.* New York: Oxford University Press.

Schumaker, J. F. (1995). *The corruption of reality: A unified theory of religion, hypnosis, and psychopathology.* Amherst, NY: Prometheus.

Schumaker, J. F. & Ward, T. (Eds.) (2000). *Cultural cognition and psychopathology.* Westport, CT: Praeger.

Schwab, J. J. & Schwab, M. E. (1978). *Sociological roots of mental illness.* New York: Plenum Press.

Schwartz, B. (1994). *The costs of living: How market freedom erodes the best things in life.* New York: W. W. Norton.

Scitovsky, T. (1976). *The joyless economy.* Oxford: Oxford University Press.

Seligman, M. E. P. (1974). Depression and learned helplessness. In R. J. Friedman & M. M. Katz (Eds.), *The psychology of depression.* Washington, DC: Winston-Wiley.

Seligman, M. E. P. (1990). Why is there so much depression today? In R. E. Ingram (Ed.), *Contemporary approaches to depression.* New York: Plenum Press.

Serpell, R., & Boykin, A. W. (1994). Cultural dimensions of cognition: A multiplex dynamic system of constraints and possibilities. In R. J. Sternberg (Ed.), *Thinking and problem solving.* San Diego, CA: Academic Press.

Sewall, L., & Swift, J. (1999). The embedded self. *Psychohistory Review, 27,* 71–84.

Seybold, K. C., & Salomone, P. R. (1994). Understanding workaholism. *Journal of Counseling and Development, 73,* 4–9.

Shaw, M. (1994). *Global society and international relations.* Cambridge, England: Polity Press.

Sheppard, M. (1994). Postnatal depression, child care and social support: A review of findings and the implications for practice. *Social Work and Social Science Review, 5,* 24–46.

Shore, B. (1991). Twice-born, once conceived: Meaning construction and cultural cognition. *American Anthropologist, 93,* 9–27.

Simon, R. C. (1985). Sorting the culture-bound syndromes. In R. C. Simons & C. C. Hughes (Eds.), *The culture-bound syndromes.* Dordrecht: Reidel Publishing.

Singer, J. (1997). *Message in a bottle.* New York: The Free Press.

Skinner, B. F. (1991). Why we are not saving the world. In W. Ishaq (Ed.), *Human behavior in today's world.* Westport, CT: Praeger.

Sklair, L. (1991). *The sociology of the global system.* Baltimore: Johns Hopkins University Press.

Slater, D. (1997). *Consumer culture and modernity.* Cambridge, England: Polity Press.

Sloan, T. (1996). *Damaged life: The crisis of the modern psyche.* London: Routledge.

Sloan, T. (1996). Psychological research methods in developing countries. In S. Carr & J. Schumaker (Eds.), *Psychology and the developing world.* New York: Praeger.

Smart, J. F., & Smart, D. W. (1995). Acculturative stress of Hispanics: Loss and challenge. *Journal of Counseling and Development, 73,* 390–396.

Smith, C. J. (1988). *Public problems: The management of urban distress.* New York: Guilford Press.

Smith, J. W., Lyons, G., & Sauer-Thompson, G. (1997). *Healing a wounded world: Economics, ecology, and health for a sustainable life.* Westport, CT: Praeger.

Smith, J. W., & Sauer-Thompson, G. (1998). Civilization's wake: Ecology, economics and the roots of environmental destruction and neglect. *Population and Environment, 19,* 541–575.

Smith, V. L. (1978). *Hosts and guests: The anthropology of tourism.* Oxford: Blackwell.

Sokal, J., Zejda, J., Pastuszka, J., Dobowski, M., & Jarosinska, D. (1996). Environmental pollution and urban health. In *Urbanization: A global health challenge.* World Health Organization.

Spector, I. P., & Carey, M. P. (1990). Incidence and prevalence of sexual dysfunction: A critical review of the empirical literature. *Archives of Sexual Behavior, 19,* 389–408.

Spergel, I. A. (1995). *The youth gang problem.* New York: Oxford University Press.

Spiro, M. E. (1984). Reflections on cultural determinism and relativism. In R. A. Shweder & R. A. LeVine (Eds.), *Culture theory: Essays on mind, self and emotion.* Cambridge: Cambridge University Press.

Spiro, M. E. (1994). *Culture and human nature.* New Brunswick, NJ: Transaction Publishers.

Spruell, G. (1987). Work fever. *Training and Development Journal, 4,* 41–45.

Spybey, T. (1996). *Globalization and world society.* Cambridge, England: Polity Press.

Stark, R. (1993). Europe's receptivity to new religious movements: Round two. *Journal for The Scientific Study of Religion, 32,* 389–397.

Stern, G. & Kluckman, L. (1983). Multi-disciplinary perspectives in post-partum depression: An anthropological critique. *Social Sciences and Medicine, 50,* 149–167.

Stone, B. L. (1989). Modernity and the narcissistic self: Taking "character" disorders seriously. *Studies in Symbolic Interaction, 10,* 89–107.

Strinati, D. (1995). *An introduction to theories of popular culture.* London: Routledge.

Suzuki, D. T. (1960). Lectures on Zen Buddhism. In D. T. Suzuki, E. Fromm, & R. De Martino (Eds.), *Zen Buddhism and psychoanalysis*. New York: Harper & Row.

Swanson, J. L. (1995). The call for Gestalt's contribution to ecopsychology. *Gestalt Journal, 18*, 47–85.

Sznaider, N. (1998). The sociology of compassion. *Cultural Values, 1*, 117–139.

Taylor, C. (1985). *Philosophy and the human sciences*, Vol. 2. Cambridge: Cambridge University Press.

Teeple, G. (1995). *Globalization and the decline of social reform*. Toronto: Garamond Press.

Thompson, I. (1991). *The American replacement of nature*. New York: Doubleday.

Thurman, R. (1998). *Inner revolution: Life, liberty and the pursuit of real happiness*. New York: Riverhead Books.

Triandis, H. C., Bontempo, R., & Villareal, M. J. (1988). Individualism and collectivism: Cross-cultural perspectives on self-ingroup relationships. *Journal of Personality and Social Psychology, 34*, 323–338.

Tseng, M. D. & McDermott, J. F. (1981). *Culture, mind, and therapy: An introduction to cultural psychiatry*. New York: Brunner/Mazel.

Turner, J. (1985). *Without God, without creed*. Baltimore: The Johns Hopkins University Press.

Tyler, F. B., Susswell, D. R., & Williams-McCoy, J. (1985). Ethnic validity in psychotherapy. *Psychotherapy, 22*, 311–320.

Valadez, J., & Clignet, R. (1987). On the ambiguities of a sociological analysis of the culture of narcissism. *The Sociological Quarterly, 28*, 455–472.

Vaux, A. (1988). *Social support*. New York: Praeger.

Vernon, G. M. (1968). The religious nones: A neglected category. *Journal for the Scientific Study of Religion, 2*, 219–229.

Vigil, J. D. (1988). *Barrio gangs: Street life and identity in southern California*. Austin: University of Texas Press.

Vilhjalmsson, R. (1993). Life stress, social support and clinical depression. *Social Science and Medicine, 37*, 331–342.

Wachs, T. D., Uzgiris, I. C., & Hunt, J. (1971). Cognitive development in infants of different age levels and from different environmental backgrounds. *Merrill-Palmer Quarterly of Behavior and Development, 17*, 288–317.

Wachtel, P. (1983). *The poverty of affluence*. New York: The Free Press.

Wallace, R., Struening, E., & Susser, E. (1993). Homelessness and psychopathology. In A. A. Ghadirian & H. E. Lehmann (Eds.), *Environment and psychopathology*. New York: Springer.

Wallace, R. A. (1979). *The genesis factor*. New York: Morrow.

Wandersman, A., & Nation, M. (1998). Urban neighborhoods and mental health: Psychological contributions to understanding toxicity, resilience, and interventions. *American Psychologist, 53*, 647–656.

Waters, M. (1995). *Globalization*. London: Routledge.

Wilder, D., & Shapiro, P. N. (1989). The role of competition-induced anxiety. *Journal of Personality and Social Psychology, 56*, 60–69.

Wilder, T. (1947). *The bridge of San Luis Rey*. London: Longmans, Green.

Wilkinson, R. (1996). *Unhealthy societies: The afflictions of inequality*. London: Sage.

Williams, S. J. (1998). Modernity and the emotions. *Sociology, 32*, 747–769.

Wilson, E. O. (1998). *Consilience: The unity of knowledge*. New York: Alfred A. Knopf.

Wilson, G., & Baldassare, M. (1996). Overall sense of community in a suburban region: The effects of localism, privacy, and urbanization. *Environment and Behavior, 28*, 27–43.

Winfield, R. D. (1991). *Freedom and modernity*. Albany, NY: State University of New York Press.

Wohlwill, J. F. & van Vliet, W. (1985). *Habitats for children: The impacts of density*. Hillsdale, NJ: Lawrence Erlbaum.

Wuthnow, R. (1994). *Sharing the journey*. New York: The Free Press.

Yalom, I. D. (1980). *Existential psychotherapy*. New York: Basic Books.

Yeich, S. (1996). Grassroots organizing with homeless people: A participatory research approach. *Journal of Social Issues, 52*, 111–121.

Zepp, I. G. (1997). *The new religious image of urban America*. Niwot: University of Colorado Press.

Zey, M. (1994). *Seizing the future*. New York: Simon & Schuster.

Index

Aborigines of Australia, 65, 129–30
Abstract systems, 1
Acculturation, 71, 75–76, 143
Acid rain, 162
Addiction, 40, 78, 91, 127–33
Advertising, 125; children and, 44, 84;
   self and, 18; unreality and, 43–44
Africa, globalization in, 49
Age of Anxiety, 71
Agitation, collective, 80–82
Air pollution, 143–45
Alcoholism, 10
Alienation, 21, 24, 41, 77, 93, 116, 119,
   121–24, 143, 171; competition and,
   72; depression and, 64–65; global-
   ization and, 47; self-interest and, 82
All-consuming society, 30
Allergies, social, 84–87
Ambiguity, modernity and, 2, 74
American Dream, 33, 38, 74, 96
Americanization, 2
Amish, 4, 165
Amnesia, collective, 157–58
Angels, infatuation with, 118

Anger, 100; depression and, 54, 56–58,
   61–62, 68; urbanization and, 140
Anomie, 123
Anorexia nervosa, 70, 79
Anthropological shock, 156
Anti-depressant medication, 53
Anti-globalization forces, 47
Anti-intellectualism, 133–37
Antisocial trends, 101–6
Anxiety, 6–7, 10, 17, 51, 68, 69–82, 122,
   143, 158; acculturation and, 76;
   across cultures, 69–71; competition
   and, 71–73; environmental, 156–57;
   existential, 20–21; future minded-
   ness and, 80–82; globalization and,
   47; moral, 19–21; religion and, 107;
   social, 26
Artificiality, 25, 30, 37, 152
Asocial freedom, 9–11, 27
Assertiveness training, 54
Atomism, consumer, 172
Aum Supreme Truth cult, 113
Australia, 38
Authenticity, 18, 27, 71–73, 86, 119
Authoritative center, 22

Autonomy, 3
Avarice, 32–33

Banality: consumerism and, 30, 121;
    modernity and, 2, 23; rarefied,
    133–37
Belongingness, 16–17, 76, 165
Bhutan people of Himalayas, 14–15
Binge eating, 40, 42
Biological diversity, loss of, 155
Body, 70–71, 76–77, 79, 106; consump-
    tion and, 42–43, 46; dysmorphic
    disorder, 79
Borderline personality, 27, 101–6
Boredom, 27, 47, 124–26
Bounded self, 14–15
Bowling alone phenomenon, 96
Brand names, 85, 115
Buddhism, 14–15, 35, 113, 115
Bureaucratic processes, 48

California self, 13, 16
Canada, 38
Capitalism, 10, 37, 46–49, 86, 150, 158,
    167; dehumanization and, 10; glob-
    alization and, 48; liberal type of, 3;
    religion and, 117–20; unsupported,
    26; working mechanisms of, 3
Caprice, 32
Cathartic release, 54, 58, 61–62, 107,
    110, 115
Celebrities, 28, 119, 157–58
Celebrity fantasies, 87
Chaos, 2, 8, 77, 79–80, 112, 124–25
Charisma, 115
Child-as-customer phenomenon, 93
Children, 57, 82, 84, 87–88, 90–94, 102,
    105, 136, 142, 174; commercializa-
    tion of, 36, 44–45; competition and,
    67–68; day care centers and, 91–92;
    depression and, 51–52, 57–60; de-
    velopment of compulsive con-
    sumption in, 41; divorce and,
    98–102; as optional extra, 99; pa-
    rental pushing of, 93; rearing of,
    90–94; undersocialized, 92, 174; ur-
    banization and, 142–43

Choice, 34, 45, 75–78, 110, 127; fatigue,
    75–78
Cigarettes, 45, 161
Cities, growth of, 139–43
Civic religion, 113
Clairvoyance, 114
Climate destabilization, 155
Cognition, 13, 44, 78, 107, 115, 131,
    150; culture and, 5, 22, 40; depres-
    sion and, 53, 58, 61–62; globaliza-
    tion and, 49; oversupply of, 78;
    pollution and, 143–48
Cognitive theories, 4–5
Collecting fetishes, 78, 88, 119–20
Collectivism, 15–17, 66, 83, 123; men-
    tal health and, 16–17
Commercial unreality, 25
Commodity: logic, 119; sphere, 10
Communal marriages, 95
Communitarianism, 21
Compassion, 21, 31
Competition, 4, 35, 84, 92; advantages
    of, 66; anxiety and, 71–73; collectiv-
    ism and, 15–16; cultural heroics
    and, 66; depression and, 65–68; fa-
    tigue, 72; trap, 73
Compulsive buying, 40–43
Conflict-free divorces, 100–101
Conformist consumption, 84
Conformity, 21, 25
Confucian family, 105
Conjugal power, 99
Consciousness, 3, 11, 13–28, 79, 108,
    114–15, 124, 128, 130, 156–57, 164;
    cultural, 165–66; externalized,
    27–28; future, 81; modern, 78, 81,
    157; unhappy, 30–32
Conservation mindedness, decline of,
    32–33
Consumer: consciousness, 27, 29–50,
    119, 121; heroics, 25, 28, 30, 85;
    trance, 159–62; vertigo, 32
Consumerism, 7, 10, 23, 26–27, 29, 84,
    104, 134, 150; evolution of, 31
Consumption, 14, 16, 29–50, 82, 84, 93,
    104, 116, 121, 149, 166, 172; body
    and, 42–43; compulsive, 40–43;
    conformist, 84; creative, 104; disor-

ders, 40–43; frenzied, 28; globalization and, 46–47; growth, 36; institutionalized, 31; instrumental, 39; intellectual decline and, 133–37; interpersonal relations and, 83–106; mental health and, 29–50; parenting and, 90–94; as a preconscious mechanism, 41–42; religious, 110, 115; ritualization of, 117–20; sacralization of, 117–20; as salvation, 117, 121; as social signifier, 29–30, 84; terminal, 39; trance and, 159–62
Consumption disorders, 24, 40–43
Contentment, 32, 176
Cook Islanders, 16–17
Coping, 15–16, 27, 38, 101, 133; collective, 25; consumption and, 41; culture and, 7, 21; depression and, 54, 63–64; religion and, 107–8; trauma and, 78–80
Corporate domination of culture, 46
Cosmic sensitivities, 82, 110
Creativity, 21, 25, 38, 72, 74, 83, 104, 106
Credit industry, 32–36
Crime, 15, 47, 91 101–2, 140, 165
Critical thinking, 46
Cults, 112–13
Cultural: blindness, 165–66; disintegration, 47, 80–81; disintegration hypothesis, 6, 10, 80–81, 129, 143; disobedience, 84; heroism, 66, 68, 75, 94, 98; neglect, 137; schemas, 18; suffering strategies, 79
Cultural reality, shared, 21
Cultural self, eclipse of, 62
Culture, 5–6, 11, 81, 103; as cognitive system, 5, 18, 40; collapse of, 80–81, 129, 143; collectivist type of, 15–16; commodification, 28–50; disobedience and, 84; evolution of, 2; fitness of, 11, 64–65, 75; intellectual decay and, 133–37; learning and, 4–5; meaning and, 124–26; as pathogen, 2, 11; personality profile of, 22; premodern, 25; ritual and, 79; as survival mechanism, 4–5, 11

Culture-bound disorders, 55
Culture shock, 47, 75
Customs, 16
Cyberpunk movement, 114
Cyber relationships, 87–88

Dandyism, 80
Datura, 131
Day care centers, mental health and, 90–94
Death, 57, 101–2, 120, 126, 171; of mind, 133–37
Debt, 34, 36
Defamiliarization, 122
Defense mechanisms, modernity and, 13–28, 79–80
Dehumanization, 6–7, 10
Delinquency, 91
Demoralization, 47, 97
Dependency, 38
Depleted self, 13
Depression, 10, 51–68, 97–98, 104, 124, 142, 165; competition and, 65–68; cultural cognition in, 58, 61–62; cultural immunity to, 56–60; cultural perspectives on, 55–58; individualism and, 62–65; pollution and, 144–45, 147; postnatal, 56, 58–60; rage and, 61–62; rise of, 51–52; social support and, 62–65; somatic features of, 55–56; theories of, 52–55; tourism and, 152–53
Designer drugs, 78
Desire, 26, 28, 30, 33–34, 36–37, 43, 45, 77, 81, 88, 95, 98, 108, 149, 171
Despair, 63, 107, 120, 127
Digestive problems, 55
Disciple, new breed of, 118
Discontent, 10, 31, 33, 84, 161, 176; future-mindedness and, 81; materialism and, 36–37; social fraudulence and, 72
Discrimination, 75–76
Disillusionment, 31
Dissociation, 17–18, 104, 127; alienated, 78–80; drugs and, 130–32; environmental, 157–62, 165; from guilt, 94; need for, 78

Distributive justice, 176–77
Divorce, 94–101, 143, 165; as con-
    sumer distraction, 99; causes of,
    100; conflict-free variety, 100–101;
    culture of, 94–95; effects on chil-
    dren of, 99–101
Drama, psychological need for, 8
Drives, homogenization of, 1
Drug companies, 86
Dumbing forces, 8, 15, 133–37
Duty, 3, 17

Easternization, collective identity and,
    3
Eccentricity, 21
Ecological: crisis, 4, 81; modernity,
    162–67; psychopathology, 144;
    sociopathy, 155–62
Economic: construction of reality, 29;
    motives, 25, 43
Economics, 72–73, 90, 96, 109, 128,
    135, 141, 154, 156, 163, 165, 170–71;
    globalization of, 46–49; mental
    health and, 43–46; of marriage, 95;
    postreligious, 108
Egocentric preoccupation, 17
Ego inflation, 35–36
Emotion, 6, 25–28, 41–43, 61, 67, 71,
    79–80, 86–88, 91, 100–101, 104, 119,
    124, 147, 171; artificiality of, 25; ca-
    tharsis of, 110; commodification of,
    25–26; consumption and, 41, 98;
    deregulation of, 26; effects of pollu-
    tion on, 143–48; estrangement
    from, 25; externalization of, 54,
    56–58; flexibility of, 16; internaliza-
    tion of, 54–55, 62; modernity and,
    2, 95; paralysis of, 126;
    undersocialized, 26, 103–4
Emotional insurance, 97–98; intelli-
    gence, 27
Empathy, 2, 102
Empty self, 34–35, 42
Enculturation, 5, 23, 33, 42, 53, 82, 90,
    92–93, 101, 103–4, 165
Ennui, 31, 47, 126, 165
Entertainment, life as, 23
Entitlement, dysfunctional, 24

Environment, 2, 4, 43, 76, 81, 139–67;
    Amish and, 165; destruction of, 38,
    47, 155–62, 164; hyperglobalized
    type of, 3; mental health and,
    139–67; pollution of, 143–48; tour-
    ism and, 150–53
Environmental: dissociation, 157–62,
    165; guilt, 156; madness, 177; stress,
    145–48, 154, 157
Ephemerality, 81
Escapism, 31
Evangelism, 114
Evil spirits, 57–58, 69
Excess, drive toward, 32–36
Exchange relationships, 94–101
Exercise, compulsive, 78
Exhibitionism, 86, 104, 106, 122
Existential: counseling, 171–77; health,
    120–38
Existential problems, 9, 17, 20–21, 26,
    34, 63, 81, 120–37; consumption
    and, 34, 84; environmental and,
    158–59; intellectual and, 133–37;
    substance abuse and, 127–33
Experience, reliability of, 80–81
Externalization disorders, 24–25
Externalized consciousness, 28
Exxon Valdez spill, 145

Faith, 108, 110, 117, 150; in abundance,
    117
Faithless religion, 109–110
False: assumptions, 44; needs, 31
Fame, preoccupation with, 86
Family, 40–41, 89–94, 101, 145, 161;
    breakdown, 105, 128, 149; urban-
    ization and, 142–43
Fantasy, 2, 41, 72, 77, 87, 99, 104,
    132–33
Fashion, 31, 39
Fatalism, 107
Fear of abandonment, 44
Feeling rules, 25
Fetishism, materialistic, 28, 39, 78
Floating communities, 90
Fragmentation, 2
Free-floating identity, 14, 18
Friendship, as symbolic, 19–20

Fundamentalism, 111–12
Future: anxiety, 81; shock, 47
Future-mindedness, 80–82, 116

Gambling, compulsive, 40
Gangs, 123–24
Gestalt psychology, 163–64
Global concerns, demise of, 81–82
Globalization, 46–49; pancapitalism
    and, 46–48; well-being and, 46–47
Global warming, 155
God, 114–15, 118, 120; as broker, 109;
    new personality of, 108–10
Goddess worship, 114
Grace, 117
Grandiosity, 61, 103
Greed, 14, 32–34, 36, 43, 165
Grief, 57
Guilt, 63, 86, 93–94, 105; environmen-
    tal, 156; self-disappointment and,
    20–21, 81
Guns, 142–43

Hallucinations, 130–32
Happiness, materialism and, 39–40
Hardiness, culture and, 16, 79
Headaches, 55
Hedonism, 16, 31
Helplessness, 53–54, 58
Herodotus, 1
Homelessness, 17, 47, 143, 148–50
Homo consumens, 80–81, 83
Homogenization: of culture, 47; of
    tastes, 1, 43–44
Hong Kong, 2
Hope, 116, 162–63
Hopelessness, 47, 107–8, 120, 157; de-
    pression and, 54, 58, 64
Humanistic: industrialization, 162–67;
    psychology, 80
Humility, decline of, 92
Hydraulic formulation, 6
Hyperbolic discounting, 33–34
Hypoactive sexual desire disorder, 98
Hysterical symptoms, demise of, 24

Ideal citizen, 32

Identity, 10, 15–16, 41, 64, 67, 105, 107,
    123, 143, 156; collective type of, 3,
    80; confusion, 91; cultural, 22, 80,
    153; globalization and, 48; loss of,
    75–76; megatrends in, 13–28; need
    for, 7–8, 10; stunted development
    of, 21
Id impulses, 22–23
Idolatry, 112
Immediacy, therapeutic value of,
    80–82
Immortality, 20–21
Impotency boom, 98
Impulsive self, 13
Impulsivity, 23, 102, 104–5
Inadequacy, sense of, 44
Indigenous people, destruction of,
    175–76
Individualism, 2–3, 14–19, 23, 83–84,
    103, 123, 158, 171–73, 175; alienat-
    ing, 17, 83; competitive, 71–72; de-
    pression and, 53, 62–65;
    psychology and, 4–5, 53, 169–70,
    173; radical, 17; reciprocal, 17; reli-
    gious, 109; self-construal strategies
    and, 15
Industrialization, 47, 49; mental health
    and, 139–43
Infinite possibility, 75–78, 85
Information, consumption of, 84–85
Initiation ceremonies, 8, 128
Insatiability, 32, 45
Institutionalized overconsumption, 31
Institutional self, 27
Intellect, 8, 45, 58, 155–56; decline of,
    133–37; environment and, 155–56,
    160; pathologies of, 137
Internalization disorders, 24–25
Internet, 38, 77–78, 85, 91
Interpersonal relations, 27–28, 79, 103,
    136, 140, 147; competition and, 67,
    72; modernity and, 83–106; poverty
    of, 93
Intimacy crisis, 87–90, 97, 136
Invisible parenting, 90–94
Isolated self, 13, 16, 64
Israel, marriage in, 99

Japan, 2
Japanese society, 52, 113
Joylessness, 35
Justice: commercial view of, 2; social,
    175–77

Kaluli peole of New Guinea, 56–58, 61
Karma, 14–15, 115
Kipsigis people of Kenya, 58–60
Kleptomania, upsurgence of, 27, 40
Korea, 2
Koro, 70

Learned helplessness, 47, 54, 58
Leisure pathologies, 73–75, 90–91
Lobby groups, 43
Localness, eclipse of, 85–86
Loneliness, 6–7, 13, 17, 25, 43, 63, 80,
    84, 98, 120–23, 136, 143, 165, 171;
    industry, 120–21
Lonely self, 13
Loss, depression and, 55–58

Madness techniques, 21, 80, 102
Magic, culture and, 23, 33, 129
Malls, as cathedrals, 119
Marginalization, 75–76, 141
Marital capital, 96
Market mentality, 18, 25, 45–46, 75, 82,
    87, 95, 98, 102, 110, 149–50
Marriage, 87, 94–101, 105, 165; com-
    munal, 95; companionate, 96; ex-
    change, 95; lifespan of, 99; as
    obsolete, 99; poverty of modern,
    97; as self-fulfillment, 94–95
Mastery, 19, 53
Materialism, 2–3, 36, 77, 84, 92, 100,
    105, 119, 161–2; happiness and, 39;
    interpersonal health and, 83–85;
    life satisfaction and, 39–40;
    nongenerosity and, 37; psychologi-
    cal effects of, 36–43
Maximal self, 13, 16, 83–84
Mbuti Pygmies of Africa, 14
Meaning, 64, 83–84, 98, 109, 122, 124,
    136, 157, 164–65, 171; consumerism
    and, 30; modernity and, 4, 171; reli-
    gion and, 108–9, 111, 115, 121;
    self-distracting pain and, 124–26
Meaninglessness, 47, 64, 120–21,
    124–26, 165, 171
Media, 44, 46, 84, 86, 120, 161; heroes,
    115; religion and, 115; self, 13; so-
    cialization, 104; suggestibility, 41
Mediation, 78
Memory, 79–80
Mennonites, 4
Mental health workers, 40, 126, 137,
    140, 148, 150, 169–77
Mesmerization, 78
Mickey Mouse, as God, 120
Migrants, 76
Migration, 47
Mixtecan people of Mexico, 65
Mobility of information, 47
Modernity, 1, 14, 103, 176–77; anxiety
    and, 69–82; corrosive effects of, 2;
    cultural foundation of, 4–6; ecolog-
    ical, 162–67; ecological pathologies
    of, 155–62, 167; emotion and,
    25–28, 54–55; environmental de-
    cline and, 139–67; as exile, 18–19;
    existential crisis and, 120–38; fea-
    tures of, 1–2; human context of,
    1–12; inner type, 3–4; interpersonal
    health and, 83–106; negative outer,
    3, 32–36; outer type, 4; parenting
    and, 90–94; as self-seduction, 85;
    spirituality and, 107–20; the final,
    177; as unnatural compromise,
    9–11; varieties of, 2–4; voyeurism
    and, 84–87; Western type of, 6
Modern person syndrome, 2
Money fetishes, 39
Monocultural societies, 22
Moral codes, 20
Moral cosmology, 21
Morality, 17, 64, 92, 98–99, 102, 110,
    112, 124, 153, 175–76; asocial, 21;
    collective, 19; globalization and, 48;
    individualism and, 19–20;
    self-absolving, 19–21
Moral net, culture and, 9–10
Motivation, 4–5, 7, 21, 25, 28, 34,
    36–37, 70, 88, 105, 111, 153; con-

sumer, 81, 93; cultural, 90, 93; depression and, 53; imbalances of, 137; religious, 112, 114
Mourning-guilt syndrome, 94
Multinational conglomerates, 47
Murder, 101–2, 126
Music, hypnogogic, 78, 84, 124
Mutable self, 13
Mutuality, decline of, 87–88
Mysticism, 19, 53
Myth of the market, 119, 121

Narcissism, 16, 23, 28, 61, 101–6, 117; depression and, 104; frustration tolerance and, 105
Nationalism, 113
National sovereignty, erosion of, 47
Need satisfaction, modernity and, 7
Neoindividualism, 14
New Zealand, 38
Nihilism, 5–6, 17
Noise pollution, 145–48
Nomadic life-styles, 90
Nonemotionalism, 2
Nongenerosity, 37
Normlessness, 64, 88, 123
Novelty, 47, 85
Nuclear: holocaust, 81; waste, 162

Obesity, 71
Obligation, 17
Obsessive-compulsive disorder, 69, 102
Ocean degradation, 155
Ontological insecurity, 133–37, 171
Orgasm, ultimate, 106
Overeffort pathologies, 73–75
Overindulgence, 23, 84
Overpopulation, 139–40, 143, 163, 174
Ozone depletion, 155

Pancapitalism, 46–49
Paranoia, 47
Passivity, 48–49, 78, 136
Pastiche personality, 18
Patriotism, 113
Personal growth, 39, 87, 99, 113, 124
Personality disorders, 101–6

Petism, 88
Phenomenological consciousness, 14
Philosophical counseling, 171–72
Phobias, 69, 86–87
Pleasant personality, 26
Pluralism, 2, 47
Pollution, 140; emotional responses to, 143–48; noise, 145–48
Population explosion, 139–40, 143, 163, 174
Postemotional society, 2, 26–27
Postintellectualism trend, 23
Postmarital depression, 94–101
Postnatal (postpartum) depression, 56, 58–60, 96
Poverty, 35, 49, 142, 150, 165
Powerlessness, 17
Pragmatism, 96
Prayer, 109
Prejudice, 75–76
Premodern culture, 25, 29, 43, 52, 102, 109, 121
Prenuptial agreements, 95
Problematic: future, 48; self, 13
Profit motivation, 17, 21, 26, 43, 93, 102, 106, 117, 160, 163, 167
Prostitution, 154
Protean self, 18–19
Pseudo-gratification, 81
Psychic: deadness, 26, 125–26, 171; homeostasis, 22–23
Psychological: defense, 13–28, 79–80; individualism, 4–5, 53, 169–70; parent, 91
Psychology, toward a relevant, 172–77
Psychopathology, 11, 26, 40–43, 105, 170–71; consumption and, 40–43; culture-based model of, 6–7; drugs and, 131–33; environmental, 177; groups and, 11; modernity and, 2, 5, 9–10; proneness to, 17; ritual and, 110–11; self and, 19
Psychosocial toxins, 49, 51
Psychotherapy, 4, 53, 169–77
Public orientations, 84–87
Pure relationships, 87–88
Purpose, 4

Quebec, 36

Racism, 47, 174
Rage, modernity and, 2, 61–62
Raging self, 13, 61
Rarefied banality, 133–37
Reciprocity, cultural theme of, 56–58
Reflexive knowledge, 1
Refugees, 76, 174
Reincarnation, 117
Relatedness needs, 24, 35, 88, 140, 165
Relativism, 7
Religion, 29–30, 39, 61, 102, 106–120,
    128, 131, 142; Amish, 165; as big
    business, 118; civic, 112–13;
    deinstitutionalization of, 109; envi-
    ronmental change and, 164–65;
    faithless, 109–110; globalization
    and, 47; individualism and, 109;
    innerness of, 109; media and, 115;
    mental health and, 107–8; private,
    108–111; psychological defense
    and, 21; revitalization of, 111, 113;
    secularization and, 113–14
Religious: cults, 111–12; fundamental-
    ism, 111–12; surrogacy, 111–17
Repression, 59; intellectual, 133–37;
    social, 83, 106
Responsibility, collective action and, 3,
    81, 97
Retail-style futures, 82
Ritual, 16, 55, 57–60, 107–8, 115,
    119–20, 128; crisis of, 110–11; disso-
    ciation and, 79; drugs and, 127–28,
    130, 133; need for, 8; religious,
    108–9, 114–15; therapeutic proper-
    ties of, 110–11

Sacrifice, 3, 118
Salvation, 117
Savings rate, 33
Secular myths, 115
Security crisis, 48
Segmentalization, 141
Self, 76, 108, 117, 171; empty, 34–35,
    171; enhancement of, 83–84, 86, 90,
    104, 106, 118, 171; impaired sense
    of, 41, 43; nature and, 156; as a

package, 25–26, 73; as public
    broadcaster, 85–86; tech-
    nique-driven, 106
Self-absolution, private religion and,
    108–9
Self-actualization, 24, 87 114; guilt
    and, 93–94
Self-betrayal, 20–21, 81
Self-destructiveness, 27, 46, 49, 101,
    126, 133
Self-divinization, 109
Self-esteem, 44, 101; competition and,
    67–68; depression and, 53, 55; ma-
    terialism and, 39–40; movement,
    67–68; unwarranted, 24, 68
Self-estrangement, 31, 43, 156
Self-glorification, 104–5
Self-hate, 40, 104
Self-interest, 36–37, 64, 83–84, 95,
    104–6, 117
Self-knowledge gaps, 28
Self-marketing, 73
Self-socialization, 124
Self-validation, 26
Sexism, 174–75
Sex therapy industry, 98
Sexual abuse, 149
Sexual behavior, 6, 70–71, 97; compul-
    sive, 40; dysfunctional, 97–99
Sexuality, as consumer right, 98; crisis,
    97–98
Shame, 18, 25–26
Shintoism, 113
Simplicity, as solution, 38
Simultaneous communication, 1
Singapore, 2
Single mothers, 101
Sleep problems, 55, 70, 74
Social: allergies, 84–87; anxiety, 26, 86;
    atomism, 62; bonds and consumer-
    ism, 7; capital, 88–89;
    connectedness, 7, 105, 107, 129, 141,
    155; conscience, 19–20; continuity,
    31, 41; entrepreneur, 86; fraudu-
    lence, 25, 71–73, 86; interest, 20,
    83–84; justice, 175–77; marginality,
    1; memory, impairment of, 2; pho-
    bia boom, 86–87; sins, 24, 93, 102,

118, 127, 148; skills, 25; support,
62–65, 79, 105; unconscious, 22–23;
utopia, 134
Societal: solidarity, 158; therapy,
170–71
Sociopathy, ecological, 155–62
Solitariness, intimacy crisis and,
88–90
Spiritual environmentalism, 164
Spirituality, 106–38, 171, 175; alienation and, 117; environment and,
164–5; modernity and, 4, 115; unconscious, 112
Sports, as religious compensation, 115
Sport utility vehicles, as
self-destructive, 159–62, 166
Stress, 15, 38, 63–64, 73–75, 77–80, 101,
116, 142–43, 174; acculturative,
75–76; as badge of honor, 71; cul-
tural, 75, 137; depression and, 54;
environmental, 144–48, 154, 157
Sublimation, 22
Substance abuse, 40, 78, 91, 108,
126–33, 143, 145, 149, 174; as
socioexistential problem, 127–33;
cultural context of, 127–30; religion
and, 130–33
Suffering strategies, 79–80, 150
Suggestibility, media, 41
Suggestion, cultural, 37, 122–23, 130
Suicide, 63, 107, 126, 165
Superego, 22–23
Superfluidity, 30, 37
Sweden, 36, 52
Symbolic interactionism, 64

Taboos, 20, 22, 68
Taiwan, 2
Tangu people of New Guinea, 65
Tastes, 1, 43–44, 85; for everything,
81
Technology, 46–47, 85–86, 156, 166,
174; attachment to, 2; consumption
of, 32, 85, 116; dependency on, 116;
encroachment of, 1; religious,
164–65; as religious surrogate,
115–16

Television, 43, 119, 125; ministries,
118–19
Temperance, end of, 24
Terrorism, 174–75
Therapeutic emptiness, 78
Thrill killing, 102
Toraja people of Indonesia, 61–62
Tourism, 4; artificiality of, 152; consequences of, 150–55; cultural,
152–53; depressing, 152; economic
benefits of, 154; negative perceptions of, 153; physical environment
and, 150–53; social disharmony
and, 153–54; types of, 151
Tradition, 45, 74; collapse of, 47, 155;
preservation of, 3; tourism and,
154–55
Trance: consumer, 159–62; facilitators,
78
Transcendence, 14, 108–110, 114,
116–18, 165; consumerism and,
118–19; need for, 8, 114; ritual and,
110–11, 115; substance use and,
128–32
Trauma, 133, 142; proneness to, 78–80;
sexual, 98
Trust, 87–88
Truth, 18, 46, 121

UFOlogy, 113–14
Ugliness, 85–86
Unconscious, 22–23, 43
Unhappy consciousness, 30–32
Universities, decline of, 135
Unreality, 25, 28, 31, 43–46, 68, 81, 109,
116, 128, 133
Urbanization, 47, 174; children and,
142–43; mental health and, 139–43;
tourism and, 154

Values, 3–4, 17, 22, 37, 39, 46, 63, 103,
105, 149, 160, 167, 172–73; communitarian, 171; globalization and, 48;
religion and, 111, 117
Variety seeking, 97
Vices, as virtues, 165
Vietnam war, 101–2

Violence, 47, 49, 101, 105, 142–43, 145,
     165
Virility, cultural theme of, 70–71
Volition, 23–24, 44; depression and,
     53–54; emotion and, 1
Voluntary simplicity, 38
Voyeurism, modern, 84–87, 123
Vulgarity, consumption and, 30

Waste, 38, 165
Westernization, 2–3, 47, 70
Whimsical parents, 93
Wisdom, cultural, 14, 58, 130
Wish, fantasy and, 41

Witchcraft, 69, 114
Work, 31, 73–75, 90–91, 94, 140–41;
     compulsive, 74
Work-family dilemma, 94
Working marriages, 96
Worry, 74

Yoruba aborigines of Australia, 69–70
Youth, 85, 149, 165; boredom of, 124–26;
     concerns of, 82; cultural fixation on,
     25; gangs, 123–24; subcultures, 124

Zen, 115
Zuni Indian culture, 65

About the Author

JOHN F. SCHUMAKER is a Senior Lecturer in Clinical Psychology at the University of Canterbury in Christchurch, New Zealand. He has authored and edited nine books and numerous chapters and journal articles. His areas of research include psychopathology across cultures, the psychological consequences of materialism and consumerism, eating disorders, depression, dissociation, human suggestibility, and the relationship between religion and mental health.